The Cinematic Tourist

Recent years have seen a radical transformation of conventional tourist marketing and experience. The use of exotic locations in Hollywood films has allowed global audiences to enjoy distant places. Simultaneously, Hollywood screening of potential 'tourist paradises' has generated new tourist industries around the world. This book takes a closer look at this new phenomenon of 'cinematic tourism', combining theory with case studies drawn from four continents: America, Europe, Asia and Australasia.

The author explores audiences' perceptions of film and their covert relationship with tourist advertising campaigns, alongside the nature of newly-born tourist industries and the reaction of native populations and nation-states faced with the commodification of their histories, identities and environments.

Drawing on a wide range of disciplines, this fresh and original book will be of compelling interest for students and scholars of tourism, film theory, cultural studies, post-colonial studies, sociology and anthropology of culture, and political economy.

Rodanthi Tzanelli is Lecturer in Sociology at the University of Kent. Her main research interests include the sociology of nationalism, 'race' and ethnicity, the relationship of tourist and film industries and representations of deviancy. Her recent publications include articles in numerous esteemed journals including *Sociology*, *Tourist Studies*, *Mobilities*, *Ethnic and Racial Studies* and *Media, Culture and Society*.

International Library of Sociology
Founded by Karl Mannheim
Editor: John Urry
Lancaster University

Recent publications in this series include:

Risk and Technological Culture
Towards a sociology of virulence
Joost Van Loon

Reconnecting Culture, Technology and Nature
Mike Michael

Advertising Myths
The strange half lives of images and commodities
Anne M. Cronin

Adorno on Popular Culture
Robert R. Witkin

Consuming the Caribbean
From Arwaks to Zombies
Mimi Sheller

Crime and Punishment in Contemporary Culture
Claire Valier

Between Sex and Power
Family in the world, 1900–2000
Goran Therborn

States of Knowledge
The co-production of social science and social order
Shelia Jasanoff

After Method
Mess in social science research
John Law

Brands
Logos of the global economy
Celia Lury

The Culture of Exception
Sociology facing the camp
Bulent Diken and Carsten Bagge Lausten

Visual Worlds
John Hall, Blake Stimson and Lisa Tamiris Becker

Time, Innovation and Mobilities
Travel in technological cultures
Peter Frank Peters

Complexity and Social Movements
Multitudes acting at the edge of chaos
Ian Welsh and Graeme Chesters

Qualitative Complexity
Ecology, cognitive processes and the re-emergence of structures in post-humanist social theory
Chris Jenks and John Smith

Theories of the Information Society, 3rd Edition
Frank Webster

Mediating Nature
Nils Lindahl Elliot

Haunting the Knowledge Economy
Jane Kenway, Elizabeth Bullen, Johannah Fahey and Simon Robb

Global Nomads
Techno and new age as transnational countercultures in Ibiza and Goa
Anthony D'Andrea

The Cinematic Tourist
Explorations in globalization, culture and resistance
Rodanthi Tzanelli

The Cinematic Tourist

Explorations in globalization, culture and resistance

Rodanthi Tzanelli

Routledge
Taylor & Francis Group

LONDON AND NEW YORK

Transferred to digital printing 2010

First published 2007 by Routledge
2 Park Square, Milton Park, Abingdon, Oxon OX14 4RN

Simultaneously published in the USA and Canada
by Routledge
270 Madison Ave, New York, NY 10016

Routledge is an imprint of the Taylor & Francis Group, an informa business

© 2007 Rodanthi Tzanelli

Typeset in Garamond by Keystroke,
28 High Street, Tettenhall, Wolverhampton

British Library Cataloguing in Publication Data
A catalogue record for this book is available from the British Library

Library of Congress Cataloging in Publication Data
    Tzanelli, Rodanthi.
    The cinematic tourist : explorations in globalization, culture, and
resistance / Rodanthi Tzanelli.–1st ed.
        p. cm.
    Includes bibliographical references and index.
    1. Tourism. 2. Motion pictures–Social aspects. I. Title.
    G155.A1T93 2007
    302.23′43–dc22   2006024739

ISBN10: 0–415–39413–9 (hbk)
ISBN13: 978–0–415–39413–0 (hbk)

ISBN10: 0–415–58132–X (pbk)
ISBN13: 978–0–415–58132–5 (pbk)

For Majid,
Gia panta

Contents

List of illustrations

Preface

It is the convention to say a few words about the way in which a published monograph has come to life, drawing attention to its academic significance. Often, however, this exercise becomes trapped in the academic vocabulary of seriousness – a performative act that, no doubt, eventually attains an objective status. As a result, scholars feel obliged to fill these first few pages with an account of the importance of their study complete with an apologia addressed to readers who invest time and energy to engage with it. I will and will not operate within these academic conventions. In reality, this book was born in a dim auditorium at Trafford Centre's cinema complex following the release of *Captain Corelli's Mandolin* in 2001. At the time, the film had caused pandemonium and rage in Greek communist circles for its association with what was considered an anticommunist novel by Louis de Bernières. All sorts of accusations were directed against Universal Pictures for encouraging this mindless commodification of Greek histories, and a war was waged against the *Corelli*-mania of global tourists. These reactions persuaded me and my friends to watch the film; later, they induced me to write the first article on it and its impact on self-narration on the island of Kefalonia, where the movie was filmed. Watching the film was, by all accounts, a rather banal experience – and mine was not much different from anyone else's. However, my academic engagement with it turned out to be more cumbersome than I expected: the Greek and foreign press, which was rife with articles on the *Corelli* phenomenon, had managed to communicate the less pleasant aspects of Hollywood's intrusion into the everyday life of island communities, an intrusion that was worsened by the international touristification of Kefalonia. These developments encouraged a reflexive process: however irrelevant my movie-watching experience might have seemed to be, it was not. As a consumer of a film that advertised Kefalonian nature and culture, I was implicated in the touristification of the island. This marked the moment at which I decided to pursue a more detailed and culturally nuanced analysis of what I have termed the 'cinematic tourist' and 'cinematic tourism'.

This monograph, then, voices an aspiration to link the process of production – of novel, films, cultural difference and authenticity – to that of consumption – of films and the ideas they communicate, of actual filmed places. As I was to find out, practices of consumption can also reinforce structures of production: they can strengthen social inequalities in tourist industries, consolidate economic hierarchies of different nation-states in the international political arena and also result in the modification of filmed identities and cultures. Sociologists of consumption, political and moral economy, culture, media and cultural studies do not communicate well. The battle for territorial monopolies has taken a toll on a discipline so rich in subject matter, but so rigid in theoretical and political approaches. The idea of studying the whole 'social life' of commodities, to adapt Appadurai's term, is still somehow inconceivable. In the case of the life trajectories of place and culture, sociologists tend to focus either on the economic structure of tourist industries or on the tourist experience. My aim in this monograph was to immortalize and analyse the whole production/consumption cycle (from the politics of filmmaking, to audience reception, to the generation and institution of tourism in filmed locations and the local, national and global reactions to the phenomenon). As happens with all ambitious studies, *The Cinematic Tourist* is, in places, incomplete or flimsy. This can be partially attributed to my attempt to do justice to all the important scholars who work in similar (Mike Crang, Sue Beeton, Tim Edensor, David Crouch and Ellen Strain to mention but a few) and other cognate areas (such as John Urry, Mimi Sheller, Don Slater and Scott Lash, again to mention very few), and to throw bridges between their work and that of more classical social theorists (such as Andrew Sayer and Michael Herzfeld). The interdisciplinarity of the book – it embraces historical studies, social theory, moral economy, critical and cultural geography, anthropology and media studies – may turn out to be an asset, but it has also complicated my theoretical approach. My empirical focus exposes the limitations of the study: tourism based on cinematic representations of place and culture is a phenomenon that has manifested its presence across the world – what with the *Harry Potter* craze of Japanese tourists photographing themselves in front of filmed locations in London, and the notorious *Da Vinci Code* court case that is on its way to generate tourist industries in the UK and Italy. In addition, the question of virtual tourism extends beyond that of cinematic tourism, on which I primarily focus. As artist and bestselling writer Euan Ferguson has intimated in a recent interview, today 'you can Google up, say, "McMurdo Base" and "party", and you'll find someone's posted digital party shots from Antarctica, and you're almost there' (*Observer Magazine* 2006). My attempt to connect cinematic tourism and Internet tourism may be interesting, but is also challenging. The fact that I did not operate within a recognized field certainly did not help, although the lack of disciplinary paradigms secured some intellectual freedom and creativity. As there is no such thing as 'cinematic tourist' studies, I have both the privilege and the terrifying responsibility to be one of the first authors who introduce it into sociology. Better informed work by more experienced academics may establish it in the discipline as an autonomous field.

Acknowledgements

Like films, books have a polyphonic nature, as they are the product of interaction with colleagues, friends, family and significant academic others. I would like to thank Martin O'Brien and Sue Penna for the challenging conversations we have had over the years and the memorable dinners that helped me digest some rather heavy ideas. Their support has been invaluable and cannot be communicated in these pages. Thanks to Bülent Diken for the symbolic smack in the head when I was seduced by pluralism. I am grateful to John Urry for his support in these early and difficult years of my career. I am also indebted to Michael Herzfeld; his intellectual influence has been formative. Thanks to Anna, David, Sandy and Jill for being so patient when I could not contain my intellectual excitement. I am grateful to my mother and father for believing in me when I did not believe in myself. Majid, thank you for all the love, moral support and intellectual engagement; *Ich bin Ich, wen Ich Du bin.*

An earlier version of Chapter 2, entitled 'Reel western fantasies: portrait of a tourist imagination in *The Beach* (2000)' appeared in *Mobilities*, 1(1), 2006. Chapter 3 was published in *Tourist Studies*, 4(1), 2004 under the title 'Constructing the cinematic tourist: the sign industry of *The Lord of the Rings*', but here some revisions were introduced and additions made. Chapter 4 is based on two articles that were published in *The Journal of Consumer Culture* ('"Casting" the Neohellenic Other: tourism, the culture industry and contemporary orientalism in *Captain Corelli's Mandolin*', (2001, 2003, 3(2)) and *Studi Culturali* (Orient(alizz)ando l'"Italia": identità italiana e industria culturale ne "Il mandolino del Capitano Corelli"', 2004, 1(1)). Ideas have been reworked and revised, however, and a whole new section was added to the chapter.

The copyright for film stills 2.1, 2.2 and 2.3 belongs to 20th Century Fox Film Corporation and reproduction was made possible via *Photofest*;

copyright permission was granted by New Line Cinema for film stills 3.1 and 3.2, and by Universal Pictures for stills 4.1, 4.2 and 4.3. Permission to reproduce them was made possible via *Photofest*. Copyright holder for image stills 5.1 and 5.2 is Lions Gate Inc., photographer Barry Wetcher, but permission was granted via *Photofest*.

1 The world of signs

Production as consumption/ consumption as production

Film and tourism

The Colosseum rests at the heart of collective European memory as a site associated with the greatness of Roman antiquity. Its international fame has compelled travellers equipped with travel guides and historical treatises to visit the monument and modern tourists to immortalize it with their cameras. At the turn of the new millennium a crisis began to brew amongst its glorified ruins: when the Italian state was repeatedly criticized for not providing the basic tourist facilities for its visitors – such as cafés, fast ticketing arrangements and museum options – the culture minister Giuliano Urbani supported its privatization (*Daily Telegraph* 2001). It seems however that the pledge to modernize the country's heritage industry has also been embraced by other Italian entrepreneurs, who have decided to exploit the monument's tourist potential in other ways. These are the modern 'gladiators' of Rome, who pose outside the Colosseum for tourists in their shiny costumes with baroque swords and other accessories from the realm of kitsch souvenir fantasy. The business of these 'warriors' picked up after the global success of *Gladiator* (2000), a Hollywood blockbuster directed by Ridley Scott and starring Russell Crowe as the gladiatorial hero who defeats the evil emperor Commodus (Joaquin Phoenix). Legions of tourists, who would normally spend time roaming the archaeological site and its museums, started visiting the monument just to be photographed with such colourful characters and take home evidence of their Roman experience.

Unfortunately, this enterprise acquired the infamy of an 'Italian job' when the costumed men were faced with numerous tourist allegations that they charge exorbitant prices for their services. The final blow was dealt when waves of complaints made their way into the press. Tourists reported that the gladiators' uniforms were cheap, their helmets plastic and 'they're not exactly Russell Crowe' (*BBC News* 2002a). As the saying goes, the customer is always right and it is fair to expect good value for money – as long as demands do not turn into an occupational hazard. Inevitably, accusations of shabbiness and lack of authenticity put immense pressure on these Italian men, forcing them to take extreme measures to respond to the challenge. In March 2002 the police arrested a gladiator who carried a real sword to look 'more authentic' to foreign crowds; traffic wardens repeatedly drove his colleagues off their patch to protect Rome's visitors from extortion; and, eventually, the city of Rome coerced these new businessmen to form a professional association and adopt a proper dress code that would appeal to their customers' tastes. Through these measures the authorities wanted to respond to comments that stereotyped the gladiators as 'just a group of men hanging around smoking', even if 'at a first glance [they] are very nice' (*ibid.*). This organized attack resulted in street conflicts, 'with tearful centurions claiming that they have families to feed' (*Daily Telegraph* 2003) and protesting that they have no money to buy fancy costumes for the benefit of foreigners. Such despair hardly fits the macho image of Crowe killing imperial villains.

The temptation to follow the gladiatorial episodes that ensued is great, but this would divert our attention from more important observations. These are: the tourists' urgency to secure the efficient performance of an act that reproduces a cinematic narrative which was never true to the historical record; the mobilization of the narrative by local entrepreneurs for economic reasons; the authorities' intervention in the controversy in order to regulate the provision of tourist services; and the city's overwhelming concern about the Italian cultural image abroad. To these obvious issues one could add some less obvious ones: what happened to those film viewers who never visited the Colosseum? How and what did they enjoy from the film? Did their desire to visit Rome lead them to learn more about its history? This book embarks on an investigation of these themes, exploring the impact that cinematic representations of place and culture have on the formation of the virtual tourist experience; the interplay between virtual and corporeal tourism following an exposure of audiences to cinematic representational apparatuses; the connections between cinematic production and the establishment of tourist industries on filmed locations; and the types of response that this phenomenon induces in host countries.

The title of the book encapsulates these themes, albeit in a rather condensed way. 'Cinematic tourism' and the 'cinematic tourist' are not uniform conceptual tools, but theoretical models internally differentiated by the moves and motions of travel through and after film, as well as the cinematic production of travel and tourism. To invoke Barthes (1993), the cinematic tourist is a Hollywood myth, a construct that emerges out of a decontextualization of the actual touring experience. The Hollywood model of the tourist exists within cinematic texts, in the movies that we watch: it suggests ways of consuming places, enjoying and 'investing in' (for educational purposes) our holiday time. At the same time, touring through cinematic images produces a second type of tourist who uses the power of imagination to explore the world. This version of the tourist corresponds to the movie viewer, who 'reads' and consumes film. The surplus meaning of a film enables audiences to travel virtually, to experience the filmed locations at a distance: thus the impulse to visit these locations originates in the imaginary journey on the screen. A third version of the 'cinematic tourist' is created when a tourist industry is established in filmed locations, through the products that tourist industries offer when they exploit the film's potential to induce tourism. There is also a fourth type of cinematic tourist that completes the imagined journey of movie watchers. This is the tourist in the flesh, who visits places because they appeared in films, and whose experience of travel may be influenced by film and the attractions that the tourist industry has to offer. The interdependency of these types is not fixed: filmed locations are also visited by tourists who never watched movies and watching a movie will not necessarily result in visiting the filmed place. However, the bonds between these types of touring and the tourist are unmistakable and command analysis.

Tourism and the media: an overview

Tourism is an established subject area in the disciplines of sociology and anthropology, with research stretching back to the 1960s and 1970s or even earlier (see for example Norval 1936). Theoretically, scholars concentrated on the nature of tourism as a quintessentially modern phenomenon (MacCannell 1973), discussing tourist (Cohen 1974, 1979; Leiper 1979; Gottlieb 1982; Pearce 1982) and tourism (Boorstin 1962; Graburn 1977; Nash 1981) typologies, the relationship between hosts and tourists (MacCannell 1973; Hiller 1976; Pearce 1980) and the structure and cultural impact of tourism as a socioeconomic system (Greenwood 1977; Nash 1977). A synthesis and critical evaluation of some of these early perspectives that transformed the subject area has been John Urry's (1990) book *The Tourist Gaze*. Drawing on Foucault's concept of the gaze, Urry maintains that there are systematic ways of 'seeing' tourist destinations, which have roots in Western occulocentric practices, central to debates that envelop modernity. Urry already acknowledges the role visual culture has in the construction of the tourist experience and tourism as an organized system of leisure, a conviction that he carries forward in his more recent research (Urry 1995, 2000). It is precisely the centrality of the visual that this book aspires to analyse from a cinematic perspective.

The literature on cinematic tourism is surprisingly thin, given the growing importance of the phenomenon in the construction of the tourist experience and the representation of identity and culture. An interesting contextual analysis is provided by Fruehling Springwood (2002), who has argued that cinematic and televisual culture has equipped Japanese tourists with preconceptions of 'America' and a desire to visit specific locations. Fruehling Springwood stresses that the process of signification is culturally embedded and that it takes place prior to visiting the filmed location. An edited volume by Crouch, Jackson and Thompson (2005), with contributions from both media and tourist studies, places more emphasis on the role of imagination in tourism. In the introduction to the book the editors stress that 'the media are heavily involved in promoting an emotional disposition, coupled with imaginative and cognitive activity' (Crouch, Jackson and Thompson 2005: 1) that carries the potential to be converted into actual tourism. However, they also argue against conflating the mediation of tourism through television, newspaper and film images with the actual tourist experience, stressing that the former retains a utopian unboundedness that may be challenged by actual tourism, resulting in 'acute consumer dissatisfaction' (*ibid.*: 5). This argument has various ramifications, but here I wish to concentrate on two important ones (included in the volume) that I have integrated in my analysis. The first is developed by Fish (2005), who maintains that the process of 'viewing' is constituted by media producers through notions of touring. Televised images reflect tourism because they operate as escapist techniques, although their reception is not fixed. Fish implies that media producers generate ideal types of viewers, a notion which corresponds to the first type of cinematic tourist of my analysis.

The second dimension of the argument that I want to present comes from Edensor's (2005) research. Edensor focuses on the Hollywood blockbuster *Braveheart* to debate the ways media representations of history can affect understandings of national heritage. For Edensor film has an active role in the social construction of place and culture, not simply its marketization for tourists. Cinematic narratives are inscribed in historical landscapes, but the ways they are appropriated or contested by visitors/tourists may differ. The theme of manipulative creation of cinematic narratives also concerns Parsons (2000) who argues that aesthetic media images are able to manipulate myths of national identity powerfully, but can also create new forms of popular identity. Like Edensor, she maintains that such representations of culture can be consumed by visitors at the destination. Edensor and Parsons highlight the shift from the first to the second, third and then fourth version of the cinematic tourist: from the film's ideal viewer to the real viewer and then the actual tourist. Other relevant studies do not stay within the ambit of 'cinematic tourism' as defined above, but explore more general connections between visual culture and tourism. For example, an edited volume by Crouch and Lübbren (2003) debates both how images inform tourist practices, form referential networks within them but are also constructed from actual tourist experience. The role of bodily presence, of 'corporeal bonding' with the new environment, is crucial in this experience (see also Crouch *et al.* 2001: 260–1). To make this observation applicable to the cinematic tourist thesis I want to suggest that film and tourism form a dynamic relationship of interaction which often has unpredictable outcomes. Unfortunately, little room is spared for an exploration of the actual tourist experience of filmed locations in this book; a few reflections are provided in Chapters 3 and 4.

Analytical differentiations of actual and virtual tourisms may be useful, but they bear the potential to obscure other important questions about the tourist experience as such. Following the trail of colonial studies, Strain (2003) identifies in tourism a romantic pursuit for authenticity that divorces the encounter with 'other' cultures from its political context. According to Strain, visual technologies have always been at the heart of these romantic pursuits, from the nascent steps of anthropology to the present endeavours of Internet, 'virtual' tourists. Cinematic technologies and the 'travel mystique' share *'the illusion of demediating mediation'* (2003: 3; emphasis in the text), the idea that certain types of experience have the power to erase the mediation of reality altogether. Travel to foreign lands is replete with demediating mediation, as it allegedly involves contact with unspoiled otherness, 'a cleansing process that renews perception' (2003: 3). Although she traces parts of her argument back to various classical anthropological and sociological studies of tourism, she concentrates mainly on the work of MacCannell (1989), who identifies in travel a search for authenticity stripped of the marketing discourse of tourism. Strain's understanding of film viewing as demediating mediation is based on the medium's power to manufacture a version of authenticity while simultaneously blocking and filtering the mechanisms of exoticization employed in the construction of cinematic imagery and narrative. Film has, in short, the power to simulate authenticity while denying that it engages in simulation (Strain 2003: 18–20). This enables the viewer to engage fully with image and narrative like a traveller who deludes themself that they have reached the core of 'other' cultural realities when they have, in fact, simply hit upon the wall of yet another representation. I agree with Strain that the demediation of representation is inherent in the cinematic experience, and I maintain that it can be marketed or sought after (by virtual or actual travellers) as 'the real experience'.

Interesting though they are, these works do not have much to say about the communities or nations used in destination images and narratives. The centre of attention is the viewer, the tourist or consumer or alternatively the producer, rather than the 'consumed' host. I would like to discuss a different approach that integrates community responses to the general picture of tourist production and consumption. This comes from *Film-Induced Tourism* (2005), the only existing study of tourist development through film by Beeton. For Beeton, film-induced tourism includes 'visitation to sites where movies and TV programs have been filmed as well as to tours to production studios, including film-related theme parks' (Beeton 2005: 11). This definition is rather broad for the purposes of the present study, but does not deviate from Strain's basic argument. Beeton recognizes the roots of contemporary tourism in the eighteenth-century Romantic movement that promoted the picturesque, idealized versions of landscape for consumer gratification. Drawing on Seaton (1998), she sees the picturesque as the predecessor of the 'tourist gaze' that idealizes nature and otherness (peasantry, noble savagery) (Beeton 2005: 5–8), a point I will reiterate in some case studies of this book. According to Beeton, contemporary media representations of place share this idealization with eighteenth century literary creations and can induce the desire to visit places and cultures. To support this thesis she has recourse to MacCannell's (1989) argument that mediated versions of tourist locations generate 'markers' of places in the form of images. Film has precisely this function: it ascribes meaning to locations through imaging, making them desirable destinations.

Beeton is concerned about the impact that tourism can have on a location and its environs. 'Tourism carries with it the seeds of its own destruction' (Beeton 2005: 12) because it can lead to environmental destruction and community disintegration. Debating the problem from a destination-marketing point of view, Beeton argues for organized sustainable development strategies. Her commitment to this community development project is admirable. Although her methodology draws upon other disciplines, mainly psychology and market studies, it also incorporates Marxist sociological and anthropological approaches to tourism, largely forgotten in contemporary research that celebrates consumerism but brushes aside its pitfalls. My approach in this book differs on one point from Beeton's: I am concerned less with the economic and more with the cultural impact of cinematic tourism (or their relationship), especially the consequences of host–guest interaction for local and national identities. But before I discuss the politics of this interaction, it is necessary to be clear about the minutiae of relations between Hollywood film and tourist industries.

The 'sign industry': from film to tourism (and back again)

The terms 'film' and 'tourist industries' take us back to the radical critique of mass consumption pioneered in the 1930s and the 1940s by a number of Frankfurt School theorists, among them Theodor Adorno (1991) and Max Horkheimer (Adorno and Horkheimer 1993). In an era of European totalitarian politics, the rise of mass media in democratic countries such as the USA was regarded as a demagogic tool that might divert collective consciousness from sociopolitical problems. Consequently popular culture – music, film, magazines – was viewed by Frankfurt School theorists as a force that could destroy the potential for a social revolution. Especially in the light of an increasing success of Hollywood musicals, Adorno and Horkheimer expressed the fear that the recipients of cinematic messages could become consumers in *abstracto* – that is, consumers who have lost their particularity and become interchangeable and quantifiable. As Kellner (1989) recently clarified, according to Adorno and Horkheimer's version of critical theory, this reification can be detected in capitalist societies in general. Quantifiability, interchangeability and abstraction may also point to what Marx described as a shift from use value (value as such, exemplified in the use of things) to the exchange value (value acquired in and through the act of exchange) in capitalist systems. This shift applies both to the consumers themselves and the products that they consume.

Compelling though this sociological model may be, it tends to underestimate the complexity of production, because it considers the manufacturers of cultural goods mere participants in a conspiracy against collective consciousness. But as Hesmondhalgh (2002: 4–6, 232) has explained, the manufacturers of cultural goods in global industries are involved in a creative manipulation of symbols to such an extent that they should be considered agents of sociocultural change. Creative manufacturers often derive non-economic satisfaction from their involvement in production processes, even though they remain dependent on basic economic planning (e.g. advertising of products) (Caves 2000: 2–4). The relationship between creative arts and commerce seems to have become closer as sectors within creative industries that were not commercial in the past (e.g. performing arts, broadcasting) have become commercial. For some scholars, most modern economies are consumption-based, and 'social technologies that manage consumption derive from the social and creative disciplines' (Cunningham 2005: 293). Pushing this argument further, Castells (1996) and Lash and Urry (1994) inform us that symbolic creativity permeates contemporary socioeconomic life, as more industries fashion themselves on the cultural model. This invites us to examine the social relations (see also Urry 1995: 129) of creativity, that is, the ways in which cinematic images of tourism are produced by Hollywood companies *and* exploited by tourist providers. There is an implicit interplay of artistic creation and market production that cannot be ignored, because it is central to the innovative aspects of commodification (Hartley 2005: 5–6; Miège 1987). These reflections point in one direction: production modes have their *own culture* (Zelizer 1983, 1988: 618) that needs to be understood before it is condemned.

The modes of contemporary production must correspond, or respond, to those of consumption. To coordinate the analysis of film and tourist industries we must, therefore, question exactly *what* film viewers and potential tourists consume. In films and film-induced tourist practices potential tourists never seem to consume *specific* objects, but clusters of signs: they are tempted to buy holidays to filmed spots because of their Hollywood aura; they are invited to relive the film through tours 'on location'; and they are enticed to buy souvenirs that refer to the mythical figures of the cinematic plot. Tourist production is made possible through film consumption only because film produces meaning in the first place (Ateljevic 2000: 381), but these cinematic messages do not develop in a sociocultural void: they comprise representations of existing consumer experiences that circulate in the realm of contemporary culture. It may be more correct to argue that mythical (Rojek 2000: 54; Shields 1991), socially constructed images and experiences of place and culture are not *directly* the product of tourist industries, but are over-determined by a variety of 'non-tourist practices, such as film, TV, literature, magazines' (Urry 1990: 3; see also Taylor 2001) and other consumption objects and processes. The interconnectedness of all these different phases and sectors of the culture industries confirms that tourism begins with cultural 'signification' (Culler 1988; MacCannell 1989; Urry 1990: 12; Lash and Urry 1994; Wang 2000).

This demands a re-evaluation of the analytical distinction between the film and tourist industries, as they both participate in the circulation of what Jean Baudrillard (1973) has termed symbolic 'sign values'. Debating the postmodern condition, Baudrillard observed that the relationship between the sign and the signified has loosened so much that all textual and visual meanings became arbitrary. The absence of a stable relationship between signifier and signified leaves the sign vulnerable to what Best and Kellner have called 'manipulation in coded differences and associative chains' (1997: 99). This manipulation refers both to producers and consumers, with grave consequences relating to the destruction, decon-struction and creation of social realities. Baudrillard is very pessimistic when it comes to these consequences, arguing that since images and representations simply succeed each other in arbitrary ways, we can talk about the 'death of the real' (Baudrillard 1983: 53) and the rise of a society that lives through simulations. His theory radicalized the analysis of the impact that the mass media have on the construction of reality, and questioned the ways in which 'dominant codes' of meaning rise and fall in Western liberal societies (Baudillard 1991; Porter 1993: 2). His approach clearly transcends the classical Marxist distinction between production and consumption (see Lash and Urry 1994: 123) on which Adorno and Horkheimer based their thesis, as the two modes become interchangeable in what I will term *global sign industries*. The term is pertinent for many reasons: first, because it does not deviate from the classical argument that we do deal with *industries* that trade in images and ideas, the intangible aspects of culture; second, these industries are *global*, because they thrive on their economic and political interconnections – a point to which I return below; finally, they are *sign* industries, because they generate, manipulate and market cultural signs. Central to the operative forces of these industries is a game of endless hermeneutics: by filmmakers (of novels on which films are based), by audiences (of films) and by holiday providers (of audiences' film readings). Even tourists engage during their holidays in the collection and appropriation of signs (Urry 1990: 12) that sometimes originate in films. Hermeneutics itself *is a mode of both consumption and production*, which constantly enriches the signifying systems of our late modern world – our contemporary cultures, in other words.

I would like to drop the singular ('industry') of the Frankfurt School approach in favour of an argument that considers the diversity of production modes: first of all, there are numerous possibilities for different cultural industries to establish strategic alliances. This book looks at perhaps one of the most pronounced cases, but invites similar research into other possible combinations. The singular is inappropriate also because a variety of cultural determinants shape the marketization of cultural products. Unfortunately, this is not always a saving grace, as powerful media conglomerates simply have more transnational power than small media firms. Hollywood and its production companies have spread their control globally by absorbing smaller companies who had less capital to finance expensive cinematic enterprises. This is not to argue that Hollywood has not been challenged by other emerging media industries. As the case of Israeli television attests, the Americanization of the media is a knife with sharp blades for both the transmitting and receiving ends of globalization. In a compelling monograph on this issue, Liebes (2003: 190) explains that although Israel's television system has embraced American technologies, genres, advertising styles and organizational modes wholeheartedly, it has simultaneously subjected all these to domestic economic and political interests. In addition to their home viewers, Bollywood films have acquired millions of fans abroad, both from expatriate Indian communities and from Western audiences. Hong Kong cinema is also spreading its influence globally (Logan 1995), invading foreign markets that were traditionally controlled by Hollywood.

This book's case studies will not discuss these emerging rivals. The reasons for this are not solely those of scholarly coherence. Hollywood rather than Bollywood or Hong Kong cinema appears as the shadowy manipulator of some travel agencies on the web. Hollywood's involvement in the provision of tourist services is irrefutable, and as the present study draws upon film viewers who review movies, book holidays and travel online, it is important to retain it as a focus. I do not argue here that such cooperation of Hollywood and tourist agencies amounts to a merging of different industries, because their relationship is regulated by contingent interests (Beeton 2005: 9). Even within film industries power and control over the production and successful marketing of a film are subject to factors that are not always predictable. Cinema corporations are always competing to secure the emotional investment of their viewers by involving film directors and other Hollywood agents in online discussions with fans (see also Ryan 1992). These actors will proceed to plan their policy independently from emerging tourist industries, although such policies may in fact benefit the latter. Convergence of interests can be 'crafted' to secure interdependencies (Castells 1996: 151–68) that will reduce risk of failure, or manage to 'silence' critical voices from without (Garnham 1990: 160–2; Hirsch 1990). The rationale of the global sign industries model refers more to the modus vivendi of the cultural industries, not the way they operate in practice.

The single 'culture industry' vision is dystopian also because it does not take into account the responses that those who are addressed *in* or *by* the signs may develop. To put it succinctly, it tends to dismiss the role of consumers as what Willis (1990) has termed 'symbol creators' of an entire universe of ideas and practices. In the case of the consumption of tourist images and ideas, it assumes that cultural 'texts' (in the form of movies, posters, internet images of tourist destinations) are prescribed from above. There is an element of truth in this argument, but when we move to reception questions we note a multiplicity of textual readings that may or may not coincide with those of the originary message creators (Abercrombie and Longhurst 1998; Golding and Murdock 2000; Dunn 2005). As Mayhne puts it 'it is one thing to assume that cinema is determined in ideological ways . . . that is, that various institutions of the cinema *do* project an ideal viewer, and another thing to assume that those projections *work*' (Mayhne 1995: 159, emphasis in the text). On most occasions it is impossible to bridge the gap between ideal and real viewers because films as 'social texts' (Turner 1999), representations and negotiations of the social world, are not uniform. Most cinematic narratives tend to incorporate contradictory and conflicting social visions, suggesting to viewers both reaction and conformism. To follow Ryan and Kellner's analysis of Hollywood production, even the most ideological films carry within their narratives 'potentially progressive undercurrents in American society by delineating . . . the salient fears, desires, and needs that make up the everyday fabric of American culture' (1990: 2).

More celebratory tones of a pluralist tradition that empowers the consumer would cover up the pitfalls of production relations and ought to be treated with as much caution as the single-industry model. It has been argued that in its extreme form the pluralist argument tends to adapt for academic purposes the free market logic of neo-liberalism: if, indeed, there are no 'core' cultural meanings, only 'signs' that can be interpreted in multiple ways, then it is easy for someone with enough power to construct a whole economic empire on an attractive collection of them (see McGuigan 1992; Gitlin 1998). The cultural studies literature around the 1990s, which found its apotheosis in Fiske's (1989) and Jenkins' (1992) analysis of the hermeneutic power that audiences possess, further obscured the question. Though admirable for its rich empirical research and theoretically original understanding of fan reception, it tended to conflate political activism with the 'hermeneutic unpredictability' (Murray 2004: 12) of television and cinematic fans. As Hill (2002) has clarified, fan cultures are inherently both anti-commercial in their pursuits and interests and commodity-oriented in their nature: one cannot join them without partaking in consumption, even if they end up contesting and challenging its restrictive modes. A distinction between fan creativity and political resistance points to a series of processes that exist independently from consumer sign-reading, and compels us to address issues of exploitation and inequality, largely abandoned in media

studies. Whereas it is important for this book to consider risk management in the global sign industries or the process of sign reading
by movie fans, Internet users and tourists, a few questions loom large:
who is affected by this process? Who hosts all these potential 'guests'
on-location? How does the local encounter with demanding consumers,
who arrive at the filmed place with certain preconceptions in their mind,
develop? What happens to screened indigenous cultures during such
encounters? These questions demand a serious engagement with concerns
that inform studies in the sociology of globalization, developmental
anthropology and moral economy.

The premises of these concerns originate in the fact that media representations do, after all, affect internal perceptions of culture. I understand
culture as the malleable and porous sets of beliefs, ideas, habits and
customs that define and order our everyday life (Williams 1958). Such
beliefs and ideas are communicated in codified ways, through signs and
symbols (Geertz 1973), and define the social order. I do not argue that
cultures exist or develop in isolation from the rest of the world. This
solipsistic approach, favoured by early work on tourist–host encounters
(see for example MacCannell 1973; Chhabra, Healy and Sills 2003)
assumes that culture is a coherent and stable system that exists a priori.
Apocalyptic theses would have it that in the era of globalization, the
collapse of national boundaries and the interpenetration of the local
by the global, identities and cultures become vulnerable and fragile
(Arnould and Price 1993: 304; Ritzer 1996). As the argument goes, the
more media conglomerates cast their shadow globally, the more likely it
becomes that the palettes of locality will be eclipsed. Other scholars,
avoiding this deterministic tone and the ethical questions it raises, explain
that the global dissemination of cultural images through the media and
in tourist business can be viewed simply as the erasure of specificities out
of their context (Tomlinson 1999). More cautiously, anthropologists and
sociologists point out that global flows generate their own resistance
mechanisms that protect cultures and identities (Foster 1991: 236; see
also Ray 2002: 5.2, 5.4). The literature on globalization is vast, but it
converges upon one issue: the future of cultural specificity.

Synthesizing from these arguments, this book constructs its own
polemics, accepting that media production and distribution have always
been resting at the heart of the culture and identity-making projects.
More than a decade ago Anderson (1991) spoke of print-capitalism as
the vehicle for ideas that gave birth to national identity, arguing that
collective imaginations are regulated by universalized (mediated)
messages of culture. In the dawn of the twenty-first century these images
and messages are not addressed only to the 'nation', or created exclusively

by its elites. The construction of popular versions of national or ethnic cultures by the media enables localities and nation-states to 'meet the world' and escape the cage of a not always happy isolation. This 'banalization' (Billig 1995) of culture, the interaction of self-imaging and external representations, triggers processes that change the face of nations and localities in unpredictable ways (Held 2000: 1–3). To reconsider Strain (2003), nations can also be caught in a process of demediating mediation, which may convince them to accept cinematic simulations of 'their indigenous monoculture' as real. To put it bluntly, externally constructed representations of a culture can attain an objective status. Often, the use of indigenous specificity by global sign industries as a valuable commodity puts massive pressure on the hosts to perform for foreigners (Nash 1977; Williams and Shaw 1998). Subsequently, it may lead to a projection of stereotypical versions of identity and the marketization of authenticity 'by the pound' (Greenwood 1977). Cultural marketization is often welcome, because it bolsters local economies and creates the preconditions for the generation of more local jobs (Leadbeater and Oakley 2005: 301), but the beneficial or damaging results of this enterprise cannot be assessed *in abstracto*, only in relation to the structural environments in which cultures live: the position they occupy in collective imaginations outside their cradle, the nation-state that hosts them and the historical and economic relationship of this state with the globe.

This is a thorny issue indeed, given that some of the book's case studies take us to less developed corners of the world. My research spans four continents (Asia, Australasia, Europe and America) and countries (Thailand, New Zealand, Greece and Cuba). Each of them has a different socio-historical and political experience that conditions responses to outside intervention, whether this be from Hollywood, tourism capitalists, or even the state. The geographic or political marginality of these countries, their peripheral role in the world economy and their colonial pasts place them in a subsidiary position when it comes to the articulation of the national or local voices that object to developmental projects originating in the economic centres of the developed West. The nature of cultural resistance to global hegemonies is narrated in the following chapters like a Hollywood story that, nevertheless, does not always have a happy ending for its hidden local heroes. Each case study will shed light on cultural specificity and national economic conditions before unveiling the theoretical universalities of resistance. Problems of structural and infrastructural development can affect the tourist sector *and* labour conditions, as often tourism in these places is 'highjacked' by foreign travel agencies, airlines and other companies that are more ready to respond to increasing tourist demands (de Kadt 1979; Shaw and Williams 2004: 44). Rapid tourist expansion calls for makeshift solutions that involve the growth of informal markets, support poor payment, and introduce or exacerbate community rivalries and competition (see Agarwal *et al*. 2000). Globally famous images of tourist destinations may be treated locally and nationally as sources of cultural capital, and opportunities for economic capital accumulation (Britton 1991), but they may also be exorcised as foreign demons that transgress the intimate space of the nation (Herzfeld 1997). The coexistence of positive and negative, or often ambivalent and indecisive, responses to the sign industries and their consumers deserves meticulous analysis. It is important, then, to look at this group of anonymous actors who clearly comprise a necessary component in the production/ consumption cycle: the cinematic tourists themselves.

The cinematic tourist

The historical origins of tourism are usually traced back to the eighteenth-century grand tour, a succession of visits to countries such as Italy, Greece, the Ottoman Empire or even the Holy Lands. Gourgouris (1996) recognized a pedagogical impetus in the peculiar habit of upper middle class and aristocratic families of subsidizing their son's adventures in unknown places. The tour familiarized young travellers with the great civilizations of the past, such as Athens and Rome (Towner 1985), and brought them in contact with foreign customs and people (Hibbert 1969; Cohen 1996: 102). The didactic element could also operate as a performative act, communicated to future audiences through travel writing. Gourgouris' analysis is interesting, but the motivation and rituals of the grand tourists were much more diverse than he suggests. Some of these travellers were indeed young students of aristocratic parentage who wanted to broaden their intellectual horizons, or artists looking for inspiration in remote countries, but others were established diplomats on political missions that propelled them to produce lengthy accounts of their experiences and observations. Work, education and leisure were coexisting modes and motivations for travel, all equally important in the history of the grand tour. Urry (1996: 120) saw in this blending of work and leisure activities the beginning of an increasing rationalization of travel that provided the modern tourist system of leisure with a *raison d'être*.

According to Urry (1990), the visual experience of touring, 'gazing upon' other cultures and environments, is a quintessentially modern act that both celebrates and domesticates otherness. Photographing, or even recording cultures and environments can be regarded as a way of disciplining otherness and producing authoritative knowledge about it (Foucault 1979). The production of such knowledge was encapsulated in the performative act of writing about one's experiences and communicating them to a readership at home. Travel book narratives became thus 'spatial trajectories' (de Certeau 1988b: 115) that clearly 'mapped' and arranged locations in imagined registers. This domestication of travel destinations was furthered by Thomas Cook's large-scale tours in the nineteenth century that offered the first organized type of travel for leisure rather than work (Urry 2000: 180). Even Cook operated within a Foucauldian knowledge regime of travel writing. Most of his tours survived in printed forms and became as popular as the numerous travel books of the era. Readerships were allowed to move, or choose, between imagined and corporeal modes of travel. Taking into account the limitations imposed on travel readers by class – working classes could not afford the grand tour – or gender – travel was not a socially acceptable type of leisure for women for a long time – we can see how print-capitalism gave birth to the modern virtual tourist. This tourist moves in the symbolic space of textual narrative, filters adventure through other people's travel exploits, and revels in mediated acquisition of knowledge about 'other civilizations'.

The nature of contemporary virtual tourism underlies the problematic of this study. Virtual tourism through old (travel book) and new (film, the Internet) media inculcates in the modern subject a much-needed utopian aspiration to become an actual tourist. The activity of contemporary tourism itself is 'an imaginative process which involves a certain comprehension of the world and enthuses a distinctive emotional engagement with it' (Crouch, Jackson and Thompson 2005: 1). This is already present in virtual tourism through film. As de Certeau has explained, voyages simultaneously 'create and destroy the paths they take. Or, more exactly, they take their own course, but wish to lose the landscape and the way. Mysticism operates as a process whereby the objects of meaning vanish' (De Certeau 1986: 37). The tourist imagination is always-already structured through ideal images of place that transcend, and often define, tourist destinations. If place and culture are mythical constructs (Rojek 2000) then virtual tourists themselves can assume the *situational role* of tourists. Since their identity as tourists can always be deferred, it is the promise of the journey to represented locations that enables them to enjoy the film. Their symbolic move from the world of the cinema to that of the Internet, where they can 'travel' without the constraints of time, space or money, replaces the actual mode of travelling only temporarily.

I have already pointed out that the concept of cinematic tourism encapsulates the move from film viewing to actual tourism. Using this generic term can be confusing, and further terminological elaboration needs to be introduced here. I will term the cinematic viewers who surf the web for virtual consumption of potential tourist destinations (the ethnographic material of the book) *virtual flâneurs*. My association of tourism with flâneurie follows Dann's recent observation that over the decades, tourism has been likened to a number of other social phenomena such as pilgrimage, sightseeing and performance (Dann 2002: 7). More meaningful metaphors are necessary, because they facilitate reconceptualizations of such an important phenomenon. Walter Benjamin's (2002) flâneur is the person who roamed the crowded city observing at a distance, yet Benjamin also saw in the flâneur the 'soul' of the mass; for him, the crowd lives though the flâneur's creativity, words and imagination (Benjamin 2002: 420). Unlike Benjamin's type, the fast mode in which virtual flâneurs engage with the world is not regulated by mere observation at a slow pace, but by the speed of their computer. The nanoseconds of transfer from one location to another ensure a 'digital' space–time compression (Lash and Urry 1994), which enables them to stay at the heart of global developments while retaining territorial distance and anonymity (Germann Molz 2004: 171). This does not prevent virtual flâneurs from dreaming, imagining and desiring the objects that films and tourist websites market. We can liken the 'arcades' of the Internet and Hollywood to the phantasmagoria of capitalism: both commodify fantasies – in the form of a desired travel, experiential authenticity and self-accomplishment (see also Rojek 2000: 58).

The passage from film to the Internet enables virtual flâneurs to tour the world anonymously but with an all-consuming desire for actual experience. The response to cinematic viewing and Internet surfing is split: on the one hand, it promotes a touring model in which an immaterial self is subjected to a camera obscura 'eye'. This eye communicates an 'objective' truth that exists independently from the observer (Crary 1992: 33). It could be claimed that the cinematic viewer's or the Internet surfer's distant engagement with other cultures (see also Turner 1993: 154) resembles Baudrillard's (1988) driver, who enjoys the American landscape through their car screen. The vast array of images that flick through the driver's eyes construct an experience that substitutes the zapping of television channels. In the hyperreal space, other cultures and landscapes are detached from their original contexts (Eco 1987) and reinvented as objects of the tourist gaze, spectacles that can be consumed or 'disposed of in much the same way as any other consumer object' (Bennett 2005: 38). But even though there are travellers and tourists who upon arrival at a filmed location begin to simulate life 'on the screen', it would be wrong to generalize. It is therefore paramount to examine a second potential response to cinematic viewing and Internet surfing, which reinserts into vision a material, embodied self (Crary 1992: 33–34). The embodied viewer is both a spectator and an actor who can challenge the objectivity of the camera. Virtual flâneurs are hermeneutic agents because they often precede any interpretation of the film's marketing value by local and global tourist providers (Inglis 2000). To be more precise, online viewers may be seen as participants in a new version of the 'public sphere' (Habermas 1989) that is performed, 'staged' with the help of the new media (Thompson 1995). At the same time the commodified objects of Hollywood and the Internet (the tourist destinations) invite virtual flâneurs to depart on an inner journey that will define them as the tourists of tomorrow. Like Benjamin's ideal type, their role is to engage in 'illustrative seeing', to match cinematic images with their own understanding of them (Benjamin 2002: 419) in a game of cultural *bricolage*. The decentralized and mobile gaze that collects and collates ideas 'conducts a flânerie through an imaginary other place and time' (Friedberg 1993, 1995: 67; Williams 1995: 8), by simulating the mobility of tourism. It matches actual with virtual cosmopolitanism, knowledge and experience of otherness with simulation of this experience, turning film viewing and Internet surfing into a project of personal development (Urry 1995: 145). Lash and Urry (1994: 5–6) attribute to virtual flâneurs an increasing 'aesthetic reflexivity', the ability to monitor and evaluate rather than passively accept a predetermined place in the social world. The aesthetic reflexivity of virtual flâneurs resembles the Romantic form of the grand tour(ist) gaze that emphasized privacy, solitude and spiritual growth through an intense engagement with the observed object (Urry 1995: 137).

Even in the case of corporeal tourism, consumers cannot be treated as part of an exploitation apparatus that functions through a gaze fabricated by a culture industry, with no critical attitudes. As MacCannell (2001) has suggested, actual tourists are conscious that what they are offered is fake. Re-examining Urry's 'tourist gaze' (1990), MacCannell does not deny that tourists can be manipulated by the tourist industry for marketing purposes. It is precisely their self-recognition as *manipulated* (and not manipulative) subjects that makes them reconsider what travel agents offer them. This 'second gaze' enables virtual and actual tourists to enjoy their encounter with new places and cultures in ways different from those suggested by tourist markets. Unlike some film studies that see 'the shape of the media [being] determined by its audiences' culturally-shaped desires' (Hesmondhalgh 2002: 83), MacCannell recognizes both the industries' work and the tourists' agency. Risking the accusation that I have turned into the devil's advocate, I would like to outline my main objection to MacCannell's argument. Although the second gaze is usually aware of the fabrication of 'induced' (industry-produced) images of tourist destination (as opposed to the 'organic', first-hand accounts of a place by visitors (see Daye 2005: 14)) the recognition of fabrication does not always guarantee resistance. The case studies of this book shed light on a rather disconcerting pattern of conformism that by no means applies to all viewers.

It would be incorrect to argue that corporeal travelling has been replaced by movie watching and web browsing (Dewailly 1999; Urry 2000). I would also like to avoid futuristic arguments that see virtual travel eliminating tourism, preserving ecologically important sites intact (Pinney 1994). I certainly do not side with theorists who separate the virtual from the real, and by extension overstress the playfulness of identity online (Rheingold 1994; Turkle 1995). Rather, I understand Internet technology as a socially shaped phenomenon (MacKenzie and Wajcman 1985; Webster 1995) that does not unilaterally determine social life but is inserted into existing forms of social interaction to mediate them (Williams 1974). For example, it can be argued that the Internet has the power to erase the boundaries between leisure and work that define contemporary tourism. Internet sites related to tourism or films that represent and advertise tourist destinations can be accessed at work. Undoubtedly, the very act of surfing belongs to the regime of leisure, but this simply reverses the argument that work has always been reflected in leisure activities (Rojek 1995: 4). It is more important to examine how Internet surfing operates as a threshold that leads into the world of actual tourism: exploring the web for more information on a potential destination, reading travelblogs and other web commentary by 'veteran tourists' before visiting a place, or even booking holidays online have become common practices. Over a decade ago Clifford claimed that tourism and television are key institutions in contemporary 'travelling cultures' (1992). Today we could add to these institutions the Internet as the space in which corporeal and virtual mobility cross and interact in manifold ways, providing the global sign industry with new customers.

The mobilization of online reviews as ethnographic material comes with its own ethical and practical baggage. Ethnography as a method of social research traces its origins in anthropological enquiry into other cultures, but in recent decades it has been applied in a wide range of fields, including the media. As a practice, ethnography is open to attacks from the disciples of a positivist tradition that supports the use of 'hard' data and still clings to the myth of objectivity. Web ethnography is exposed to critique for the absence of face-to-face interaction between observer and observed and – given that web ethnographers deal with texts and images – the danger of imposing meaning on the available material (Hine 2000: 43–4). Some of these concerns fall within the ambit of a more general anthropological distrust in ethnographic research as a discursively opaque practice of cultural representation (Clifford and Marcus 1986). Indeed one of the main problems I faced in my web analysis was the lack of immediate interaction with the groups of Internet users. This physical distance is responsible for a paradox: on the one hand, it gave me the opportunity to observe web group discussions, while avoiding my demarcation as a 'stranger' in the community. As a user of the main websites I draw upon in this book, I achieved a combination of self-effacement and participant observation. On the other hand distance and anonymity valorized my status as an author, raising a number of questions regarding the finished product of my research (but see also Van Maanen 1988: 7–10).

My review pools are the two biggest and most popular online film databases, the Internet Movie Database (IMDB) and Amazon.com. IMDB is the global online market for films and television programmes, whereas Amazon.com is a virtual market that trades in a variety of media, including books, films, music and much more – an exemplary result of global sign trading. Both sites are consumption domains with their own customer review facilities. Their customer reviewing domains strategically create the preconditions for the establishment of 'active trust' (Giddens 1994) in virtual environments that are often regarded by users as unsafe when it comes to regular economic and social transactions. The reviewing process itself makes the customers feel that their opinion is valued. Review domains can also generate virtual communities of consumption (Kozinets 1999; Hill 2002) that exist more as 'a complex of ideas and sentiments' (Calhoun 1980: 107) than structured and fixed entities. These communities interact in neotribal ways (Maffesoli 1996) because their members do not comply with the social conventions of familiarity and tight solidarity; on the contrary, they favour the commonality of ephemeral interests (e.g. liking or disliking the same film or actor). Therefore virtual communities can be understood not as 'a *thing* [but] a process' (Fernback 1999: 217), as they emerge out of contingencies and mediated interaction.

Not all these developments are new. Global telecommunication systems such as the Internet may deterritorialize socialization, but they also reinforce established patterns of exchange for fans. Virtual worlds should not be located solely 'in some enclosed cyberspace: they exist in human culture, knowledge, and values as well' (Kellogg, Carroll and Richards 1991: 430). As in the case of other fan cultures, interaction in the virtual consumption domains I use assumes a textual nature: chat and message lines, available on IMDB and Amazon.com, are the primary media of communication. Texts are often reproduced within the community and acquire a life and authority of their own. Henry Jenkins has explained that fan reading is 'a social process through which individual interpretations are shaped and reinforced with other readers . . . [expanding] the experience of the text beyond its initial consumption' (1992: 45). Some film viewers are anxious to conform to popular readings of the film (Brooker 2003: 207) and simply buttress discursive tropes on it. Others assume the voice of the critic who shapes collective opinion, and tend to produce deliberately provocative analyses to that end (Hill 2002: 41–2). As Nancy Baym (2000) has suggested, the presentation of a coherent identity online involves both manifestations of commonality through identification with others, and claims over uniqueness of opinion through dissociation with the wider community. The poetics of authorship are very complex, given that fan texts are 'polyvocal' rather than 'univocal' (Geertz 1986: 13–15). Moreover, we cannot know if the review itself is the outcome of more than one viewing of the film or an impressionistic account of the story written on a Saturday night after an evening at the cinema. Perceptions and readings of a film change over time, and are shaped by a variety of external factors – reviews by critics, magazine and newspaper articles – often unknown to the researcher. Lest I claim that I will provide an accurate picture of fandom, I will state in advance that I deal with fragments of the whole viewing and reception experience.

The absence of a coherent ethical framework for web ethnography makes Internet research a controversial enterprise, and I decided to follow some guidelines set by conventional fieldwork (Mann and Stewart 2000: 42–7). IMDB and Amazon.com review pools are publicly available for use, but for reasons of identity protection I avoid the disclosure of personal information about my reviewers. As a result all reviews are referenced and dated in the following chapters, but the names of the reviewers are missing. Given that the content of all posted reviews is intended for all web readers (see also Homan 1991), whether they be registered users of the site or not, I treat this type of material as deliberately intended for public access and consumption (Herring 1996; Cavanagh 1999). The international make-up of these reviewer communities did not allow me to complement online reviews with actual interviews (for an example see Correll 1995). Using web material can sabotage one's ability to think in terms of variables such as ethnicity, gender or sexuality. I was left with echoes of the reviewers' identity or with the task of recovering it through hyperlinks or from hints in their reviews. Most IMDB and Amazon.com customers choose to state their country of origin, their ethnicity and cultural affiliations – valuable information for a study that looks into consumption in the more developed countries of the West, such as Britain and the USA. Although review pools always contain comments by viewers from the less developed world, the vast majority of online comments originate in Western countries. One cannot dissociate this from the fact that the Internet is still a fairly rare commodity: a very small number of the global population owns or has access to a computer (Lax 2004: 226). The reviewers of the study are amongst the most privileged individuals on our planet. It is easy to lump together all these 'Westerners' into an amorphous mass of consumers when one departs on these observations. Luckily, the vast majority of my reviewers are British or American; when they are not, I elaborate on potential ways their cultural affiliation might have affected their opinion. A recovery of the viewers' gender or sexual identity proved to be more difficult, mainly because in most texts it does not seem to play an apparent role. Because I was not in a position to infer how gender or sexual dispositions might have shaped opinions and ideas, I did not pursue a further investigation of the question.

Internet reviews were complemented with other websites, especially those maintained by holiday providers. They were not chosen randomly. I mainly drew upon those websites that either were consulted by my reviewers or established and maintained by the most important global sign industry actors – namely Hollywood and their tourist collaborators around the world. As Mitra and Cohen (1999) have suggested, web texts have an intertextual nature due to the presence of hyperlinks or other implicit links within their structure. This implies that I was not simply yet another reader of web reviews, but their *second order* author: by following my reviewers' suggestions, or by connecting their comments to ideas that originate in other websites I mapped their trajectory through my own movement in cyberspace. Most of the websites I use include imagery that refers to the film by which their business is informed. In a book that aspires to explain how visual culture structures the ideal tourist type the value of these images is more than decorative. It is also important to examine how viewers (my reviewers) relate to some of these images and their accompanied texts. All in all, my aim was to place web imagery, like film imagery, in its wider cultural context (Becker 1999) while examining whether it has an impact as such (Rose 2001: 3).

The organization of the book

As the title implies, one of the book's central concerns is the generation of global, national and local resistance to the establishment of film-induced tourist industries. The main part of the study follows this rationale, moving from the global to the national and then the local scene, with each chapter concentrating on one of these three levels and taking one film as a starting point. Within chapters I have adopted a more holistic approach that covers the main phases of the production and consumption cycle; these precede my examination of host responses to the phenomenon. I follow the politics of film production in Hollywood in order to discuss the use of place and culture as cinematic backdrops. Such images of place and culture may be referents to established holiday resorts or unknown corners of the world with the potential to become tourist destinations. Hollywood bestows these undeveloped locations with a reputation that invites their infrastructural development for tourists and other visitors. In the second stage of analysis I examine the reception of such films by international audiences – the virtual and future corporeal tourists of the filmed place. Looking at cinematic fans that produce online reviews of the films and the exploitation of these films by tourist providers, I explore the construction of ideal models of the 'tourist'.

The mobilization of filmed countries by holiday providers on the web and beyond contributes to the consolidation of local tourist industries in filmed locations, but also generates competition between local and foreign markets. In the third stage of analysis I consider the emergence and consolidation of local tourist industries and their investment on the locality's image as a cinematic attraction. I debate the competition for market primacy when the localities' potential is claimed by external, foreign actors and industries. I also provide some reflections on what is actually consumed by real tourists on location, although the corporeal experience of travel and tourism never becomes the focal point. The last phase of analysis is concerned with the reactions (local, national and global) that such developments generate. Reactions and responses to Hollywood and tourist interests lie at the heart of the globalization project that transforms identities and economies in multiple, uncontrolled and not always desirable ways. Although my aim was to excavate the formulas of local, national and global resistance to film and tourist industries, I wanted to maintain a degree of respect for the specificity of each case. I will not contend that this is an exhaustive study of film and tourism, or even of resistance to globalization; more modestly, and working through cases that developed in the first five years of the twenty-first century (1999–2004), I will offer some reflections on the nature of cinematic tourism, its politics, poetics and consequences.

In Chapter 2 I look at the construction of the tourist gaze in *The Beach* (2000) and the reception of the film in fan sites as a 'traveller's utopia'. The turning point in the politicization of this enterprise was the exploitation of Thai natural resources by Hollywood. A strategic alliance of 20th Century Fox, the Hollywood production company and the Thai authorities that wanted to promote national tourism through the film offended local, national and global environmental sensibilities. 20th Century Fox was allowed to modify the filmed location to conform to preconceived images of tropical tourist paradises despite the fact that the site was protected by national conservation laws. Independent environmental and tourist agents also played an auxiliary role to this end, promoting their own economic interests in the region and suppressing local and national criticisms. The chapter follows the organization of Thai and international ecological protests against the alleged destruction of the Maya Bay national park by 20th Century Fox, arguing that resistance to the 'sign industry' can assume global dimensions.

Chapter 3 examines the generation of a massive tourist industry in New Zealand following the global success of *The Lord of the Rings (LOTR)* cinematic trilogy (2001, 2002, 2003). Drawing on responses of reviewers and the nature of the *LOTR* commodification by online tourist providers, I argue that the *LOTR* trilogy promoted a type of tourism based on simulation of the films' mythical structures. I also investigate the shift from the commercialization of the *LOTR* tourist locations by individual tourist providers to state control, questioning whether the state-sponsored, 'organized', form of the *LOTR* capitalism indicates a New Zealand resistance to a global tourist economy or a battle over branding control. It is significant that in an effort to secure tourist monopolies, the New Zealand government had recourse to national myths and nationalist practices that bestowed the enterprise with the aura of cultural specificity.

Chapter 4 will examine the creation of a tourist industry on the Greek island of Kefalonia following the global success of the cinematic adaptation of Louis de Bernières' novel *Captain Corelli's Mandolin* (CCM). I discuss the commercialization of Greek Kefalonian and Italian history in the film, suggesting that we find its counterpart in Western practices of cultural tourism in Greece. I argue that sightseeing, display of interest in the history of Greece and Italy and in the Mediterranean 'folk' life is inextricably linked to Greece's orientalization in Western political and travel imaginations. These ideas also permeate some online reviews, consolidating the link between visual representation, tourist commodification and political orientalization. The development of the actual tourist industry on the Greek island of Kefalonia was rather disorganized and led by individual holiday providers. The chapter visits some of the filmed locations and examines the ways in which they became reference points for cultural tourists. Following that, it explores Kefalonian reactions to Hollywood and tourist intrusion, and the ways these changed with time. The chapter shows how the economic tourist boom on Kefalonia after the film's release gave way to a progressive decline in international interest, providing some reflections on state-led and locally organized development of local tourist attractions.

Chapter 5 explores the marketing of Cuban culture in the West through *Dirty Dancing: Havana Nights* (*DD2*) (2004). More specifically, it discusses the exoticization of Cuba in film fan sites, suggesting that it is related to recent Western appropriations of salsa dancing as lifestyle. Taking into account the fact that *DD2* was filmed mainly in Puerto Rico but used to advertise holidays to Havana, the chapter debates the construction of place and culture by Hollywood. This last case study deviates from the pattern established by the other three. In *DD2* we do not deal with tourism generated by a film, but with cinematic internalization of tourist practices that are then reappropriated by tourist providers. It is important to consider this reverse process, as *DD2* in particular does not hide its implication in the politics and poetics of Caribbean consumption. This case study will debate the unpredictable, risky and flexible relationship between film and tourist industries. At the same time, Western consumption modes of Cuban culture touch upon questions of imported (mobile) and appropriated lifestyles (from the Caribbean to Western countries) that enter our everyday life. This questions the theoretical argument that tourism as a practice stands apart from leisure and 'work time'.

The final chapter draws on the political, cultural and economic dimensions of cinematic tourism to debate the nature of resistance or accommodation to foreign capitalist and cultural hegemonies. I mainly examine the extent to which resistance to the global sign industries is generated from the urgency to protect cultural and natural versions of authenticity. More specifically, I maintain that a dialogical production of authenticity through forced encounters with sign industries and their consumers informs national representations but does not unilaterally define collective identities. National politics, which are aggravated by the presence of sign industries, are also involved in their articulation. Thus the book aspires to avoid the trap that Herman and McChesney's (1997) 'cultural imperialism' thesis constantly sets for students of globalization. Revisiting the argument, I argue that truly, whether they be positive or negative, the effects of globalization cannot easily be divided into economic and cultural, because the two domains of human experience interlock. At the same time, however, we need to understand *how* they interlock – a question largely neglected in Herman and McChesney's analysis. To this end, we need to examine the moral reasoning of local and national resistances to sign industries, which is informed by local cosmologies. Underneath the cultural specificity of these responses, however, there is a universal pattern that will provide the book with a conclusion.

2 Pitfalls of the 'tourist gaze'

Ecotourist dialogues and the politics of global resistance

1996 saw the global success of *The Beach*, a novel by Alex Garland that has been translated into 25 languages and sold millions of copies around the world (Gluckman 1999c). A decade later we may claim that the book has become a contemporary classic. It did not come as a surprise that in the second half of the 1990s Hollywood expressed an interest in adapting the story for global cinematic consumption. The core narrative encompassed the trajectory of travel experience, the pain of unrequited love and the horrors of social dysfunction – fantastic scenarios in a powerful combination that would normally appeal to movie viewers. The finished product, however, did not enthuse audiences, because it failed to live up to the magical story that Garland had contrived. The manipulation of the novel's plot was received by many viewers as a manifestation of Hollywood's cultural imperialism: in the film the protagonist, a British backpacker, was turned into an American who is looking for adventure in an exotic land. Such revisions were deemed to be addressed exclusively to American viewers and offended the sensibilities of Garland's fans. The diversity of responses that were registered online by audiences form a wealth of material for this study. Central to reviewer comments were questions that modern travellers often ask: how is it possible to gain an authentic experience from and through travel? When is an inner, spiritual, journey 'authentic' and how is it complemented by corporeal travel?

Although the film deviated from the novel, it still followed the original narrative in brush strokes. Richard, a young American traveller, decides to visit Thailand to escape the monotonous and repetitive life of his homeland. In Bangkok he meets Mr Daffy, a drug addict who speaks of a spectacular beach hidden away from the eyes of Western tourists. The idea of visiting an unspoilt paradise lures Richard, now equipped with Mr Daffy's map, to search for this legendary place. Together with two young French travellers, Étienne and Françoise, they trace the island of 'the beach'. There, behind a marijuana plantation maintained by Thai drug dealers, they find a self-sufficient community of Westerners who live on the island, but the joy of arriving at their destination and joining the group will soon be replaced by disillusion and terror. Nothing is as it seems. While a series of mishaps lead to the collapse of communal solidarity, Richard's sanity is in danger and the dream of inhabiting an earthly Eden falls apart. When sharks attack two members of the group, the group leader refuses to allow their transportation to the city, fearing that the secret of their island will be disclosed. This decision affects community morale and brews conflict and resentment among its members. Richard, who had shared the map with two fellow backpackers, watches them being murdered by Thai plantation guards when they track the island down. Finally, the drug dealers turn against the community and demand its departure so that they can be rid of foreign intrusion and further trouble from newcomers. The survivors of the ensuing tragedy find their way back to the civilized world, bearing with them the scars of memory for the rest of their lives.

If the cold reception of the film was unexpected, the film's impact on Thai tourism was not. The island that figures in *The Beach* (Phi Phi Leh, Maya Bay) eventually became a popular tourist destination for Leonardo DiCaprio (the cinematic Richard) fans and for deluded travellers who sought to reproduce his cinematic adventure by visiting the island. Moreover, *The Beach* assisted in the promotion of tourism in the Phuket region by international holiday providers, especially those who maintain websites. It must be noted that Garland's story itself was intended more as a satire of backpack travel (see *Wall Street Journal*, 1999; Gluckman 1999c) and counter-cultural tourism, an alternative type of tourism that emerged in the later part of the 1960s and the 1970s (Cohen 1988b). Counter-cultural tourism was popular among the hippie communities and involved long-term visits to underdeveloped Asian countries for spiritual betterment and experiential authenticity. Many such countries were consequently added to the itineraries of backpackers, for whom travel was more a way of living and a shared value (Schwartz 1991) than a brief break from work. It has been argued that backpack travel to Asia and beyond differs from conventional tourism in that its disciples operate outside the structures of organized tourism: even if they have a list of desired destination visits in their diary, they do not follow an organized programme decided in advance (Feifer 1986: 2). More controversially, it has been argued that travellers always express an interest in the values, customs and ideas of the host culture, although they never manage to 'live like the locals' (Westerhausen 2002: 6). However, as some viewers observed, the cinematic adaptation of Garland's novel had a more ambiguous agenda, because it promoted a confusion of backpack travel with the pleasures of conventional tourism, uncovering their implicit connections.

This implicit cross-reference of travel and tourism was exploited by global sign industries for the establishment of a tourist site that was also packaged and presented as a destination for prospective alternative travellers. These developments were shadowed by a controversy over the film and the very presence of the Hollywood production company, 20th Century Fox, on the island. After achieving an agreement with the Thai authorities, Fox decided to 'modify' the natural backdrops because they did not fit the fantasy of a tropical idyll. These blatant interventions in an area protected by environmental laws generated a great deal of reaction locally, nationally and globally, and angered environmentally friendly viewers. Under pressure to retain 'high consumer satisfaction' and complete the production process that stumbled upon protests, Fox embarked on a publicity campaign to counter accusations of ecological destruction. Both director Danny Boyle and DiCaprio were involved in interviews, published online, in an attempt to turn the tide in their favour.

In this chapter I am going to follow the controversy and Hollywood's response and discuss the development of cyberactivist communities that invited film viewers and other fellow activists to partake in boycotting the film. Cyber-activism, I claim, contributed to the organization of *actual* activism 'on location', because it enabled local and other international environmental pressure groups to identify a cause and present a coherent political agenda that then made its way back to online publications. It could be said that *The Beach* online wars exemplify recent developments in the field of social movements, but I do not want to support the idea that a change in the medium of communication radically altered the nature of the movements, only that it multiplied their appeal. Activist websites, rife with publicly available material on the episodes, provided global, national and local environmental groups with a 'marker of stability' (Germann Moltz 2004: 171), a symbolic home which the activists needed to counterbalance Fox's publicity campaigns. I will not claim that the Internet 'materialized' the activist groups of *The Beach* wars. Information networks linked up already established activist communities that meet regularly on a geographical basis (Lax 2004: 225). Subsequently, the 'network' nature of actual activist communities was mirrored in their use of the Internet, which has 'technologically and culturally embedded properties of interactivity' (Castells 1996: 358). The main burden of this campaign was shouldered by international campaigning organizations such as Greenpeace that customarily use the Internet to complement their existing organizational structures (Gibson and Ward 1999). Another question that follows from these developments is how pivotal were external activist initiatives (on and offline) for the local Thai cause. To answer this I will examine the anti-statist nature of Thai environmental movements and the responses of state agents to local reactions. Following Urry (2003) I argue that *The Beach* protests activated a process of 'glocalization' (2003: 85) that drew the Phi Phi island communities into global tensions and flows of ideas, sustaining a phenomenal relationship of solidarity and interdependence between foreign and domestic activist cultures (Melucci 1996: 113).

Authenticity, *communitas* and travel

Tourism activates a spatiotemporal segregation from organized work (Urry 1990: 2–3), because the routines that define our everyday lives grind to a halt and we live in suspended time. 'Taking time off work' to travel is, after all, often associated with seeing new, non-ordinary places and cultures (Urry 1992; Chaney 2002). At the same time travel, just like leisure literature, performs a compensatory function, providing the individual with the opportunity to avoid standardized practices and lifestyles (Burch 1969). *The Beach* narrates a story that follows this logic, because it takes as its starting point Richard's decision to escape his depressing life in America in favour of adventure. His first experience of Bangkok is rather frustrating. The camera here replaces the traveller's pen, capturing a dazzling array of city images including clubbing, traffic congestion, drug dealing and sex trade that despair and confuse the young Richard, who was looking for something different. This produces a spectacular sequence of 'tourist glances' (Urry 2001: 4), equating mobility of vision with travel. Richard's true 'escape' begins when he takes possession of Mr Daffy's map and departs on a quest for authenticity. The authenticity that the film promises is double: on the one hand travelling invites Richard to explore difference and test the limits of his knowledge. This he eventually achieves by joining the small international community of 'the beach'. This type of authenticity partakes in the project of self-fulfillment and emotional transformation – what Wang has termed '[a preoccupation] with an *existential state of Being*' (1999: 359, emphasis in the text). At the same time the film engages the viewer with the 'object' of travel, the 'paradise' of the island, to use the viewers' vocabulary. Although I concentrate on the first dimension, which received more attention in online reviews, I will not neglect the social construction of the toured object, which I discuss later in the chapter.

It is interesting that in film reviews experiential authenticity was translated into an engagement with youth culture. 'The beaches, the bars, the snake blood, the dope, the parties', a mixture of Richard's urban and communal experiences, belong to the performance of youth identity. 'Many from New Zealand head off in their late teens/early twenties on "The Great OE" (Overseas Experience). The same is undoubtedly true for many Australians and Brits, if not so commonly for American youth' (IMDB, 24 January 2002), says a viewer from New Zealand. Another viewer calls the film 'a narcissistic youth fantasy' (IMDB, USA, 30 September 2000) whereas an American found the 'sharp contrasts between the Beach and the town . . . very true about young westerners in Thailand' (IMDB, 20 December 2001). Young viewers even treated the film as a documentary worth seeing before catching a flight to an exotic location (see for example IMDB, California, 1 February 2004). Backpack travel is, of course, an established ritual in Western societies for young people. It marks the passage from adolescence to the world of independent and self-sustained grown ups with professional occupations. Before entering the realm of work youths enjoy prolonged leisure by visiting foreign countries and familiarizing themselves with other cultures (see also Bell 2002).

Figure 2.1 Richard wanders in the touristified streets of Bangkok.

Source: 20th Century Fox/Photofest. ©20th Century Fox Film Corp.

Some reviewers discussed the community of the secret island as a sub-cultural enclave. Following Garland, a viewer is surprised to find out that 'the paradise' is 'full of hippies' and wonders whether this is an allusion to the 'Vietnam era' (IMDB, US, 5 December 2004). An Australian suggests that the film leaves behind 'pop culture' 'for an alternative culture' (IMDB, 20 August 2001), and an American sees in the island community the model for a 'pacifist, anarchist society' (IMDB, 8 March 2004; see also San Francisco, California, 10 September 2002). Travel is thus for viewers a *rite of passage* (Van Gennep 1906) that accompanies a process of spiritual change. Rites of passage used to be performed in pre-industrial societies in order to consolidate changing positions (marriage, puberty, change of political status) in the social order. They involved the ritual separation of the initiate (or the group) from the social, their existence in a stage of 'in-betweenness' (what Turner [1969] termed *liminality*) and finally their reaggregation to the social fabric as carriers of new identities. However, rites of passage also occur in postindustrial societies, especially in subcultural contexts. Their function is to establish boundaries between the inside (who belongs to the group) and the outside, securing the distinctive identity of the group. Victor Turner employed the term *liminoid* to describe these phenomena, differentiating them from the liminal, as they are 'not obligatory ritual[s] [but] a play-separated-from-work' (Turner 1974: 74). The liminoid phase is voluntary, unlike the liminal, which is prescribed from outside, the structural environment. Turner operationalized this concept in his examination of various subcultures, among them the hippies, who construct their own system of beliefs in opposition to given norms and values. Despite the fact that their liminoid state of being is not recognized or 'classified' by outsiders, such subcultures develop their own patterns of collective self recognition – what he termed *communitas*.

These anthropological models can be mobilized in our understanding of reviewer comments. On an individual level, Richard's journey to Thailand resembles a puberty rite. After his pilgrimage to the beach, he is an adult, alert to the dangers of transgression. At the same time the viewers recognize in the island group to which Richard belongs the anti-structural element of communitas that tourists enjoy while traveling. The dramatization of the story on a beach further stresses this: as Shields (1991) has argued, the beach is the 'locus of an assemblage of [. . .] behaviors and patterns of interaction outside the norms of everyday behavior' (1991: 75). I must stress here that for some viewers the communitas of the island enclave *does not* belong to travel but to the tourist experience. Holiday time is free from everyday constraints and voluntarily spent in enjoyable ways (Wagner 1977; Jafari 1987). As we will see below, many viewers believe that all the work-related activities and the division of labour in the community (very central to Garland's narrative), are written out of the cinematic plot. What is left is a group of young people on a beach who dance in pop rhythms while smoking marijuana that they stole from the plantation. Divorcing subcultural activities from their historical and social context enables, in Roland Barthes' terms (1993), the mythologization of these 'hippyish' Westerners. On the second order, mythical level of the story, the young group of the beach embodies the archetypal community of tourist experience.

The scenes of leisure bear a striking resemblance to stereotypical perceptions of hippy culture as decadent and apolitical, popular in foreign discourses of the West as the place of vice and lack of moral order. This discourse, present in some reviews, becomes the backlash of 'occidentalism' (Carrier 1995), a response to Western denigration of the Orient as the place of disorder, lack of civilization and immorality (Said 1978). It forms the voice that attacks tourist orientalizations of countries from within the rigid structures of Western discourse. On a structural level, Thailand exists in Western consumption practices only as a tourist brochure, an embodiment of hedonism and a promise for initiation into the secrets of the Orient. Young Western tourists often visit the place because of its promised sensual qualities; the country has been hosting hippy communes for decades. This transposition of Orientalism into experiential tourism complements its exposed political counterpart, because it promotes discursive fixities *through* emotional fixation and investment. The comments of viewers who praised the film for 'tak[ing] a concentrated look at the misery of urbanity', and 'offering up clever images of mechanization, population, and capitalization' (IMDB, Los Angeles, 7 February 2001) and 'antimaterialism' (IMDB, USA, 10 October 2001) confirm that this project can influence the ways in which film is read. At the same time viewer comments uncover the Western desire for a rediscovery of the self away from the stresses and pressures of everyday life and function as a lamentation for the 'loss' of authenticity. So, despite their conformist nature, which is promoted through the film, these comments highlight the alienation and fragmentation that plagues modern societies. Online discussion of cultural contrasts between the urban environment of Bangkok and the serenity of the beach bears witness to a paradox: the very industry that produces conformity promotes the idea of the authentic Self as an ideal 'that acts to resist or invert the dominant order' (Wang 2000: 60).

The complaints of some other viewers that the island community is full of 'spoiled teenagers' with no social skills or 'political convictions and principles' (IMDB, 23 October 2003) echo these discourses of Western decline from which committed travellers want to escape. Here we move away from the notion of organized, package tourism, favoured by young clubbers, and enter the domain of travel as a form of 'pilgrimage' (Graburn 1977), an individual project of spiritual change that lost its religious connotations with the advent of rationalization (Bell 2002). This invites us to differentiate modern organized tourism from travel, an earlier form of acculturation that found its expression in the grand tour (Urry 1990). Travel experience is transgressive and destabilizing, unlike organized tourism that operates as 'a system for managing pleasure and keeping danger and destabilization at bay' (Chard 1999: 208). Travel of course provided the economic and ideological framework for the development of tourism as an escape to peripheral and exotic countries (Brodsky-Porges 1981).

A brief history of travel and tourism in Asia supports the analytical distinction between them: in the late 1960s many young Westerners followed the 'Hippie Trail' to Asian countries in search of a different lifestyle. By the early 1970s this type of travel had acquired the character of a youth culture, replacing the hippy endeavours of the previous decade. The new travellers would use means of transport that were safer than those of the previous generation, resembling in their exploits and travel styles the wealthy youths of the grand tour (Westerhausen 2002: 25): organized enough to avoid unpleasant surprises along the way, yet free from parental constraints and able to enjoy the 'unknown' (often with parental financial contribution). More importantly, the popularization of travel flights during this decade consolidated the institution of a structured tourist system that by the 1980s had overtaken youth, drifter-style, travel. Although backpack travel survived these Western socioeconomic changes, conventional tourist visits to places like Thailand are the rule today. Historical changes in travel and tourism in Asia were registered in the film by viewers, because backpack travel and tourism still coexist in Western societies. Preferences to either vary: for some viewers travel is regarded as a rite that must be performed properly, without deviating from the protocol. For example, a viewer disliked the uncivilized attitude of the island group, exclaiming that 'if this is what would happen in a paradise setting with so-called "civilized" people, I'll take savage headhunting tribes any day' (IMDB, USA, 25 July 2000). Another explained triumphantly that 'the best part of the film is the ending when all these pathetic, craven softies from civilization, who fancy themselves rugged individualists, get their final comeuppance' (IMDB, USA, 30 September 2000). Conclusively, the absence of the trials and tribulations of travel from the cinematic story was unacceptable for some viewers – mostly Americans. According to them, not unlike Adler's 'anchorite pilgrim' (1992), who looks for spiritual growth in the wilderness, Richard should have been educated through hardship, not debased socialization.

This categorical dislike for Richard's and his friends' liberation from the constraints of organized time and work deserves closer examination, because it comprises an extension of the debate on the liminoid phase of travel. The film left many viewers with a bitter taste of disappointment, as the island community fails to realize their desire for authenticity. The failure acquires two dimensions: the first one involves the inability of the community to master nature, as sharks devour its members. The second involves the grip that dissonance and hatred take on the group when their leaders decide that they cannot sacrifice the secret of their paradise in the name of humanitarian purposes (e.g. to save the shark-bitten members of the community by providing proper medical help). It is interesting that despite protestations from the makers of *The Beach*, many viewers compared the story with *The Lord of the Flies* (1990), a cinematic adaptation of a novel by William Golding. *The Lord of the Flies* follows a group of youngsters who, trapped on an island, begin to degenerate into savagery – a classical exponent of the Hobbesian state of nature in which social solidarity collapses. A viewer confirmed the comparison, explaining that both films are stories about the way 'people would behave in a state of nature (i.e. away from civilization and the political institutions that accompany it), and as such [they] reveal a great deal about our collective psyche' (IMDB, UK, 9 August 2003). For others, the movie's moral message exposes 'the dangers of separated communities, the disappearance of rules, regrets, the little value human life has in extreme situations' (IMDB, Oxford, UK, 14 April 2002; IMDB, Dublin, Ireland, 18 February 2002; IMDB, Anonymous, 18 May 2000; IMDB, Calgary, Canada, 12 February 2000; Amazon, Oxford, 28 November 2000).

We could claim that what disturbs these viewers is the liminoid anomaly of the island community: their lax mannerisms, their pot addiction and their disagreements. There is, however, another subtext to the comments: once they are settled in the island, the utopian beach ceases to be the unattainable and *becomes more like home*. This paradox did not escape attention and was recorded in some reviews. The community of the island begins to resemble more what a viewer calls 'a microcosm of todays [*sic*] society' (IMDB, California, 12 February 2000) rather than a carefree touring of different places. As another viewer wittily argued,

Having gone travelling from my point of view this film is utter drek. You go travelling for two reasons: 1) to go and see and do different

things 2) to go home again. Cos [*sic*] you see, if you don't go home
then in fact you are NOT a traveller. You have stopped travelling.

(IMDB, Cardiff, UK, 29 May 2001).

The viewer recognizes that travel involves change, and is incompatible
with the stability that the protagonists of the film aspire to establish
(Amazon, Berlin, 14 August 2005) – a complaint that travellers constantly
voice against tourists (Westerhausen 2002: 57). Consequently, the anti-
structural element of Richard's journey is quietly replaced by mere
conventionality. The viewer implies that the film reproduces conventionality: the conformism of following orders by a more 'experienced'
group leader is complemented by regular trips to the civilized world of
holiday resorts to stock up on all the goods that cannot be provided by
nature. The food is nicely cooked, yet nobody appears to do any cooking
– a miracle that can only take place in the back regions of a regular
restaurant (Goffman 1987). Last, but not least, the young community
members seem to enjoy their time playing soccer, as if they had stepped
out of their hotel in a tourist resort. As a viewer pointed out, the film

Figure 2.2 A relaxing break in Thailand: the island commune enjoys the crystal-
clear waters of 'the beach' while the food cooks itself.

Source: 20th Century Fox/Photofest. ©20th Century Fox Film Corp.

'failed to show isolation' at all because it looked 'just like a normal tacky beach resort' (Amazon, UK, 28 February 2001).

Isolated, these details are not so striking, yet they do converge upon one point: the experiential authenticity that the film itself markets has an artificial flavour. Another group of reviewers are so upset by the cinematic interpretation of the novel that they renounce the idea of travel as a personal transition to a more authentic state of existence and welcome standardized tourist offers by commercial providers. A viewer explained that 'those of us who have long ago freely capitulated to the lure of all our assorted modern amenities get the last laugh' (IMDB, USA, 30 September 2000). Another remarked that there is 'too much order' in the story, as its heroes are 'unable to give it up . . . to leave [their] comfort zone' (IMDB, Cobham, England, 14 February 2000). An American viewer is even more critical, accusing 'Westerners, who have gone to the remote corners to escape their own cultural imperialism . . . But [they] cannot run away from [themselves] or [their] culture' (IMDB, California, USA, 13 April 2000). 'As surely as human nature seems to require both projects and play in equal measure, life skewed toward recreation alone is bound to become a boring and unfulfilling existence' (IMDB, 31 July 2000), argued a sophisticated viewer from Ohio. It is interesting that the harshest critique comes from the United States, despite Richard representing the average American traveller. Even non-American commentators value Richard's travel only as a short-term commodified activity, welcoming standardized tourist offers that they enjoy every year. A viewer explained:

> I guess if you are a student or a hippy then you would understand how idyllic it would be to live in a small community with few responsibilities and most of the day spent playing in the sun. But most of us work and struggle from day to day to pay the bills . . . Most of us would have the island developed with hotels and every latest amenity for a 2 week break.
>
> (IMDB, 3 July 2004)

This viewer welcomes tourist offers stripped of any pretensions that they involve fakery and the staging of experience.

This could be regarded as the ultimate undesirable prediction that Adorno and Horkheimer (1993) theorized over half a century ago: not only do modern consumers not resist cultural replicas, but when standardized products are not available they demand them. Such a pessimistic claim would not take into account active rejections of so much standardization. There was, for example, a lot of criticism of the cinematic background (the island and its location), which was deemed too contrived.

Someone from Vegas laughs at the fact that the island 'seems to be . . . visible by binoculars from a tourist beach (come on!)' (IMDB, 14 April 2000), translating 'emotional accessibility' into measurable distance. A viewer from Texas notes that 'the community's compound was reminiscent of a luxury resort, not a slacker hangout' (IMDB, 4 August 2000). 'This is like a Club Med resort without room service' (IMDB, USA, 30 September 2001), exclaims a rather angry viewer. 'I felt I was seeing a travelogue or a Club Med ad' (IMDB, Canada, 10 October 2000), added someone from Montreal. Although this and the previous group of viewers' comments occupy the two ends of the critical spectrum, they both acknowledge that the film corresponds to tourist practices. The recognition that the film functions as a preliminary tourist experience is not confined to the IMDB community of viewers, but extends to readings of the film by the creative actors of global sign industries, as the following discussion suggests.

The cryptocolonial condition: cinematic signs for the tourist gaze

Genealogically, the emergence of a Thai tourist industry can be situated in the early twentieth century. Akin to the grand tour ritual, travelling to Thailand was a Western elite activity that involved visits to cultural attractions, such as temples and palaces, and recording or photographing sites. English-speaking elites had acquired their own special travel guide to Bangkok published by the Siamese Royal State Railway Department, which provided a wealth of information on cultural sites (Peleggi 1996: 434). The production of travel guides for unknown, peripheral, countries in Europe has a special place in the history of Western scientific knowledge (Graik 2000: 119). Recording, describing and domesticating unfamiliar places that international politics shunted outside the civilized world was a practice analogous to that employed by renowned (French or British) Orientalists, who complemented the actual colonization of the Orient with a symbolic subjection of its culture into scrutiny, cataloguing and scientific examination (Tzanelli 2003). The link is subtle, yet unmistakable: the non-European Thailand was becoming an exotic destination ready to be 'tamed' by the tourist gaze.

Thailand's exoticization satisfied political dilemmas. From the outset, the country occupied an atypical position in the Orientalist order, because it was regarded as a 'buffer zone between the colonized lands and those as yet untamed' (Herzfeld 2002b: 900–1). Thus, following the example of other semi-Oriental countries such as Greece, Thailand lived in a peculiar stage of non-recognition from Western imperialist powers as

Figure 2.3 Representing the virtual flâneur: Richard and Françoise getting a good suntan.

their equal. One of the major obstacles in this recognition was the alleged Siamese racial difference, which went against the European purist project. The country may have managed to escape the net of Western colonialism – indeed, it was the only one in the region to do so – but still strived to conform to the Western civilizing project in the same fashion that colonized countries did. Thai–Western relations were regulated by a form of *cryptocolonialism* (Herzfeld 2002b), whose predicament was destined to have long-term consequences for Thai identity. One of the major Thai dilemmas has been how to accommodate imported models of progress and civilization (*kwampen araya prathet*) to claim membership to the community of 'superior races' without compromising cultural difference.

The emergence of Thai tourism as a system of organized leisure became complicit in the economics of Western cultural imperialism (Nash 1981: 467). Initially, it secured the dependency of the Thai economy upon Western capital, as most tourist-generating countries coincided with the metropolitan centres of global political and economic domination (see Nash 1977): Britain, France and later, the United States. As the Thai tourist industry evolved, tourist practices themselves began to contribute to the exoticization of a country whose sociopolitical institutions still negotiated a way out of structural underdevelopment. A milestone in the history of Thai tourism was the programme of economic development launched by Prime Minister Sarit Thanarat, who achieved the establishment of the Tourist Organization of Thailand in 1959; this was followed by infrastructural changes that would assist in the accommodation of tourists (hotels, roads). Significantly, Sarit Thanarat's civilizing project was encapsulated in his use of the term *khwamsahat* or cleanliness (Peleggi 1996: 434) – a neat correspondence between purity and order that followed the paradigm of Western Orientalist discourse.

Less than a decade later, in the context of the Vietnam War, Thailand received American economic aid that boosted the growth of its tourist sector. It was precisely over this period that Thailand's tourist crypto-colonial status was consolidated. First, the establishment of American military bases led to the development of nightclubs, bars and restaurants, and the expansion of sex trade to cater for soldiers' demands and needs (Ryan 1991). Second, in the context of hippy subcultural movements (an offspring of American sociopolitical problems), and later countercultural movements that dictated liberation from Western ideological practices, Thailand became an escape from the iron cage of Western progress. By the 1980s, the country was a major world tourist destination that bore the stigma of decadence, as it was strongly associated with gay communities, AIDS, and the promise of sexual pleasure (Craig-Smith and French 1994; Hall 1995). The Phuket region, in which *The Beach* was filmed, became internationally famous for its hectic nightlife that simply replicated Western lifestyles in exotic surroundings.

In this part of the chapter I explore how *The Beach* turned out to be a cinematic transposition of past orientalist themes into the matrix of global sign industries. Further analysis of online reviews will expose the survival of such themes and practices in contemporary milieus. Thereafter, I look at the tourist promotion of Thailand in online sites, often quoted by the same viewers that I use in the chapter. I do not claim that hedonistic or mystical images of Thailand eliminated cultural tourism in the country. Clearly, there is a split in the history of Thai tourism between the original expression of interest in cultural sites – still present amongst those who visit the country to become familiar with its distinctive, long, history – and drug tourism and backpack travel, types of tourism to which the film alludes. *The Beach* generated the preconditions for their coexistence in virtual and actual tourist markets.

A general observation that one can make about online reviews is that they do not really discuss Thai culture: on the contrary, they are mostly preoccupied with the film's commune and Richard's adventures. This absence reflects and is reflected in Richard's cinematic narration. Richard's experience is told through the camera's lens in a detached pseudo-anthropological fashion: wandering in the streets of Bangkok, he encounters more tourists than locals; the locals that cross the threshold of his spectrum are pimps and druggies. Bangkok seems to be a Western colony for tourists, and the few Thais that walk its avenues do so in the service of Western consumer desires. Even when Richard finally leaves this urban havoc behind, he enters a white world, because the island commune does not really include non-white members, with the exception of Americanized Keaty (Joseph Paterson). The Thais of the island are yet another group of malicious creatures, who guard their plantation while killing foreign intruders. They are in fact the only hint to the harrowing political background – a feeble reference to Thailand's involvement in drug trafficking and distribution *for* its Western guests. We can liken their plantation to Mary Pratt's 'contact zone', the domain of interaction between colonizers and colonized. Contact zones are traditionally 'the space in which peoples geographically and historically separated come into contact with each other and establish ongoing relations, usually involving conditions of coercion, radical inequality, and intractable conflict' (Pratt 1992: 4). In the film, the promise of violence lurks in the background, as the plantation workers patrol their dominion ready to fire at Western intruders. But whose violence is superior here, theirs or that of cinematic technology? If Richard represents the global tourist, who traverses continents to reach the fantastic place of his innermost desires, the natives of the story are the ugly savages of his teenage travel narrative: devoid of manners, mores and humanity. The so-called 'international community' of the island is a mirror for Western tourist imperialism: the message of the film is that yesterday's guests are now the true natives. The domestication of the beach is complete and unquestionable.

Once emptied of life, 'Thailand' is nothing more than a neutral plane, ready to be replenished with a plethora of new meanings. It is small wonder that some cinematic viewers of the film discussed so extensively 'things Occidental' – offshoots and representations of Richard's experiential trek – and almost nothing 'Thai'. Angry protestations that the story was 'a racist dope' (IMDB, Frankfurt, Germany, 14 April 2000) were isolated incidents. Auxiliary to this silence are hundreds of reviews that separate historical and social context from place. An anonymous viewer concludes that *The Beach* 'could have been a silent film and the photography of Thailand's pristine Maya Bay would have been enough to hold most viewers' attention' (IMDB, 26 March 2000). Others decide that 'the beauty of the backdrops and settings' is characterized by 'sheer artistry' (IMDB, Alberta, Canada, 5 November 2001), implying that cinematic representations of Thailand may be the product of an over-polished lens, but they are still appealing. 'Kudos to the cinematographer of this movie' says another, on vacation in Thailand at the time (IMDB, 11 April 2001). 'If you like nature and paradise . . . pictures then rent or see this one', suggests someone from Sweden (IMDB, 15 October 2001). For others the camera was 'brilliant' (Amazon, Devon, 28 December 2001), 'spectacular' (Amazon, UK, 18 January 2001) and 'worth spending millions for a perfect result' (IMDB, Vancouver, 12 August 2000), as it advertised Thailand's 'incredible settings' (Amazon, UK, 16 June 2004) in the best possible way. The cinematic and photographic lenses are identified by other viewers (Amazon, Brighton, 13 January 2001), who find the film's picture 'outstanding' (Amazon, UK, 6 September 2001). I do not reject Mike Crang's (1997) argument that visual experience of tourist settings involves a process of interpretation and must be considered in relation to the making of subjectivities. However these film (re)viewers are more constrained than actual tourists, since they are trapped into the visual world of Hollywood. Their comments run against the grain of Crang's argument, suggesting that *some* viewers can be affected by externally produced 'signs'.

The obsession with visual perfection betrays symmetry between literary narrative (Garland's fictional travel account) and cinematic representation (its filming), and takes us back to the genealogy of European travel. When the wheels of 'progress' set in motion the institutionalization of Western scholarly knowledge, travel experience ceased to be recorded exclusively in travel books, and began to find expression also in drawings, sketches and, later, photography (Adler 1989; Pratt 1992: 201–7). At a later stage, scholarly interest in the 'other' was separated from tourist adventure, although the two never stopped interacting in cultural tourism. The admiration that viewers expressed for the cinematic scenery is one of the most recent developments of the phenomenon: cinematic tourism is the 'safest way' to observe and survey sterilized otherness, caged 'behind the bars' (Crawshaw and Urry 2000: 178) of Hollywood's cinematic Panopticon. As a viewer explained, 'any idiot in that region would just pick up a camera and roll' (IMDB, Toronto, Canada, 15 February 2000). This is not to say that none felt that the film was characterized by 'antiseptic travel-brochure prettiness' (IMDB, Paris, 22 March 2000; IMDB, Italy, 23 August 2001), 'pictures full of clichés' (IMDB, Germany, 19 January 2000), which 'you can get . . . on the travel chanel [*sic*] for free' (IMDB, Wisconsin, 16 October 2002). 'Maybe it is meant to be, but an advert for the Thailand Tourist Association it ain't', retorts a viewer (Amazon, Middlesex, UK, 24 June 2002).

Sporadic reactions confirm that the use of cinematic technologies of this kind have become an institution that promotes the circulation of signs from film to tourist markets and back again. An essential intermediary in the distribution of signs is the cinematic audience itself. Some viewers were inspired by the scenery and 'wanted to sell [their] car and go to Thailand in search of an Island somewhere with white beaches' (IMDB, St Paul, MN, 26 March 2000), disregarding the specificity of place. Others were 'consumed with the idea of a lost paradise . . . and considered finding a beach of [their] own' (US, 20 February 2005). More to the point, many viewers 'saw the "Beach"' and planned their 'dream vacation' (IMDB, Bellevue, WA, 12 August 2003; IMDB, UK, 26 August 2000; IMDB, Scotland, 23 June 2002). Others used the film as an illustration of their past experience of Thailand. For example an 'Englishman living in Spain' explains that *The Beach* 'acted' on his behalf: it convinced his girlfriend that Thailand 'is amazing', something he did not achieve although he lived for years in the country (Amazon, Spain, 6 February 2001). Needless to add that the Thai authorities thought along the same lines when they gave Fox permission to shoot the film in Maya Bay. But before we examine the politics of *The Beach* we should have a look at the ways in which the film was mobilized by the global sign industries.

It all started with the online marketing of the film. The official website is designed as a digital travel book with hyperlinks to different aspects of Richard's journey, one of which is a colourful gateway to his travel trajectory. This is accompanied by a subsection ('Travelers' Exchange') in which hundreds of viewers discuss the utopian messages of the film, drawing on their own travel adventures, or inviting readers to visit Thailand and any other corner of the world that they like. The function of this gateway is double-layered: participants may be assuming it is the space of fandom that they share, but when we peel off this layer, we come across a sign industry that is using them as promoters of the film or tourist resorts. Why else does the official website figure in most online tourist markets? The most remarkable aspect of the website is its main page, complete with an invitation to 'enter the site, as a tourist or a traveler' (*The Beach*, 1999–2000). The text that accompanies this invitation is also suggestive:

> The wonders of modern technology, like computers, video games, cell phones, pagers and the Internet were designed to make our lives more enjoyable and facilitate communications. Yet for many, the complexity of the digital world is overwhelming, leading to a feeling of unreality . . . of being disconnected.
>
> The desire to find something real . . . is what drives Richard . . . a young American backpacker who arrives in Thailand with adventure on his mind. Travel, he asserts, is *the search for experience, the quest for something different*.
>
> (*ibid.*, emphasis in text)

The 'invitation' is built on a paradox: the hyperreality of the digital world that the site inhabits is classified as inauthentic – we can only be led to consider it a fabrication of the Hollywood machine for the virtual tourist eye. The text seems to deconstruct its own role, to deal a blow at the value of its travel simulation. At a first consideration and in Baudrillard's terms (1973, 1983), we can argue that *The Beach* is a reproduction of fiction (the novel), a simulacrum of the real travel. In the same way that film viewers denounced the stresses of modern life, the website denounces the technological age – a reference to Richard's own words and actions at the beginning of the film. But while the text makes us aware of the 'structural impossibility' (Baudrillard 1998) to look for experiential authenticity, it celebrates the simulation of this quest in Richard's cinematic journey. Hence, the very website that accuses technological progress of human alienation, *proceeds to valorize its practices*. The gallery of postcards from the 'beach' that the site hosts, constructs a place that exists only in the virtual flâneur's imagination. It is not the pictures themselves that count, but what they stand for in the phantasmagoric world of consumption: the fetishized object of the film, the alleged paradise.

This simulatory game found application in the websites of holiday providers. Beaches in the Phuket region appeared in different websites and were marketed in different ways. I will provide one example here, because it is mentioned in film reviews as an alternative to Phi Phi Leh. Thaipro.com, a Thai search engine, advertised the Koh Pha Ngan island from the Phuket complex as an upcoming holiday resort. It is, of course, omitted that Koh Pha Ngan has been a resort for a while and that its sister island, Koh Samui, inspired Garland to write his novel. 'In the gulf of Thailand is everything you ever dreamed about for a faraway paradise', the site claims. What follows is a long list of Ibiza-like, clubbing activities *combined with* images of unspoilt beaches. Interestingly, some of these images are almost identical to those we find in the official movie website. Koh Pha Ngan is described as a 'castaway secret of backpackers', which has just acquired a 'booming tourist industry' complete with 'a Buddhist retreat' for those seeking spiritual experience. The virtual advert leads us to establish connections between cinematic subcultural activities (already recognized in film reviews) and actual products for tourist consumption. More importantly, for marketing purposes the engine cites a travel account by Marie-Thérèse Le Roux, a replica of Richard and Mr Daffy, who worries that we will not manage to 'keep the story a secret' and word of mouth may crowd the island 'of our dreams' with tourists who have expensive 'imperial tastes'. Surely, millions of web surfers would never do such a thing.

Travel accounts that promote the 'authentic stage' of the film's official website began to appear on the web during the filming of the movie. I will analyse one that appears on *Wanderlust*, a website that publishes travelogues from different parts of the world. A backpacker and reporter who ended up in Phi Phi Don, Phi Phi Leh's sister island, narrates a colourful story. The traveller is upset: he does not belong to the paparazzi tribe, and he is not DiCaprio's fan; he 'simply yearned for adventure'. Unfortunately, he was caught in the furore of protests against the filming of *The Beach* and the invasion of the island by 'screaming pubescent females' who want to have a close look at their teenage idol, DiCaprio. He has read every single tabloid on the politics of the film, and an idea began to take shape in his head: months before travelling to Thailand, he had read Garland's novel and toyed with the idea of copying the plot (look for 'his own' island). Now that he found out what is going on in Thailand, he changed plans:

> Why not live 'The Beach' in reverse? Instead of seeking out a secret, untouched island, why not explore the most scrutinized island in all of Thailand? Why not try washing ashore the movie set itself?
>
> (Wanderlust Salon)

He soon finds out that his original paradise 'expired years ago' anyway, when urban Thailand was taken up by the 'aliens' of the West. This is where his reflexivity ends, and he passes in silence a rather important detail: once upon a time Westerners wanted to visit unfamiliar lands in order to expand the borders of their knowledge. 'Rolf Plotts', as the narrator signs himself, may have started his journey on the same premise, but he ended up looking for the Thailand of Hollywood. Like other contemporary tourists, he only pursued the 'stage' that someone else invented for him.

On the global scene, one of the lasting consequences that *The Beach* has had was the promotion of Edenic fantasies for those who can afford a truly unique experience: to rent, or even buy, their own island. Private Islands Online, the largest Internet directory of private islands for sale, hosts today a long list of 'Movies for the Island Enthusiast' (see Private Islands Online). Among them is *The Beach*, with hyperlinks to the plot and the background of the film. The story is surrounded by pictures of islands from different continents and seas available for purchase. The website erases the identity of these places, as their location is blinded by their visual radiance: what prospective buyers – or even virtual flâneurs with no money to spare for such luxuries – consume is a postcard from Richard's destination. The film has joined a global economy of signs that has no respect for, or interest in, cultural specificity. The website's entrepreneurialism is echoed in the use of images that repeatedly appear in the travel prospectuses – green crystal clear lagoons and beaches full of palm trees in the middle of nowhere.

The visual marketization of the region has picked up over the last two years, with many international tourist providers using high angle shots of Phi Phi Leh's famous beach on their websites. DiscoveryThailand.com for example, advertises the island, stating that these days Maya Bay, 'the spot where the movie *The Beach* was filmed' is a '"must do" item in its own right'. The website encourages travellers and tourists to visit the region, explaining that regular boat trips are run from Krabi to the islands. It also stresses that although Phi Phi Leh and Don are officially part of a national park no admission fee is charged for the tours. A standardized advertisement for visits to the islands has been reproduced in many other websites maintained by foreign tourist providers. Accompanied by lustrous photographs identical to the cinematic images of *The Beach*, the suggested itinerary includes Maya Bay, apparently 'very busy in high season' and 'famous' because of the film (see for example South Orchid, KrabiTourism.com and PhiPhi Phuket.com). Unpopulated, high angle shots of the islands reproduce the now familiar cinematic signs of *The Beach*, consolidating the appropriation of these 'paradises' by the commercial providers of the tourist gaze. Even when the websites are addressed to committed travellers, they rely on the same sign order. Travelfish.org, an independent backpacker's guide to Indonesian islands, includes similar photographs of the region in its 'Phi Phi Travel Guide'. However, most of the description and guidance offered does not involve these sister islands but hyperlinks to Koh Samui, Garland's initial inspiration. The specificity of the region is erased from the electronic references.

As opposed to all these foreign tourist providers and guides, The Tourism Authority of Thailand website modestly promotes the islands as ecotourist destinations that belong to a region 'less developed' than Phuket. This modest advertising is a curious move, given that the Thai government fought a battle to legitimize Fox's production project. In early 1999, the Royal Thai Forestry Director General Plodprasop Suraswadi cheerfully declared that the film has been 'the perfect commercial for the park [the islands] and for Thailand', claiming that they 'couldn't buy better publicity for a *tourist destination*' (*Wall Street Journal* 1999; emphasis mine) – an illuminating *lapsus linguae* that betrayed the appropriation of a national park in tourism structures. Beyond any shadow of doubt the formation of a global sign industry with a Thai epicentre had already begun with the filming of the movie in the late 1990s. The second step that was taken in the same direction originated in the domestic political arena. In 2003, a Film Commission was formed in Thailand. Looking at its opening policy statements we realize that the initiative did not aim to prevent despoliation, but to support changes in the taxation on 'foreign actors and corporate income-tax holidays', as well as to 'make Thailand Asia's "film-making hub" via joint ventures' (Miller *et al.* 2005: 167). Although this aimed to consolidate Thailand's global image by advertising its 'cultural distinctiveness' through film, it may end up encouraging foreign labour flow (see also Sum 2003). In 1999 the Thai government was already happy to open wide the national gates to foreign (especially Hollywood) capital, as long as this boosted the country's tourist image, but as we will see below, Fox was to find out that a place which identifies with the tourist archetype comes at price.

'We will fight them on the beaches': cyberactivism and Thai responses

Films and their by-products (including tourism) are designed to meet and shape consumer demands. Yet what affects the finished product, its distribution and general socioeconomic consequences – what we can call 'the politics of the big screen' – may be concealed from audiences. Unlike other films, whose politics stayed securely shut in Hollywood's forbidden archives, *The Beach's* records were disclosed. This happened because the film became involved in national politics and international concerns about Western capitalist hegemony. For once Hollywood had touched a rather sensitive nerve locally, nationally and globally. This section examines direct and indirect connections between local, national and global reactions to the production and distribution of *The Beach*. The analysis will not be confined to the film itself, but will move on to debate the establishment of strategic agreements between Hollywood and tourist providers for the maximization of profits, often at the expense of Thai localities. The most interesting part of the conflict took place on the web, where both sides (on the one hand the activists and the Thais who partook in environmental campaigns, and on the other hand Hollywood actors and tourist providers) publicized their cause (see also Moore 2002). Not only did the Internet become a subsidiary medium in the activist cause (Cere 2002: 148), but it promoted a convergence of local and global concerns regarding environmental sustainability.

The Beach 'wars' began in 1998, when Fox decided that the location chosen for the filming of the story, Phi Phi Leh island of the Krabi complex, was not pleasing enough to the tourist eye. It was agreed that planting some 50 to 60 coconut trees on Maya Bay, cleaning the rubbish that the sea washed ashore from other locations and bulldozing a few natural dunes would produce the desired result (see Gluckman 1999b). In November 1998 the Thai government gave its consent to the project, especially in the aftermath of rumours that Fox was planning to spend US $10 million in Thailand, and in expectation that the film itself would attract international tourists and DiCaprio fans. The company needed official permission to make these alterations because Phi Phi Leh belongs to a national park and is protected by Thai laws. The fact that the company agreed to pay 4 million baht (US$111,000) to the Royal Forestry Department of Thailand, which is responsible for conservation issues, and to provide a deposit of 5 million baht (US$135,000) as guarantee against damages at Maya Bay, exacerbated the political tensions that Thai governmental decisions generated. The donation was understood as a bribe by Thai and other international environmentalists, who accused the Royal Forestry Department of 'selling out' Thai laws and destroying the country's environment (*The Nation* 2000).

Local protests started shortly before the shooting of the film on Maya Bay, when villagers and local representatives of civic groups from all over Thailand camped on the island, obstructing the film crew's work for more than two weeks until the police and the military were called in to disperse them (Third World Network 2000). These protests were complemented by the involvement of Greenpeace, the Wildlife Fund Thailand, the Confederation of Inshore Fishermen and the Phuket Environment Protection Association, whose representatives crowded Patong Beach in Phuket to demonstrate against the 'colonization' of the island by foreigners and Thai vendors (*International Herald Tribune* 2000). From the outset there was global involvement in the cause, which raised participant numbers and bestowed the protests with international glamour. On 11 January 1999 the Civil Court accepted a lawsuit filed by residents and assemblies from the Krabi province against Fox and Thai government officials for encroachment on Thai natural resources. A new theatre of conflict emerged at a waterfall in Khai Yai National Park, where Fox planned to shoot more scenes from the movie. Local environmental groups sent an open letter to the provincial governor, demanding a dialogue on the terms of the contract that the authorities signed with the company. When their demand was not met, they distributed a documentary on the destruction of Maya Bay by the film's production team. The crisis heightened when several protest groups filed yet another complaint against the filmmakers for violating the 1961 National Park Act and the 1992 Environment Act. The story was discussed in the international press: on 29 October 1999, the *Guardian* published an article in which it exposed extensive environmental damage at Maya Bay after the 'alterations' that 20th Century Fox had made to the natural landscape. The Internet was swamped by anti-Hollywood manifestos (*Boycott The Beach*), both Thai and international, and the film became famous in every corner of the globe for all the wrong reasons.

I should point out that the cause of the controversy may not be the turbulent marriage of tourism with environmental conservation *stricto sensu*. Despite the active involvement of international activist groups in *The Beach* controversy, the cause acquired meaning for the communities in the Krabi region because it captured in a nutshell a burning social problem: the lack of regional and local involvement in decisions that may affect the everyday life of local communities (Prudishan and Maneerat 1997; Herzfeld 2003). The violation of environmental laws is a phenomenon with a long history in Thailand; political monopolies by those in power raise concerns about the future of Thai civil society. The presence of militia on Maya Bay and the threat of violence (see *The Nation* 1999a, b) exposed an authoritarian regime that forecloses any possibility for democratic dialogue. This was the first time that a government sector was summoned to court over environmental issues; as such, the case constitutes a turning point in the history of Thai social movements.

In this hostile climate, Fox tried to counter accusations that it had destroyed the island. The most effective weapon in its counter-campaign was Leonardo DiCaprio, who appeared in interviews with a serious demeanour and wounded pride. In an interview he claimed that everything 'had to do with the political propaganda that was going on in the country', and that environmentalists used the film as a 'lightning rod for attention' (*Toronto Sun* 2000). Unsurprisingly, in the wake of Thai opposition DiCaprio declared an ethical investment in environmental issues (*Bangkok Post*, 26 January 2000). Producer Andrew MacDonald and director Danny Boyle also appeared on the film's website claiming that the protest simply helped Thai social movements to gain an international profile (see also Gluckman 1999b). With what was deemed to be unjustified arrogance, MacDonald also claimed that the film was raising local environmental consciousness, ignoring the fact that there was no appropriate American legislation to handle an environmental dispute in the US, while Thailand had a legal framework in place (Miller *et al.* 2005: 167). Andrew MacDonald stressed the financial returns from the film for Thailand (*Asiaweek* 1999), whereas Boyle claimed that the island itself is meaningless compared to what is going on in the country (*The Beach* online). Andrew MacDonald even figured in Women's Voice and Greenpeace websites, asking activist groups to write to him with suggestions for a solution (Women's Voice). Such declarations were intended to alleviate international pressure and regain the support and interest of millions of viewers. It is no coincidence that some IMDB viewers' knowledge of the debate (IMDB, USA, 20 April 2000; IMDB, Melbourne, 8 February 2001; IMDB, London, 23 March 2000) is conditioned by what appears on the official website of *The Beach*. This does not mean that *The Beach* website dominates cyberspace; the Internet 'war' has urged the most environment-aware viewers to visit other sites (IMDB, USA, 19 February 2000; IMDB, Germany, 14 January 2000) and familiarize themselves with other views. But Fox's public presentation certainly satisfied vested capitalist interests. In fact, this case presents us with a wonderful, though largely contingent, alignment of interests of the tourist and film industries: the argument used by the filmmakers was that they wanted to help Thai tourism without harming the environment.

An interesting addition to these cyber-dialogues was the site www. thaistudents.com, allegedly maintained by Thai students. When we take a closer look, however, we realize that the site does not articulate the voice of university students who joined the boycott: the actual developer of the site is Richard Barrow, a Western teacher at Sriwittayapaknam public school in Samut Prakarn. The young pupils of the *secondary* school in which he teaches are merely a façade. The website seems to be more like an advert for Thai tourism than a critical and fair assessment of the controversy. Not only does it contain numerous hyperlinks to Phi Phi islands' emergent hotels, scuba diving courses and reviews of Phuket holiday experiences, it also recommends Garland's book, the film and the soundtrack (Thai Students.com 2000). The site may be posting all developments on the protest, but it also makes a declaration that the 'students' aspiration' is to assist in the development of the tourist economy. Predictably, the initiative was praised in the official DiCaprio website and by various Hollywood actors, including producer Andrew MacDonald (also quoted on the website), DiCaprio's media consultant Richard Ehrlich and production consultant Dave Walker.

The hidden agendas of the global sign industries infuriated activists, who began to expose internal weaknesses and profitable alliances between them, subverting their interests. Third World Network (Third World Network 2000: New Frontiers, 4(6) (1998) and 5(1) (1999)) attacked Joe Cummings, traveller and writer of *Lonely Planet* publications on Thailand, for arguing that after the bulldozing Maya Bay looked better. It was explained that in his article to *International Herald Tribune*, Cummings concealed *Lonely Planet's* engagement by Fox as a consultant on travel and filming in Asia. Cummings' relationship with Fox is more significant than it may seem to be. An ethnographic study of Western travellers in Asia published in 2002 pointed out that because inexperienced backpackers regard *Lonely Planet* guidebooks as alternative travel books they frequently consult them before they start their journey (Westerhausen 2002: 78). Obviously Fox was consciously trying to communicate to the travel book industry its own cluster of global signs for commercial purposes.

Commercial interest guided the pen of Cogen and Miller from international conservation group Reef Check, who inspected Maya Bay and found the environment better than before the 'alterations', the activists argued. Reef Check pride themselves on the establishment of a non-profit global project to monitor coral reef deterioration, which spans over 40 countries and is endorsed by the United Nations. What was not discussed in this controversial report (published in the *Bangkok Post* 1999a), but was pointed out by activists, was that Cogen and Miller run an ecotour company based in Phuket, which offers explorations to 'romantic uninhabited tropical islands' (InDepth Adventure). Not only did In Depth Adventure use Reef Check's report to endorse 'environmentally friendly' travel to the Phuket region, it also included a picture of its operation managers together with DiCaprio during his stay in Thailand. On DiCaprio's twenty-fifth birthday in November 1999, the US-based website geocities.com prompted international DiCaprio fans to donate money to their idol's 'environmental favourites' – among them, Reef Check. The web material was removed when cyberactivists pointed out the link between the ecological group and DiCaprio. Cogen and Miller's report on Maya Bay was also supported by former director of Environmental Tourism Consultants in Phuket, Noah Shepherd. Owner at the time of a tour company, Shepherd posed as Cogen's 'friend', and endorsed Reef Check's expertise in an article he posted to a renowned tourist website.

The saddest aspect of this lobbying is represented by EcoLert, a website repeatedly quoted by American tourist organizations such as www. ecotourism.about.com that would rather promote Phi Phi islands as a destination unspoiled by mass tourism. The choice of EcoLert by American tourist providers was careful: in its own environmental report, the website had dismissed the protests because they allegedly concerned 'uninhabited' places (Thai Students.com 2000). The statement replicates tropes that were discussed in previous sections of the paper: Richard's whitewashed travel account, in which the Thai appear only as a minor background nuisance, and the viewers' construction of Thailand as an empty plane. The suggestion was that behind the protests there were only a few trouble-makers. As J. Ginsberg of the Wildlife Conservation Society's program (WCS) stated, 'the local people of Phi Phi, the sea gypsies, no longer exist in the area' (Media-Culture Organisation 2000), implying that the islands have no populations who can claim rights to protect the island. Ginsberg was previously condemned by human rights and other environmental groups for having an active involvement in the development of locally damaging 'ecotourist' projects in Laos and Burma (*Observer* 1997).

It may be just too convenient to forget the locals and the impact the Hollywood storm had on their lives. Nationally, Ginsberg's comment had a racist subtext that few would acknowledge without shame. Against WCS claims, Phi Phi Don is indeed populated mainly by Muslim groups from the south who started moving into the area from the 1950s. In Thailand southern Muslims generally have civic rights. In contrast, the hill tribes of the north have been denied full citizenship and classified as 'jungle people' (*chao pa*), beings whose humanity is incomplete. Perversely, however, these jungle people have become representative of pure 'Thai-ness', of 'civilization' in Thai nationalist discourse (Herzfeld 2002b: 904–5). Despite their exclusion from civic rights, and perhaps because of their value as 'national progenitors', the northern Muslims are not discussed as politically subversive elements. The state presents southern Muslims as troublesome elements, because they allegedly harbour a separatist cause. Ginsberg's statement killed two birds with the same stone: it covered up the national embarrassment of hosting ethnic-religious trouble that can expose the Thai state's dirty laundry internationally *and* denied the locals any agency.

At the same time, international journalists explained that most islanders had discounted the protests as 'a silly stink raised by the urban folk' (Gluckman 1999a). Of course, despite representations of social movements in Thailand as a phenomenon that encompasses all social groups and classes, the truth remains that it is not so. The benefits of exaggerated environmental awareness could also be questioned: strict policies on national parks can have adverse consequences for farming, promoting the exclusion of whole communities from effective use of natural resources (Forsyth 1995; Hirsch and Lohmann 1999). But the conviction that no locals participated in *The Beach* 'wars' omits the active involvement of villagers from the Phi Phi islands in the destruction of temporary crew shelters on Maya Bay while the company was still shooting the film (*Bangkok Post* 1999b). Also, Western journalists were more likely to be approached by those villagers who were not hostile to the film because of the short-term profits that they extracted from the crew, the paparazzi and DiCaprio fans. Inevitably, the controversy would divide the local community into those who were 'disgruntled over missing out on a slice of the film's budget' (Gluckman 1999a) and those who got themselves 'on the payroll'.

The division of local communities into rebels and conformists flags another issue – namely, the extent to which Western activist forces were driving or simply assisting in a local/national cause. We may begin by noting that state agents were as unwelcome as Hollywood 'capitalists'. Thus both those who came from abroad (production crews and, subsequently, travel agents) and those who represented the Thai state (the government, the Royal Forestry Department) were identified by Thai activists as 'outsiders'; protests and lawsuits directed against the former also attacked the state and its undemocratic policies. As already noted, Western intervention in Thailand is a thorny issue because it is the site of cryptocolonial oppression. But what was the position of the government in this game? Herzfeld (2002b) has already explained that the power of cryptocolonial discourse resides in its twin nature: as both oppressive and enticing to emulate Western models of progress. The involvement of international environmental organizations might have attained the form of 'symbolic capital' (Bourdieu 1984) for local and national activists, because it presented the episode as a case of 'foreigners against foreigners', legitimating their anti-statist activities in general. Forsyth (2002) also suspects that the underlying cause of these Thai protests was not so much environmental issues per se, but that they were used to strengthen criticism of the state. If anything, by flagging environmental destruction the Thai activists managed to catch the attention of Greenpeace and other satellite organizations in the West. The environmental angle of Thai activist discourse is 'epiphenomenal' (Hajer 1995), because it nicely conceals pre-existing problems concerning the nature of the Thai nation-state, its policies and its place in the international political arena. On the one hand *The Beach* 'wars' brought Thai localities into contact with the globe, transforming them into sociocultural agents; on the other hand, they shed rather unwelcome light on the global forces that shaped the Thai nation-state.

It may be useful to further distinguish between local participation in the protest and protesting against foreign capitalist invasion. We gain valuable insight on this distinction from Ron Gluckman's report from the Krabi area. Gluckman was attentive to the tensions that Thai encounters with tourists generated, and found some locals rather rude. Villagers in the Krabi region are definitely not impressed by the 'backpacker cult', he states, and call foreigners *farang kee-nok*, literally foreign bird droppings. Lest I am accused of linguistic games, I will note that the phrase works as an anthropological spyglass, because it exemplifies the effective use of rhetoric by local actors who may be disempowered on a decision-making level, but still remain politically minded. In other words, I look for ways to analyse how Thai resistance was *mediated* in this case through language (Joseph and Kavoori 2001: 1004). *Farang* (also pronounced *falang*) is the Thai word for guava, a fruit produced from a tropical tree that makes white flowers. The word often denotes colour, although on its own it is rather neutral; combined with *kee-nok* (bird shit) it refers to a particular type of guava, which is not as juicy as other varieties. The combination of words is used metaphorically to describe a type of foreigner, the stingy backpacker who lives on breadcrumbs and forgets to change his clothes and wash his body.

The obsession with cleanliness, which occupied a significant place in Sarit Thanarat's modernist discourse, figures as a pervasive characteristic of Thai encounters with tourists. Backpackers are regarded as the great 'unwashed' of the Occident – or, to use Cohen's expression, 'nomads from affluence' (1973) who pretend to be poor in order to live their dream of escape. Their value for Thai communities is equal to that of excrement, waste from the sky that bears the potential to pollute, to violate cultural boundaries (Douglas 1993). The allusion to foreign stinginess is equally important. Thais also use the expression *farang kee-nok* to describe prospective sons in-law who fail to produce presents for them (they are not as 'juicy' as others). Although traditionally the value of the 'gift' is equivalent to the bride's dowry, the gesture itself denotes respect and is duly reciprocated with another present by the in-laws at a later date. To name your prospective son in-law 'white bird shit' hints that the act of reciprocation never took place, because there was no gift giving in the first place. If we are to believe Mauss (1954), the gift and its reciprocation activate a system of 'total services' that could seal relations between rival parties and secure cooperation. The locals know that this is impossible when it comes to tourists. Put simply, just like future sons in-law, who are still outsiders for the family of the bride, tourists refuse to properly recognize the host's services. In the eyes of the Thai hosts, recognition was never present: 'Westerners' and 'dirty hippies' are supposed to cherish a fixed idea of Thai 'others' as objects of consumption with no life of their own. The tension is aggravated by the fact that backpackers always operated as a sub-cultural enclave, spending most of their time with peers and less with locals (Westerhausen 2002: 24) reasserting in the eyes of the latter their 'outsider' status. In return, the hosts refuse to recognize them as anything other than shit that needs cleaning. I did not apply the distinction between travellers and tourists here for good reasons. In the case of tourists, encounters with locals are even more restricted because tourists spend limited time in the country and mostly indulge in leisure activities. Moreover, as Brunner (1991: 248) has explained, distinctions between tourists and travellers may be important in Western contexts because they are burdened by the grand tour's history, but they are meaningless in local contexts. Stereotyping is not a Western 'privilege', but a two-way dynamic process that often legitimates local exploitation of foreigners. As an Australian backpacker put it, travellers are nothing more than 'wallets on legs' (Westerhausen 2002: 95) for impoverished Thais.

On a sustainable development front, the Internet 'war' simply recontextualizes an old question: will Phi Phi Leh, initially the ideal backpacker destination, be expropriated by international mass tourism? (Cohen 1995). The tsunami disaster left Thailand struggling to rebuild its reputation as a travel destination. In the early days after the earthquake it was reported that Phi Phi Leh and its adjacent Phi Phi Don, made famous through a James Bond film, had taken the full force of the tsunami. The island of *The Beach*, which had in the meantime become a popular excursion from Phuket, was declared by the UK Foreign Office 'off limits' (*Sunday Times* 2005) and Ton Sai, the backpackers' enclave on Phi Phi Don, was claimed to be devastated. The owner of two resorts on the islands stated that 200 bungalows were swept out to sea together with his customers and his employees (*Sydney Morning Herald* 2004) – hardly an advertisement for the place. In the face of such complete devastation, a spark of hope survived on *The Beach*: foreign backpackers and their aid groups tried help the region recover from the shock (*CNN* 2005). Internet cafes and chat rooms, the foremost acomplishments of Western hegemony, worked for Thailand in the absence of any official aid programmes. It is ironic that this humanitarian movement was assisted by the popularization of cinematic tourism, as calls for international contributions were supported by the mythical status of the Phi Phi islands. The humanitarian aid did indeed assist in the recuperation of the island communities to such an extent that today the region is 'functional' again. Yet this may be brewing new problems: in July 2005 Sarah White of *Lonely Planet* published a new report on local developments in the *Los Angeles Times*, which today figures on the web amongst a series of e-brochures for tourism in Thailand. The report, titled 'Phi Phi's charm is entirely intact' (*Los Angeles Times* 2005), reassures prospective travellers that it is safe to visit the location and provides a long list of airline and accommodation suggestions. With so much pressure placed upon the Thai state to conform to the standards of Western markets, the local voice was subdued. What remains to be seen is whether the battle for sustainable development was fought and lost or whether it has just begun.

3 'National elf services'

Organized capitalism as resistance

A few years ago, a local travel agency in a Lancashire town put on its window a makeshift brochure that foretold the future of destination advertising for New Zealand. The 'brochure' figured the digitized image of Gollum, one of the mythical creatures that appear in the *Lord of the Rings* (*LOTR*) cinematic trilogy directed by Peter Jackson (2001, 2002, 2003). The image of Gollum itself was not so much a surprise to me – these mythical creatures are advertised across the UK attracting the attention of young and adult fans, and as Beeton (2005: 137, 138, 181) has observed, they did overflow New Zealand's urban landscape and media headlines for a long while. The message of the brochure, which invited British travellers to 'visit Middle Earth', was another matter. The *LOTR* trilogy was filmed in New Zealand, but any reference to the country itself had been overwritten by a fictional story. I was sufficiently intrigued to step into the agency and talk with the manager, who turned out to be a recognized 'Aussie expert' with half a dozen certificates on the walls of his office. When I mentioned the picture, he was distraught and explained that he does indeed cater for tourists who want to visit the Antipodes because of the films. The makeshift advertising that intrigued me was a means to attract as many holiday buyers as possible. Problems began every time potential tourists descended upon him with unreasonable requests: to book for tours in filmed locations, have a family break in a place like the Shire (another mythical location that appears in the film) at the wrong time of the year, or visit inaccessible mountainous areas that put their life in danger. It was evident that yet another group of films had produced a chain effect leading to the construction of a new sign industry.

The present chapter reconstructs the profile of this sign industry, which from the outset invited its consumers to 'simulate' (in Baudrillard's [1983] terms) the *LOTR* cinematic adventure. I argue that the *LOTR* tourism is characterized by simulation of a fantasy to such an extent that we must reconsider the notion of authenticity 'on location'. More insight is gained in this direction when we explore reactions of film viewers who discuss the virtuality of the three films' content and occasionally their tourist potential. Even though some of their reflections correspond to those we encounter in backpack fan cultures, especially in those travel enclaves that value adventure tourism and ecotourism, the two are by no means identical. Backpackers are, as I explained in the previous chapter, obsessed with nostalgia for a lost authenticity, whereas simulation tourists seek to experience a fictional condition with no 'real' core. The way that commercial tourist providers used the films in the manufacturing of the tourist experience catered mainly (but not exclusively) for the second type of tourism, promoting the image of New Zealand as the 'Home of Middle Earth'. To avoid any misunderstandings I would like to clarify again that my virtual flâneurs are not identical to actual tourists, who might have enjoyed their holidays in New Zealand in ways different from the ones the *LOTR* sign industry suggested. All the same, the viewers' responses to its stimuli verify the power sign industries have over collective imaginations.

More importantly, in this chapter I explore the nature of the New Zealand state responses to the *LOTR*'s global success. The intense competition of foreign and native tourist providers aimed to secure the control of the *LOTR* branding that was coveted by other countries and businesses around the world. The initial generation of 'unco-ordinated [tourist] circuits' (Lash and Urry 1987: 208) sidelined New Zealand's economic action and seemed to have introduced a phase in which capitalist interests would flourish outside the state's jurisdiction. The New Zealand state's dramatic comeback did not necessarily cancel or alter these fragmented economic pursuits; rather, it assisted in reinstating the country's status as a global economic competitor. The ebbs and flows of capitalist competition do not comprise the focus of this chapter as such. Although the proactive attitude of New Zealand state agents (especially government actors) can be read as a form of the nation-state's submission to a progressive decentralization of economic control, their creative manipulation of the *LOTR* sign industry betrays some resistance to the *LOTR* global plundering. What I want to argue is that those subjected to the demands of the sign industries can also manipulate the signs at their disposal. As we will explore below, while (or perhaps because) state agents and other auxiliaries to New Zealand interests were trying to appropriate some *LOTR* cultural artifacts for tourist consumption, they were involved in the production and projection of a new New Zealand cultural image abroad.

The Lord of the Rings: a cinematic biography

The *LOTR* adaptation process is typical of Hollywood's global control over cinematic production. The venture to film the story was undertaken by New Line, a Time Warner subsidiary largely unknown before this breathtaking success, which nowadays figures in every DVD home library. Luckily for the small company, the *LOTR* trilogy won more Oscars than any other trilogy in the annals of cinematic history and made those involved in the creation of the films globally famous. We know now that New Line gambled US$300 million on the three films and the talent of young director Peter Jackson, risking bankruptcy. The story had a happy ending, but an agonizing trajectory. Landmark in this trajectory proved to be the decision to film the story in Jackson's native country, New Zealand, in order to control the costs. Jackson himself claimed that he was struck 'by the similarities between New Zealand's unspoilt terrain' and Tolkien's depiction of a 'rugged Middle Earth' (*Guardian* 2001b) a comment which shows that from its inception the *LOTR* cinematic saga started taking on a life of its own, blurring the boundaries between imaginary and real worlds. Unfortunately, Jackson's decision provoked the English fans of the novel, for reasons that deserve examination.

First, it is important to look at the original story, which was written by the British author J. J. R. Tolkien (1892–1973), twice Professor of Anglo-Saxon ('Old English') at Oxford University (see The Tolkien Society undated: prgs 1–2). The story, which spans many 'prehistoric' centuries, explores the end of the 'Middle Earth' cultures of Elves, Dwarves, Orcs, Trolls and Hobbits (all Tolkien's literary creations), and the accession of 'Men'. It does so through Frodo Baggins' and his friends' heroic decision to challenge the plans of the newly awakened Dark Lord to rule Middle Earth, by destroying the powerful ring that will make him invincible. The story, which was originally published in three volumes – *The Fellowship of the Ring* (1954), *The Two Towers* (England 1954, US 1955) and *The Return of the King* (1955) – captured the English imagination. At the time there were rumours that Tolkien derived inspiration from his World War II experience, but this was vociferously denied by the author in his foreword to the second edition of the novel (Tolkien 1999: xvii).

In this fantastic story Tolkien captures the life of a rural world that was slowly sinking into oblivion. To look at *LOTR* through a sociological lens, one may claim that Tolkien provided a Weberian understanding of 'disenchantment', mirrored in the end of Hobbit and Elvish eras and the dawn of warfare and appropriation of natural resources – the beginning of rationalization in human history, in short. But Tolkien's work was

influential in ways that the imaginative professor could not have anticipated: for example, in the 1960s the *LOTR* was happily adopted by an
emerging counterculture that politicized environmental concerns
(implicit in Tolkien's presentation of the war industry of the Dark Lord
and his ally, Saruman the White, that destroys the idyllic Shire and the
universe of sentient trees). More importantly, the *LOTR* mythology
became part of English *cultural* heritage. If we take seriously the *National
Geographic*'s (undated) recent comment that the *LOTR* has provided a
consistent and coherent narration of the English past (since English
history stops abruptly in the era of Viking colonization), then we may be
able to understand the angry English responses to the filmic transposition
of the story to New Zealand.

From the outset Peter Jackson tried to differentiate his films from the
book. His relationship with the Tolkien Estate, which manages *LOTR*
profits and interests, was restricted to an initial consultation regarding
permission. The Tolkien Estate distanced itself from the venture, allowing
Jackson to innovate and 'interpret', as he said in an interview with fans
(see FortuneCity 2000). He spent three years with screenwriter Philippa
Boyens and his wife adapting the novel and debating the visual
presentation of Tolkien's numerous characters. The aspiration was to
create something that 'felt much, much more real [than standard fantasy
films]' (Jackson 2002). A quick look at the official *LOTR* website
convinces us that Jackson achieved much more: not only is the site
copyrighted by both New Line Productions and New Zealand Tourism,
but it also hosts a number of computer games, toys and other items
modelled on the cinematic representation of the *LOTR* characters. The
three films created a massive tourist industry in New Zealand ('Home of
Middle Earth', as the website states), as well as a microcosm of consumption practices.

The initial scepticism that Tolkien fans expressed for Jackson's creation
had other ramifications that take us deep into the catacombs of
Hollywood's politics and economics. Jackson's courteous communiqués
to fans online were in fact part of an organized attempt of media conglomerates to simultaneously 'tame' fan networks (potentially dangerous
for corporate interests) and use them for the maximization of profit. In a
critical take on cultural studies approaches to fan cultures as sites of
resistance to established consumption modes, pioneered by Jenkins
(1992) and Tulloch (1995), Murray (2004) explained that in the case
of the *LOTR* trilogy fan opinion was successfully streamlined to serve
New Line's project. With the first signs of fan reaction to the novel's
appropriation by New Line, it was arranged for Peter Jackson to participate in two online question-and-answer sessions with Henry Knowles'

highly influential film update website *Ain't it Cool News*. These 'sessions' gave Jackson (and indirectly New Line and Time Warner) the opportunity to monitor public opinion on the films by offering fans a few glimpses of the project in advance. This was followed by the moderate, yet unmistakable, control of fan sites exclusively dedicated to the trilogy (among them the well known TheOneRingNet and Ringbearer.org) and other enticing offers (such as including fan names in the DVD credits) (Murray 2004: 19). In conclusion, the manipulation of Tolkien fan groups neutralized the risk of New Line's failure to appeal to global audiences.

Naturally, such background information casts a shadow of suspicion when one visits online film reviews from IMDB and Amazon.com. Both sites have an increasing number of reviews that today exceeds 7,000 in total. As in the previous chapter, I organized the analysis of their content by arranging them in tropes of consumption (of the film, the filmed locations and other cinematic paraphernalia). These tropes often matched the marketing practices of the New Zealand tourist industry – a result that echoes the successful outcome of New Line's fan appropriation. More specifically, I use tropes I identified in the reviews to argue that the *LOTR* tourist development in and around New Zealand was based *on an anticipation of the viewers' cinematic reception of the films*. I examine the type of experience that these holiday providers, mostly based in New Zealand, promise through brochures and other online materials. My aim is to offer a theoretical understanding of how the authentic is constructed in these marketed 'experiences'. In tandem, I look at other *LOTR* paraphernalia that complete the imagined journeys of *LOTR* fans. Finally, I investigate state-driven responses in New Zealand to the whole phenomenon, to shed light on the changes that the *LOTR* introduced in New Zealand's self-perceptions.

Hyperreality and CGI

I have already pointed out elsewhere that the mythical element 'is unavoidable in discussions of travel and tourism' (Rojek 1997: 52), as place is always a category socially constructed though an index of real and imagined references. The construction of New Zealand's natural backdrop as Middle Earth in the *LOTR* films and film reviews is an excellent example of this process. Numerous film viewers claimed that the cinematic scenery is located in a fantastic world (see for example IMDB, Annapolis, Maryland, 19 April 2004) whereas others completely identified New Zealand's 'sheer beauty' with Middle Earth (see for example IMDB, Annapolis, Maryland, 19 April 2004, Yorktown, Virginia, 6 March 2004). As one viewer put it, in the *LOTR* films we experience:

[A] mystical journey though places that seem ripped off a fairy tale. Every location . . . is so detailed and rich, that it can lead some to believe that these locations actually exist – all locations are so fantastic, yet have an incredible historic undertone to them.

(IMDB, Montreal, Canada, 23 March 2004;
see also Amazon, 7 December 2001)

The identification of the historic and the fantastic allegedly originates in Tolkien, who wanted his work 'to match other great epics like the Iliad' (IMDB, Stoke-on-Trent, England, 9 February 2004). We note that viewers move from literature to history and then to cinematic technology, making them interchangeable terms. It may be worth recalling de Certeau's argument that history writing insists on the exposition of the 'false' and 'error' in the past and not with reality as such (1988b: 200). Historians' main interest is in the mythical elements of storytelling which are often granted arbitrarily with an objective, real, status in order to become meaningful carriers of a society's past. More correctly, for some viewers the New Zealand scenery is integrated into the cinematic narrative though what Lévi-Strauss (1964) has termed 'totemism': it is transformed from *nature* into a *cultural* product that audiences consume, just as storytelling becomes socially meaningful history when it manages to conceal its fabulist origins.

The cinematic consumption of New Zealand incorporates some striking sensory experiences that we encounter in actual tourism. My reference to the senses does not take us back to an analysis of the tourist experience through universal aesthetic categories, as Harrison (2001, mobilizing Porteous [1996]) has claimed; on the contrary, it examines senses in the specific context in which they operate. In general, some viewers' comments are occulocentric, as they seek ways to visually encapsulate the *LOTR* background (see for example IMDB, 17 June 2003; Amazon, UK, 31 December 2002). Interestingly, 'gazing', subjecting landscape to scrutiny and enjoying it as a tourist commodity, is often equated with the specific cinematic technologies that the makers of the *LOTR* use. As a viewer explains:

Certainly the most breathtaking scenes in the movie are the moments of patient observation, when the camera spins around and captures the beautiful settings of Middle Earth.

(IMDB, Chicago, 11 April 2004)

Such cinematic scenes are numerous, and involve long distance and high angle shots of mountains and valleys from helicopters, often with the story's heroes in focus. It may not be an exaggeration to argue that especially the two Hobbits, Frodo Baggins (Elijah Wood) and Sam Gamgee (Sean Austin), whose trek to Mordor unfolds in the trilogy, enable viewers to enjoy the whole tourist experience: not just to see, but also to taste, touch, smell and actively partake in adventure (see Langkeek 2001). Frodo and Sam are, in other words, *virtual tourists* with whom the viewer is invited to identify. Watching the film becomes more real than actual touring, as the following viewer claims:

> For a student who lives by the suitcase and the airplane . . . as a way of life, it is a joy to have these films accessible to watch everywhere I go. And not because I carry my laptop and DVDs always, but because I find equally enthusiastic and cheerful fans who are willing to share the happy viewing with me, whether it be in Frankfurt, New York . . . and yes, even Auckland.
>
> (IMDB, Annapolis, Maryland, 19 April 2004)

The viewer encapsulates dramatic changes on the global social map. The community of *LOTR* fans in which he places himself is a highly fluid formation. It is not defined in relation to belonging, but in terms of a commonality of temporary interests that some sociologists attribute to youth culture (see for example Bennett 1999; Hetherington 1998). Maffesoli's (1996) analysis of tribalism (or neotribalism) applies here, not least because the viewer seems to traverse urban space and cultures in which social cohesion is under threat and new forms of socialization emerge. In this new social landscape the traveller is the viewer and imagined journeys are inscribed onto the image-text of the film:

> Hobbiton is perfect. The houses have flower patches and old fences, and roads look worn and made through decades of travel. And the Old Mill spins with the laziness of a quiet town. Every color is vibrant and every moment looks as though it was taken from a picture book.
>
> (IMDB, Chicago, 11 April 2004;
> Ottawa, Canada, 24 January 2004)

'Travel' here becomes an extension of the ways in which *LOTR* fans index the fantastic, but it is the consumption of this fantastic world that never refers to reality as such that dominates the film reviews. Currently, there is a battle on IMDB and Amazon.com around the artificiality of the movie images, which is quite revealing. On the one hand, there are viewers who welcome Computer Generated Images (CGI) because they enhance the novel's 'futuristic space setting' (IMDB, Sweden, 3 January 2004), enable the camera to play the role of the 'Rough Guide to Middle Earth', staying 'wholly true to the original's aesthetic' (IMDB, UK, 23 April 2003) and making Middle Earth 'a real place' (IMDB, Greece, 10 November 2003 and 11 April 2003; IMDB, US 25 November 2002; IMDB, Oakland, Canada, 24 October 2002). For this group of viewers, New Zealand becomes a footnote in the cinematic text: the role of the exotic landscape becomes auxiliary to the reproduction of a fantastic narrative. To quote two more IMDB commentators: 'the landscape is foreign enough and without twenty-first century hindrances as to make it a believable substitute for Middle Earth' (IMDB, Canada, 14 September 2004) and gives a 'touch of mystery' to the movie (IMDB, Wales, UK, 29 August 2004). Given that the *LOTR* films are a fiction constructed upon fiction, reality as such disappears from the plane and is replaced by a universe of images that appear to be real but never refer back to a 'real' world. Following this analytical path, we cannot speak any more of cinematic *representations* (as they should always refer back to a reality they represent), but about *simulation* of a non-existent place. It is nevertheless worth pointing out that even within the hyperreal regime of the *LOTR*, viewers recognize the use of representational modes of simulations (e.g. CGI of

Figure 3.1 Gandalf on horseback: in this multilevel composite, a miniature element of Minas Tirith is combined with a matte painting of Mordor, sky replacement and a CGI mist while the foreground comes from a practical element filmed on a New Zealand landscape. This is a perfect simulacrum of the 'host' country.

Source: New Line Cinema/Photofest. © New Line Cinema

the Middle Earth). This point is further supported by almost 100 viewers from Amazon.com, who recommend the DVD version of the trilogy because of its extended 'special effects' documentary that deconstructs the New Zealand 'digital experience'.

Another, smaller group of viewers, nevertheless criticized the digital technology that the *LOTR* makers used to mediate Middle Earth imagery. This group is infuriated by the whole 'cgi-induced hypnosis' of the films, which pays no attention to the plot and the idea of 'a well-told story' (IMDB, USA, 23 June 2003). Here the literary (the novel) is separated from the pictorial (digitized images), although the fact that both have no 'real' referents remains the same. More critical was another viewer who rejects the whole enterprise together with its simulatory value:

> [These] movie[s] . . . appeal to those of us who are sheltered, sub-urbanites or are urban individuals caught in an urban struggle and want to escape through some loser's imagination. . . . That is the whole movie right there, nothing more, nothing less, overall it's a movie, that's right a movie, not a way of life.
>
> (IMDB, Thunder Bay, Ontario, 22 September 2003)

The viewer condemns the pathological aspects of *LOTR* consumption, highlighting its concealed links with modern lifestyle (see also Slater 1997: 99). He or she claims, in effect, that the *LOTR* films offer escapism to their fans from the everyday and the mechanic, while at the same time they conceal the fact that the very experience is standardized, mechanical and inauthentic – a mere simulation of a simulation. Interestingly, the writer also situates this form of misrecognition of the artificial for real in urban milieus, providing another link between the 'loss of the self' in consumption and modern life in the developed world. As Strain (2003) has explained, the transformation of travel in search of authenticity into a safe holiday package for tourists has simply found an extension in virtual travel (computer games and online). Both 'safe' tourism and virtual travel insulate and protect us from the dangers of experience, while they 'both attempt to make the environmental bubble as invisible as possible' (2003: 260). The aforementioned reviewer recognizes the analogy and, often, the continuity between organized tourism and mediated experience of simulated landscape in films. This observation may explain why a critique of *LOTR* simulation is already inherent in the comments of other viewers, who do not necessarily oppose CGI but value the natural beauty of New Zealand as such. In these reviews Jackson is criticized for 'going over the top' with the aesthetic 'enrichment' of the landscape, making it artificial (IMDB, Australia, 1 October 2004; London, UK, 18 September 2004).

The fear here is that the viewer's imagined travel on the screen can be contaminated when the authentic, natural, landscape of New Zealand can offer a pure visual experience. On this occasion, the practice of demediating mediation is concealed: and viewers deny that watching a movie is not identical to visiting the viewed place. Others move even further, stressing the 'bucolic peaceful setting' of the film (IMDB, 21 February 2004; Maidenhead, Berkshire, 27 January 2004; IMDB, New York, 27 December 2003). It is true that even here the reproduction of 'natural' authenticity (or nature as authentic) is mythologized (IMDB, Helsinki, Finland, 13 September 2004), but this is, as I have already explained, an element constitutive of the tourist experience.

References to urban life make one suspect that the aestheticization of *LOTR* natural backdrops maintains its links with the romantic turn in travel and tourism during the nineteenth century. The need to escape from an increasingly industrialized world, which offers no possibilities for the redemption of a unitary self but promotes fragmentation, rationalization and self-discipline, was part of the romantic project. The authentic and the sublime merged in the age of romanticism, and were pursued though an interest in nature and an increasing valorization of peasant, agrarian ways of life (Stocking 1987). Agrarian life acquired value within the context of nationalist movements in which the 'folk' came to represent the origins of the 'nation'. For some viewers the Shire is seen as 'a fairy vision of England' (IMDB, Chicago, 21 January 2003), for example. The idea of representing the Old English way of life was thought to be implicit in Tolkien's story. The little Hobbit houses with their gardens and the small Shire community occupied some space in English reviews of the *LOTR* trilogy (see for example IMDB, London, UK, 20 November 2004). Here, although the controversy was over the 'appropriate' simulation of a fantastic community, the idea of an authentic 'way of living' (which is British, not from New Zealand!) persists, constructing a form of cultural resistance that originates in the very genealogy of travel and tourism.

Contrariwise, New Zealanders welcomed the films, rediscovering their country in the cinematic (natural) background. '"The Fellowship of the Ring" is a film that makes me appreciate my home of New Zealand so much more. I always loved it, but the success of this film has changed New Zealand so much and made it a lot better known' said one reviewer (IMDB, 25 December 2004). 'Thanks to the film everyone can see the beauty of my country and one day I hope they have the chance to come here and fall in love with it as I have', cunningly stated another New Zealander (IMDB, 28 April 2003). We note that even in reviews New Zealanders recognize the economic avenues that the films opened up. They were not the only ones: another viewer exclaims that 'the New Zealand tourist board must have love[d] Peter Jackson!' (IMDB, Dublin, 5 March 2003). A second commentator feels tempted to visit the country, stating: 'I never knew New Zealand was SO beautiful!! What a great advertisement this film makes for the director's home-land!' (IMDB, Northern California, 21 January 2003). 'It works as a very effective commercial for New Zealand tourism', said a third (IMDB, 30 December 2003) and a fourth viewer (IMDB, Australia, 25 December 2001). 'A bunch of New Zealand-born people [e.g. the makers of the *LOTR*] eventually put the world at their feet' (IMDB, 15 December 2003), concludes another one. Bearing in mind the virtual role that the vast majority of viewers attributed to New Zealand landscapes in the film, what kind of world did the makers of the *LOTR* actually create? In order to answer this question we will have to examine how the exploitative potential of the films was mobilized by the tourist industry.

Welcome to *Orc*land: from 'staged authenticity' to the authentic stage

New Zealand was largely unknown to the rest of the world before the mid-1800s, when it was colonized by the British (1840 Treaty of Waitangi) (Belich 1986). Independence came after just over a century and a half, when the demographic make-up of New Zealand had already changed: today, the country has approximately 3.6 million people, with only 15 percent of native, Maori stock. The rest of the population is of British and northern European origins (Perkins and Thorns 2001: 193). The New Zealand economy was traditionally agricultural. The country has only five urban enclaves with the Auckland area leading in numbers of residents (almost 1.5 million). Historically the country attracted adventurous European and Australian travellers (Watson 1993), but internal mass tourism is situated in economic changes that took place from the 1960s regarding the regularization of paid holidays and urban development. The generation of ties between the local and global capitalist economy also contributed to an influx of foreign tourists, notably ecotourists from Japan, Taiwan, Korea and Germany (Pearse and Simons 1997). Jackson's *LOTR* trilogy certainly complemented (or often 'reinvented') ecotourism, when a number of local and international tourist providers began to offer holidays that were framed on the cinematic trilogy. The shift from an appreciation of wild nature, scenery and indigenous Maori culture (of which some New Zealanders are very proud and which often constitutes a tourist attraction in itself) to tourist trajectories that follow those of the *LOTR* films exemplifies a breakdown of Dean MacCannell's (1973) differentiation between front and back stages of the tourist experience.

In his ground-breaking essay MacCannell drew upon Goffman's analysis of the performative nature of self-presentation in everyday life (1987[1959]: 114). Following Goffman's identification of an 'offstage', a secret space in which the 'self' is prepared before it enters the public domain, MacCannell (1973: 596) explained that tourist destinations are divided by locals into two different regions: the front and the back. In the front region, the tourist watches a series of magical performances that the locals conjure for consumption by visiting 'others'. These performances are, in effect, interpretations of tourist understandings of local authenticity (the 'unique' and 'unspoiled' qualities of alien cultures that we presumably want to experience during our holidays). What is concealed from the tourist-observer is the chaotic 'backstage' where the cultural masks are tried on and colourful costumes still hang on the rails. The backstage of local experience is the intimate space of a culture, which the tourist is not allowed to enter. Some sociologists have criticized MacCannell because his assumption that something authentic has been tragically lost fosters an 'imperialist nostalgia' (for a critique see Crang 1997: 148–9). Cultures are not watertight compartments: on the contrary, they are always dialogically constructed through encounters with the 'other'. Another comment, which will lead straight to my argument, is in order here: we cannot assume that the differentiation between authentic and staged is present in all tourist destinations. Indeed the *LOTR* tourist experience does not require a distinction between front and back regions, as the *LOTR authentic is always-already the staged*. In other words, the authenticity that *LOTR*-related holidays offer is the enhanced locales in which the story was filmed.

To illustrate the point, I will examine a number of holiday offers by commercial providers. First in the list is Air New Zealand, one of the major *LOTR* sponsors, which operates through Concorde International, an integrated travel company. Before the Wellington premiere of *The Return of the King*, the company unveiled another in a series of its themed aircraft, featuring images of two major *LOTR* stars, Liv Tyler (Arwen) and Miranda Otto (Eowyn) (B&T 2004). At the same time it offered two special package deals to New Zealand with extended tours of the regions in which the motion pictures were filmed. The first package ('Christchurch – Lord of the Rings Escape') included 'a full-day Lord of the Rings location tour at Geraldine, where Edoras was built for the filming of the movie'. The second one ('Queenstown – Middle-Earth Explorer') included visits to:

Some of the locations used to film significant scenes in The Lord of the Rings . . . Nomad Safaris operates 4WD tours into the heart of New Zealand's high country, which embodies Middle Earth brought to life in the films.

(Concorde International 2004)

The company assumes that visitors are more interested in the places in which the *LOTR* films were staged than in the natural beauties of the country. Positively Wellington Tourism, another tourist agency, has an even more detailed website with archived footage from the world premiere of the *LOTR* films and two detailed tour options. Significantly, it warns potential customers that 'conservation and legal requirements mean no film sets from the Lord of the Rings remain. Yet, there is still a lot of Middle Earth to see' and that 'a Rover Rings or Flat Earth Tour will take you to the best former filming spots' (Positively Wellington Tourism 2003). The tours also include visits to some of the actors' favourite places and cafés, as well as many *LOTR* signposted locations (especially related to the Shire 'rural' area). Again, we are invited to visit the 'stage', on the assumption that this is what we look for. The practice of highlighting filmed locations is exemplified by Matamata's signpost 'Welcome to Hobbiton', in front of which many visitors are photographed. Drawing on MacCannell (1989), Beeton (2005: 4) identified such signposts as markers of tourist locations, constitutive of the tourist industries' sign-making process. Another holiday provider based in New Zealand, Hassle-Free Holidays, replaces such itineraries with photographic images of the glacier-carved valleys that figure in the film, relating them to the story (Hassle-Free Holidays undated). In addition to such visual attraction 'posts', Wanaka Sightseeing promises reviews of the scenes on the spots and 'the opportunity to handle and try on items featured in the movies' (Wanaka Sightseeing Lord of the Rings Tours undated). The archetypal consumer that is constructed by these holidaymakers is the 'post-tourist' (Rojek 1993: 177; Ritzer and Liska 1997: 107) who indulges in merchandized fantasy: in simulacra.

The question of marker-making calls for more attention here. GINZ.com, a well-known online travel shop, suggests to prospective travellers a 4–6 or full 15-day tour through New Zealand to visit all the famous *LOTR* locations. The travel shop includes a map of the country which is pencilled with all the important *LOTR* markers – an excellent example of the ways in which the fantastic creates virtual journeys. The site also suggests that travellers to New Zealand obtain a copy of Ian Brodie's *The Lord of the Rings Location Guidebook* (Harper Collins 2002 exclusive edition; 2003 revised edition) that is already available globally through all the important online bookshops and other online commercial providers. The book is highly recommended by those readers who have already visited the country (see Review Centre undated). Ian Brodie is curator at the New Zealand Fighter Pilots Museum in Wanaka (one of the *LOTR* cinematic locations) and he is currently advertising his work through the Museum's official website. Not only is this companion a popular version of the middle-class oriented Rough Guides (with comments and maps on the films' set locations and B&B's), but it is also an effective advertisement for the films, as it contains movie photographs, before-and-after CGI photos, and sections written by Peter Jackson, Alan Lee (*LOTR* designer), Barry Osborne (*LOTR* producer) and some of the actors. More importantly, each *LOTR*-related region that Brodie presents in his guide is symbolically signposted by its mythical name: the Edge of Lothorien is 554 39.442'; the Pillars of the Kings is S45 00.711- E 168 53.567'; and so on. The suggestion that the sign industry creates a self-referential system in which ideas and imagery circulate between the cinematic and tourist regimes seems to apply in this instance. Journeys mythically create the place that we visit, according to de Certeau (1986: 37), just as writing recreates its object. In this *LOTR* companion the fantastic journey that we make is already prescheduled and lived through the films and the *LOTR* companion. It must be noted that the almost devotional advertising of the *Location Guidebook* by GINZ.com is a reciprocation of Brodie's repeated reference to this particular online agency in his guide – nothing surprising, since both belong to the same sign industry.

GINZ.com also invents an imaginary guide who takes us across *LOTR*-land. The site invites us to 'immerse in Mordor', to 'experience River Anduin' and to 'drift though the scenery'; it takes us to the home of the *LOTR* crews and makers, and offers us Harrington beer 'brewed for Hobbiton and the scenes from the Prancing Pony' (GINZ.com 2004). Finally, it suggests a 45-minute 'Middle-Earth helicopter explorer tour', which will take us to all the inaccessible locations of the films. We do, indeed, deal with the creation and recreation of the tourist gaze and the tourist himself as a whole person, who can smell, taste, gaze and participate in the *LOTR* adventure. This has created some very unusual problems for UK tourist providers, who are currently scratching their heads on how they can 'provide accommodation at Bag End' and how to explain to their customers that 'the Mines of Moria live only in the director's computer' (*Guardian* 2002). How can it be otherwise, when we note that in GINZ.com holiday packages the tourist is identified with the little Hobbits, the virtual tourists of the films, who walk through Hobbiton, sleep in the Prancing Pony and drink their special beer.

Moreover, the helicopter tour places the visitor in the position of an *omnipresent* cameraman who encapsulates the spectacular *LOTR* world 'from above' – a technique that is constantly employed in the films.

The argument concerning the emergence of an authentic stage in New Zealand has other ramifications. One of them is concerned with hiking as adventure tourism, an established type of tourism in New Zealand (Cloke and Perkins 1998), which is less passive than helicopter sightseeing. This option cannot be identified as an organized (package) holiday offer, but must be examined for three reasons: the first is that it takes us to the lower budget end of the holiday range. Yet it is not necessarily the less well-off who prefer this option, but those most infatuated with the movies. The second reason, therefore, is that it allows us to gain interesting insights into the *LOTR* fan culture: and the third is that it highlights the impact of the *LOTR* trilogy on pre-existing holiday options in New Zealand.

Following the tenth death of a foreign mountain climber, the New Zealand Mountain Safety Council's executive director Ian Nicholson complained about the marketing of the country's mountainous areas as what he called 'an adventure playground' that 'lures adventure seekers'. He warned that 'more deaths are likely to follow' if precautions are not taken by 'Lord of the Rings' would-be hikers (*USA Today* 2004). It must be stressed that adventure seeking here is not intended as an ecotourist ritual that connects the visitor with the environment. The religious sublimation that may overwhelm Adler's (1992: 408–13) 'anchorite' pilgrim, who looks for spiritual purity in the wilderness, or the 'ascetic' subject who rejects the homely comforts, are more useful starting points. We should not forget that Tolkien's story (the viewers of the film and Peter Jackson himself inform us) is that of a battle between good and evil. The undertaking of a dangerous venture by *LOTR* fans becomes thus a re-enactment of Frodo's heroic journey to Mount Doom – but with no ring to destroy and with a tragic twist in the story's cinematic ending. On the one hand climbing transforms the *LOTR* viewers into mythical participants and their experience into myth-simulation; on the other hand, it redramatizes an experience of purification (from the Dark Lord, the source of evil). However, this adventurous option coexists with package tourism, available to others who may want to visit the Ruapehu region (part of fictional Mordor) under safer circumstances: tours to Tongarino National Park are very popular, and they come in various combinations (see Forest Lodge 2005).

The last example shows that further emphasis on the simulatory nature of the *LOTR* tourism may obscure some other promotional developments that take place alongside it in the filmed locations. For example, other tourist providers in Ruapehu do not hesitate to fuse *LOTR* tours with an exploration of the Maori culture. In this case, it seems that the *LOTR* success is manipulated for the expansion of cultural tourism, which is less popular in New Zealand (Ruapehu Tourism undated). There are other occasions on which this happens. For example, Rings Scenic Tours Ltd, suggested in Brodie's book to the *LOTR* fans, may be specializing in tours to the original locations of the cinematic Hobbiton, but it also advertises the 'Shire's Rest'. This centre is similar to ecotourist retreats but also serves for social functions and conferences. The company claims to be offering access to a 'tranquil setting', surrounded by 'stunning landscapes and far-reaching views' of mountains, designed for 'breakaway groups', conferences and private social functions (Rings Scenic Tours 2005). Thus, the advertising of this retreat in Matamata (the real 'Shire'), which is addressed to traditional tourists and travellers as well as to natives, suggests a return to the discourse of authenticity similar to that which we noted in the case of *The Beach*. Other websites for tourists and travellers also list Matamata's Shire in Waikato, but are careful to add that 'the movie set was returned to its natural state' (*Backpackers Ultimate Guide* 2005). Backpacker site GoNomad.com has even posted an article in which the senior editor discusses her experience of travelling across New Zealand with her daughter. The account of their visits to filmed locations (among other picturesque stops) reads more like ecotourist travel recommended 'for kids' than an exercise in simulation. 'More than Middle Earth' (GoNomad 2003), the title of the article states. One may conclude that the *LOTR*'s simulation tourism may have overwhelmed the global market, but it did not replace ecotourism or cultural tourism in the country.

A general point one can make about these developments is that the New Zealand *LOTR* tourist industry begins as a decentralized and, by and large, private enterprise. It was simply that local and global commercial providers rushed to grasp the opportunity for profit-making without worrying too much about state control – with the exception of natural preservation regulations that everybody, including the *LOTR* makers, had to respect. Following Lash and Urry (1987) one may argue that global *LOTR* tourism in New Zealand was rather 'disorganized', as it was characterized by independence of monopolies from state regulation and regional, rather than national growth initiatives (the Wellington and Christchurch examples are prominent). The authentic stage of the *LOTR* can be understood within the framework of a local and global battle for brand monopolies. Nowadays, countries are increasingly using brands to secure a 'place' in the global markets – or, alternatively, they produce their own brands to compete in global markets: Cuba is the place of salsa dancing; Ireland is the land of Guinness; and New Zealand has become 'the home of Middle Earth'. The process often involves a number of factors and actors (state and private), as the case of New Zealand itself proves (Ryan 2002), but we may also note here that there are signs that the networks of branding initiatives in New Zealand may change. As I will explain below, the recognition of the *LOTR* films as part of New Zealand's legacy brought some state initiatives back into the picture.

It's mine! (my precious): contested monopolies, emotional investments

Thorns (1997) called for more attention to the development of New Zealand urban tourism in the last decade. According to Thorns, the need to compensate for an internal decline in manufacturing advanced the development of new urban attractions that are also available in other parts of the world (night clubs, casinos and museums) and which are 'addressed' to global urban tourists. The *LOTR* success contributed even more in this direction, as *Guardian* correspondent Matthew Brace informs us (*Guardian* 2003a). The city of Wellington in particular has become a paradise for *LOTR* fans who want to visit all the places at which the film crew have been spotted in the past three years. There are clubs, cafés, restaurants and bars that are advertised as 'the favourites' of *LOTR* actors Elijah Wood, Ian McKellen, Billy Boyd, Liv Tyler and Viggo Mortensen. Alongside these attractions, Wellington boasts its theatres, galleries and its national museum, inviting *LOTR* fans to visit these places as well (there is a long list of Wellington 'Places to Visit' in Brace's article). Wellington is a case of destination branding in the making: the celebrity aura of the *LOTR* actors and the trilogy itself certainly contributes in this direction (Beeton 2005: 184). As New Zealand's capital city, it follows the policies of creative industries around the world by turning itself into a cultural centre that may attract inward investment and international tourism (Leadbeater and Oakley 2005: 304).

Until recently New Zealand's urban space was not embedded in the *LOTR* experience; it was only after the launch of the *Lord of the Rings Exhibition* at Te Papa National Museum on 19 December 2002 (just before the New Zealand Premiere of *The Two Towers*) that this was achieved. Te Papa representatives had previously travelled to Los Angeles to discuss the possibility of an exhibition of *LOTR* costumes with New Line. In fact it took them two years to prepare a colossal show, which embarked in 2003 on an international museum tour that would last until 2005 (*New Zealand Herald* 2004b). The exhibition opened in the Science Museum in London just before the release of the last instalment of the *LOTR* trilogy, *The Return of the King*. It admitted fans from all over Europe and sold more advance tickets than any previous exhibition at the Science Museum (Talking Pictures 1 2003a). The exhibit showed in Singapore before visiting the Museum of Science, Boston in August 2004 (which announced ticket sales from 1 June 2004) and then Sydney (Museum of Science Boston 2004).

Before we move on to discuss this initiative, it is worth having a quick look at the content of the exhibition. It features film footage, props, costumes and artifacts from the films, including armoury, animatronics and miniatures. An interview with the cast (all dressed in the original costumes), the crew and the director also features amongst the exhibits. It is striking how much the *experiential* and *interactive* aspects are stressed, as first and foremost the exhibition enables visitors to enjoy and participate in some of the special film effects. Visitors are not there to be instructed in history, but to immerse themselves in popular culture (Featherstone 1991: 24) – to touch, for example, Orc armoury. A section that deals with 'scaling down' (of the Hobbit actors who are supposed to be smaller than humans) involves interviews with the filmmakers, but also facilities for the visitors who want to be photographed in a film set (see the Te Papa website for more). It is significant that demonstrations of special effects 'including the combining of "real" and "digital" action and CGI' (Talking Pictures 1 2003a) predominate. We do indeed deal with an 'implosion' (McLuhan 1964) of reality – to be more precise, the *LOTR* digital becomes more real than the real.

The museum exhibition has attracted various categories of what a *Guardian* reporter calls 'races' of fans (the neotribes to which I refer in the second section of the chapter). She is particularly impressed with the die-hards: 'those who know the book by heart, have bought special edition DVDs, audio tapes and art-work, camped out Wimbledon-style for the premieres . . . spent an embarrassing amount of money on collector items' (*Guardian*, 22 October 2003b). She is fascinated by the cries and shrieks of those who encounter for the first time the 'shard of Narsil', the 'phial of Galadriel' and the 'one ring'. She is also impressed by the type of 'collectomania' that possesses them: 'Jim' has bought a 'Sting' (Frodo's sword) for 120 Euros from a website, Heleenniuman wears his stick-on Elf ears and two girls from Denmark are dressed as Elves. A party of Japanese teenagers walk out of the gift shop with 'two life-sized cardboard cut-outs of Legolas and Aragorn', explaining that 'they will put them in their bathroom' (*Guardian* 2003b). There is no doubt that these items begin their life as consumption objects within the system of capitalist exchange. Yet what they signify for *LOTR* fans *sacralizes* them, because it bestows upon them an emotional value that contributes to their de-commodification (Kopytoff 1986; Weiner 1992). This parting of the commercial and the sacred/symbolic can be read as symptomatic of a general tension between consumer communities and markets that Kozinets (2001: 81–5) has identified elsewhere. The idea of sacralization applied even more to the original costumes and props of the *LOTR* films. As Peter Jackson stated, he will never put original items on auction and he would hate to see them on websites such as eBay, as this would damage their 'value' (*Guardian* 2003c). Jackson refers to the sign value of the *LOTR* objects, but he does not differentiate between their representational (they were worn by the celebrities of the *LOTR* trilogy) *and* simulatory (they refer to the ways the characters of the novels were conceptualized) association with humans (see also Kopytoff 1986: 85).

From the outset, the problem Te Papa Museum encountered was the difficulty of claiming *The Lord of the Rings* enterprise as part of New Zealand's 'heritage' in order to better exploit it for financial purposes. Even Peter Jackson despaired in an interview in 2003:

> I'm hoping to open a Lord of the Rings museum down there, which we can't at the moment because of the Tolkien Estate. But I'm hopeful that it will happen. A lot of tourists come to New Zealand because of the films, but there's nothing for them to see in terms of sets and so on. We've kept everything – every costume, every prop (in anticipation of a museum).
>
> (*Guardian* 2003c)

This battle for securing the *LOTR* branding for New Zealand could be explained on a purely commercial basis. In this respect, it is worth pointing out that reaction boils under the surface in Britain against a commercial success which put New Zealand on the global map but ignored the English origins of the novel. Quite a few British online reviewers of the *LOTR* trilogy expressed discontent with the 'repression' of these origins, and some attacked Peter Jackson ferociously for 'privileging' his home country. We note then that British viewers and fans understand the controversy over the *LOTR* rights as a national and cultural issue.

In reality, competition over the appropriation of the *LOTR* culture often assumed a local character, as the case of Canterbury in the English county of Kent proves. Situated in one of the lush regions of England, Canterbury is known for a rich local history inscribed onto its architecture. The western entrance to the town centre is framed by a medieval (1377–81) fortified gatehouse, which formed part of the town walls. This gatehouse includes two towers united by an arch (the Westgate Towers). In 2004 the advertising board next to the entrance of Canterbury City Library figured small posters designed by the local council to attract tourist attention. The posters, primarily advertising the Canterbury Roman Museum, also depicted the Westgate Towers. The iconography of the monument in the poster is telling: the two Canterbury towers appear as a painting taken out of the *LOTR* cinematic adaptation. The font in which the accompanying caption (Step inside and Explore the Westgate Towers) was printed is identical to the one used for the titles of the three *LOTR* films. Local gossip often situates Tolkien's Shire in Kent, as I was told in a conspiratory tone by locals and residents. For once we notice a reversal of the hyperreal condition which dictates that images have no real reference: in Canterbury's case, a significant 'site of memory' (Nora 1989) for the locality (the Westgate Towers) is replaced with a simulation (The Two Towers). Yet its replacement does not lead to the erasure of historical reality, only to a clever tourist commercialization of cultural authenticity. It is expected that the use of brand imaging in the advertising of Westgate Towers will bestow the monument with additional value (Lury 2004: 37–8) for the visitor – just like it does for the locals. This is one of the two cases of appropriation of the *LOTR* cultural capital worth mentioning

Figure 3.2 Raising emotional claims over the *LOTR* 'heritage': the Westgate Towers of Canterbury in the United Kingdom.

Source: © Rodanthi Tzanelli

from Canterbury. The second case exemplifies how independent local entrepreneurs mobilized the trilogy's success. *Café des Amis*, a restaurant situated within walking distance from the Westgate towers boasts that Orlando Bloom, a 'pure' Canterburian and *LOTR* actor (Legolas), declared that the food served there remains his favourite. Replicating Wellington initiatives, the director of the restaurant verifies this by quoting interviews in which Bloom discussed his culinary preferences. Bloom's alleged confession to have emotional attachments to Canterbury is used to raise the local profile in the eyes of visitors.

The same competitive attitude reappears in other regions of England. Again, this is accompanied by a claim on Tolkien's literary creativity. In a *Guardian* article (2003c) Jonathan Hewat, marketing and admissions manager for Stonyhurst College in Ribble Valley, complained that New Zealand would be taking all the glory when Tolkien allegedly had the green Lancashire in mind when he was writing the story. In a cunning entrepreneurial move, the *Guardian* reporter links the article to numerous suggestions for weekend breaks and holidays in Lancashire, following the commercial logic of the *LOTR* tourist industry. The logic mirrors New Line's attempt to cultivate and police a global fan community devoted to the *LOTR* brand. Strangely, although the official *LOTR* website registers all rights to the films and its products as New Line's intellectual property, it was the unwritten concern about the emotional devotion of fans that became the focus of corporate media attention. One could claim that, after all, emotional attachment to a unique creation forms the basis for the recognition of intellectual production ownership (Garnham 1990: 38). We could, therefore, consider the search for local recognition (as Tolkien's inspiration) an extension of the phenomenon of branding competition. It is simply that a *legal* battle has been transmuted into an *emotional* struggle. Celia Lury has explained that postmodern consumers operate as reflexive agents who adopt the 'semiotic logic of value' (Firat and Venkatesh 1993; cited in Lury 2004: 38) in their encounters with intangible products. This happens because the products themselves have a 'semantically autonomous' (*ibid.*: 98–9) presence constantly in need of fixity. Their occasional and often arbitrary attachment to events and activities generates a surplus of meanings that correspond to the social groups and the sociocultural orders in which they appear. The semantic autonomy of the *LOTR* representations (the 'intangibles' of corporate brands) thus invited various parties to play the role of the interpreter. Emotional monopolies were expressed elsewhere and in other ways. For example, we may read a tinge of competition in the London Film Critics' Circle awards in February 2004: with fury, *The New Zealand Herald* reported that the final instalment of the trilogy 'was overlooked by 100

British critics', despite the fact that it had won 'four US Golden Globe Awards' (2004a). With the Tolkien Estate retaining copyright of the novel and some commercial goods, global competition over the *LOTR* industry becomes even more fragmented and difficult.

The New Zealand state decided to take some initiative to protect commercial interests in the country. The stakes are high: early on, the New Zealand Institute for Economic Research, an independent economic forecast group, predicted that 'tourism will be the "star" of the country's export sector in the next two years', attributing this change to the *LOTR* success (CNN 2004). Between September 2002 and 2003, *LOTR*-induced foreign tourism earned NZ$6.4 billion (US$4.4 billion) and the amount has been growing since – something that pleased the Tourism New Zealand chief executive, George Hickton. Opinions converged behind one observation: New Zealand, a country that historically was seen as 'the dullest place on earth with more sheep than people' (*Guardian* 2002) attained a new identity as the exciting Middle Earth of Tolkien and Jackson. Beeton (2005: 137) has already remarked on the country's need for international recognition and the bolstering of local and national pride after the success of the trilogy. Exploring mainly Matamata's (Hobbiton) investment in its tourist profile, Beeton (2005: 88) highlights the emotional investment of New Zealanders in their newly acquired *LOTR* identity. It is this identity that the New Zealand government decided to defend, *appropriating the LOTR culture as New Zealand's new heritage.*

State initiatives, announced in 2003 by the Minister of Arts, Culture and Heritage, Helen Clark and Economic Development Minister Jim Anderton, involved a '$10 million annual funding boost for the NZ Film Commission, a review of the sector's funding agencies and the establishment of an industry led Screen Council' (Ministry of Economic Development, NZ 2003). Jim Anderton proudly added:

> A strong screen production sector helps strengthen our sense of national identity, our sense of ourselves as New Zealanders and internationally helps differentiate New Zealand, its people and its products by promoting our very special New Zealand brand.
>
> (Ministry of Economic Development, NZ 2003)

Interestingly, the New Zealand state contributed heavily (NZ$7 million) (Beeton 2005: 182) to the world premiere of the last film of the trilogy, *The Return of the King* (2003). In addition, the government had already put a minister in charge of *Lord of the Rings* in 2002 to fund studies of how 'it was enhancing Brand New Zealand' (Institute of Economic

Research, NZ 2002). The decision to have the film's world premiere in Wellington, and the encouragement of extensive global publicity of the event shows how committed the New Zealand government was to raising the country's international profile. In this conjunction of circumstances, Te Papa was used to host a series of events and exhibitions of national produce, sidestepping any questions of the *LOTR*-related competition and copyright ownership. Anderton's interview alone suggests that the expansion and modernization of the country's sign industry is not simply a response to global economic competition, but a long-term investment in New Zealand's self-perception and global image.

To further expand on this point, I will outline the results and consequences of this investment in the country's film production. In an attempt to capitalize more on the *LOTR* success, Economic Development Minister Trevor Mallard announced in December 2005 a series of promotional events linked to the forthcoming releases of several films that used New Zealand natural backdrops. Among them, *King Kong* (2005) and *The Chronicles of Narnia: The Lion, the Witch and the Wardrobe* (2005), are perhaps the most interesting cases. *King Kong* was directed by Peter Jackson who, keen to replicate the *LOTR* phenomenon, adopted a marketing strategy identical to that of the *LOTR* promotion by releasing the production diaries of the film well before the movie's completion. Unfortunately, the strategy did not work this time, as it led some *King Kong* fans to complain that Jackson 'is ruining the magic of the moviegoing experience' (*Empire* 2006). Nevertheless, in the summer of 2005 both *King Kong* and *The Chronicles of Narnia* had already created a sensation in Hollywood circles, as Film South Executive Director Jaqui Wood, who attended numerous meetings in Los Angeles, claimed (Film South NZ 6, 2005a: 4). *The Chronicles of Narnia* was also modelled on the *LOTR* paradigm: like the *LOTR* trilogy, the film was based on a children's book, inviting the use of CGI for the story's cinematic simulation. The film is already on its way to creating its own sign industry, whose first steps I outline below.

In December 2005 Film South, a film office that provides location permit and resource information to companies that want to shoot in the Canterbury and West Coast regions of the South Island, formed a marketing alliance with Film Wellington. The aim of this alliance, which was 'blessed' by the national government (Film South NZ 1, 2002: 2) and Ashburton District Council, was to develop the idea of using the stunning rocks at Flock Hill in the movie, under development at the time (Film South NZ 2, 2003). Two locations from Canterbury, Mount Sunday at Mount Potts in the Ashburton district (Edoras) and Ben Ohau Station in MacKenzie (Rohan) figured in the second and third movie of the *LOTR* trilogy, and became international tourist attractions (see online Tourism Guide Christchurch – Attractions and Maps; Film South NZ 3, 2003: 4). Obviously, the target of the local and national governments was to further develop the region's tourist sector through film. The collaboration of the two film offices led to an exhibition of the original location photographs in Selwyn Gallery, in nearby Christchurch (Film South-Latest News 2005). To celebrate the release of the film, Selwyn District Council and Film South gave the collection of photographs the title 'Our Land Speaks Volumes'.

So too did the production of an exhibition poster that appeared as a full-page advertisement in *Locations* magazine. The issue of *Locations* was distributed globally throughout 2005–6 at international screen festivals. In a triumphant tone, Film South's newsletter named Canterbury the 'land of Narnia' and noted that Flock Hill's rural community had already 'played host to the biggest filming experience in the district's history – the shooting of the climatic battle scenes' (Film South NZ 7, 2005b: 3). Moreover, in an attempt to match the international praise for *The Return of the King*, the film's premiere in Auckland (8 December 2005) received extensive media coverage. Finally, Ian Brodie, author of *The Lord of the Rings Location Guidebook* began to write *Cameras in Narnia: How the Lion, The Witch and the Wardrobe Came to Life*, an 'ode' to Flock Hill's 'memorable location' (Film South NZ 7, 2005b: 3). The communication of different sign industries is striking and incontestable: much to the New Zealand government's delight, Christchurch seems to be an up-and-coming tourist destination created in Narnia's hyperreal regime. In fact, despite concerns raised about the breaching of conservation laws, in 2005 Film South made an argument for the launch of the New Code of Practice that allows filming on public conservation lands (Film South NZ 7, 2005b: 3).

We may conclude that the state-controlled form that capitalism seems to have taken in New Zealand is a response to the challenges of globalization – a form of state agency from within the global capitalist structure, as it were. Of course, we should not over-emphasize this domestic response to external pressures without looking at the wider picture: the *LOTR* venture 'made a courtesy of tax loss to the host government of NZ$217 million' (Miller *et al.* 2005: 139), even though the country's tourist industry was sufficiently supported to present a sixteen-fold growth. The contrast between excessive expenditure and long-term investment presents us with a New Zealand state that follows global patterns of capitalist growth, while still caring too much about its international reputation. This conflation of national recognition in the international arena and brand monopolization haunts other initiatives too. The story was repeated for example with the launching of the first New Zealand *The Lord of the Rings* collector coins by the Royal Mint in conjunction with official licensee, New Zealand Post (Talking Pictures 2003b). National currency has always been a representational device for nation-states: even though these are commemorative coins, what is engraved on them traditionally tells us something about the history of the nation. The 'Rings Coins Sets', which circulated in 2004, may be depicting fictional characters, but on the obverse side they 'feature the official effigy of Her Majesty the Queen' (Collect Tolkien 2004). Things come full circle here, as one myth (of the *LOTR*) served to promote and revise another (that of the nation). On the economic front the initiative cannot be read as a pure expression of nationalist consciousness, but as a mobilization of practices of nationalist self-promotion for economic returns. Simply put, the myth of the nation, implicit in this project, is a clever recourse to established understandings of cultural identity that may assist in New Zealand's tourist growth. At the same time, self-promotion retains traces of a need for international appreciation. This need is expressed through self-stereotyping that even government agents claim. 'New Zealand is a nation of new ideas and new thinking', stated Helen Clark during a visit to Mumbai, where she discussed New Zealand's attractiveness as a filmmaking destination.

> New Zealanders are independent, creative, innovative and quick to embrace new technologies. These qualities are evident in the success of New Zealand films, which have won international accolades far in excess of what one could expect of a country of four million people.
>
> (Film Factory 2004)

Note that here Clark advertises the 'resourcefulness' and 'do-it-yourself attitude' that some academics have also recognized as part of the New Zealand 'character' (Tarrant 1998, cited in Perkins and Thorns 2001: 198). Again, we observe a shift from economic promotion to national representation – or, to use the Althusserian terminology, a self-imposed 'interpellation' (Althusser 1971) of New Zealand that draws upon a dark colonial past. Unlike the old New Zealanders, who conformed to the stereotype of the dull sheep farmer, the poor and uncultured European relative of colonial times, New Zealanders are independent and innovative, ready to be admitted into global politics and recognized as strong economic and cultural competitors. This image, which seems to be gaining ground in the light of the *LOTR* economic development, strategically essentializes New Zealandish identity. Curiously enough, what started as a game of simulation for economic returns transforms itself into voluntary, state-regulated, representation: Middle Earth's projection in the Antipodes has assisted in New Zealand's relocation in a fast-moving world.

4 *Corelli* goes to Hollywood

Cryptocolonial histories and local resistance

Much like Garland's novel, Louis de Bernières' *Captain Corelli's Mandolin* (1994) mesmerized international readers. The adaptation of the book into a Hollywood epic (2001) was met with brutal reactions from critics for its shortcomings and generated a controversy on the Greek island of Kefalonia, where the story was filmed. The foreground of de Bernières' book was the love story between a mandolin-playing Italian soldier and a Greek Kefalonian woman. It was, however, set in a historical background comprised of the Axis Occupation of Greece, the operation of Greek resistance, and civil strife between the Greek communist fighters of EAM/ELAS (National Liberation Front/Greek People's Liberation Army) and anti-communist forces. The cinematic adaptation stripped the story of most of its sociopolitical context, presenting it as an anodyne love affair, an unorthodox union of two cultures. It is telling that de Bernières refused to be associated with the movie: CNN rumours held that he was unhappy with the casting of Nicolas Cage as Corelli because he wanted 'someone smaller and more lively', that he hated the script-writer's (Shawn Slovo) adaptation and was disappointed with Hollywood's decision to ditch the complexity of his historical narrative (CNN 2001a). In the end the venture was not very successful and many agreed that director John Madden, known at the time as the great auteur of 'such beloved films as *Mrs Brown* and *Shakespeare in Love*,' could not 'go away unscathed' (CNN 2001a): *Captain Corelli's Mandolin* (*CCM*) was judged even by critics to be yet another expensive Hollywood flop.

It would be useful to have a glimpse of the film to contextualize the controversy. The story presumably begins in 1940 on the Greek island of Kefalonia. The shadow of war is cast over Europe and Italy, allied with Nazi Germany, invades Greece. Dr Ioánnis (John Hurt), a Kefalonian, is the father of beautiful and educated Pelagía (Penelope Cruz). Pelagía is in love with a local fisherman, Mandrás (Christian Bale) whom Dr Ioánnis does not consider her equal. Ioánnis' reservations about Mandrás do not, however, prevent the lovers from getting engaged. The situation changes with the arrival of Italian troops on the island. A young captain, Antonio Corelli (Nicolas Cage), with a 'typically Italian' conciliatory attitude, bewitches Pelagía. Corelli prefers to sing and play his mandolin instead of making war, and when he settles in Dr Ioánnis' house the eternal triangle seems inevitable: Pelagía, first repulsed by the idea of living with an Italian invader, subsequently falls in love with him. Mandrás, who becomes leader of the communist resistance on the island, reluctantly accepts the breaking of their engagement. Later, when in an unexpected turn of the war the Germans arrive and attempt to disarm the Italians, he even cooperates with Corelli against them. Corelli's life is saved by Carlo Piero Guercio, an important character in the book, but his homosexual love for Corelli, so lyrically described by de Bernières, is effaced from the film's plot and no adequate explanation is given for his self-sacrifice in the film. Corelli manages to escape and leaves the island with the promise to return for Pelagía after the end of the war. Indeed he does: shortly after liberation he appears on Pelagía's doorstep and the indispensable happy ending is granted.

Because many humane or historical aspects of de Bernières' book were repressed (for example, Dr Ioánnis' uneven narration of the history of the island, Mandrás' ideological commitment to communism, Mussolini's self-important monologues on the nature of fascism), the characters are less persuasive and well-rounded than in the novel. One might have assumed that the book's success motivated people to see the film, if one did not take into account that many online reviewers claimed not to have read it. Despite the *CCM* controversy in the world of critics and later in popular online film databases and other websites, the film was watched by hundreds of thousands, especially when it was released on DVD and VHS. War films still attract history lovers, and quite a few make millions of dollars. Epics such as *Pearl Harbor* (2002) and *Saving Private Ryan* (1998), frequently mentioned by IMDB and Amazon.com reviewers of *CCM*, relied on the formula of wartime plot that their directors and scriptwriters enriched with a love story and patriotic overtones. Likewise, *CCM* drew on the German–Italian confrontation on Kefalonia and the massacres of Italian soldiers when German troops took possession of the island.

The most enduring outcome of so much interest has been that the island of Kefalonia, off the beaten track for decades and largely ignored by holiday providers, became established as a holiday resort. To be cautious, I will say in advance that the historical episode de Bernières used in his novel and Universal Pictures-Corelli Films Ltd 'adapted' provides only a small part of the picture. Kefalonia is an island rich in history and culture, but also unusual in terms of physical attractions. Landscape, historical memory and politics complemented the ways in which the island was marketed as a tourist destination abroad, online and on location. These 'sign' factors often worked altogether in the cinematic imposition of *CCM* to generate an ambiance of virtual uniqueness served ready-made on the plates of international viewers. But Kefalonian interaction with outsiders, especially tourists, uses a mixture of *CCM* and local signs whose birth precedes the film's success. The *CCM* venture generated and reinforced modes of local self-presentation. Some of them belong to the colonial order of things and are an essential aspect of local resistance to foreign intrusion. My use of the term 'colonial' is extended so as to cover Kefalonia's integration into the Greek nation state, another imposed presence in the region. During and after the *CCM* controversy, both foreigners and the Greek centre were represented as aliens to Kefalonian culture and identity.

Even de Bernières, a foreigner interested in producing a novel rather than history, was aware of this interplay between local self-narration and resistance to powerful outsiders, and registered this in Dr Ioánnis' (the local historian of the story) meditations on the island's past which are interspersed at crucial points of the narrative. In the first few pages de Bernières mobilizes this fictional character in order to provide his readers with reflections on the Kefalonian character. Ioánnis becomes thus a meta-narrator of his ancestral origins. In the book, while he destroys his manuscripts to start anew his 'New History of Kefalonia', he informs us about the beauty of its women, its merry but tormented people, its ancient legends and its Hellenic and Christian gods. In a blast of anger he decides to 'forget about leaving out the loaded adjectives and the ancient historical grudges, [and] be vitriolic about the Romans, the Normans, the Venetians, the Turks, the British, and even the islanders themselves' (de Bernières 1997: 5). Dr Ioánnis' 'hot temperament' and his presentation of the Kefalonian historical legacies provide de Bernières not only with an infallible tool to romanticize local identity, but also with a concise postcolonial context: the nineteenth-century British occupation of the Ionian Islands. This context frames the British discovery of the Ionian Greek 'character' long before travel agents and package holidays.

The combination of British colonial history with war action could partially explain the enthusiastic reception of the story in Britain and other countries – notably by Americans, who display an interest in revisionist pseudo-historical films. Perhaps de Bernières' wartime framework was not original, but the burden of the Kefalonian past and the peasant, picturesque present of the story gave his tale an element of originality. Madden struggled to grant his protagonists a Mediterranean folk authenticity, with little interest in Kefalonian specificity. At the same time a different kind of romanticization was promoted, which reproduced universal stereotyping of the Mediterranean characters while dehistoricizing the island and its wartime struggles. As will become evident, cinematically Kefalonia did not operate as a watertight and autonomous category in the film; on the contrary, it represented a hidden totality – Greece. The identification of these two categories resembles orientalist oversimplifications of identity (Said 1978: 21) that inform representations of cultures in tourist industries. The single, uniform Orient of Western imaginations is homologous to the substitution of Kefalonian with Greek culture in the film and later in tourist advertising. This particular case of Orientalism has its own long history, which is replete with discontinuities (Foucault 1997: 127–8). It is necessary to briefly examine these discontinuities in the sequence in which they occurred, in order to situate responses to John Madden's film.

Orientalism, past and present: Kefalonia, *not* Greece

Unfolding the colonial histories of Kefalonia alongside the cryptocolonial histories of Greece is not a futile exercise but an essential clarification that illuminates cinematic representations, local self-presentations and present tourist policies. For a while these histories run parallel lives, but after the incorporation of the Ionian Islands (to which Kefalonia belongs) into the Greek state they took different courses. In reality, Kefalonia and Greece present us with two intertwined instances of orientalization by colonial powers. The history of Greece's orientalization began with the scholarly objectification of Hellenic civilization, an offshoot of the scientific study of the Orient and its objectification by Westerners (Bernal 1991). The academic multidisciplines of British and American classics and German *Altertumswissenschaft* (the study of science and knowledge of ancient history) promoted the study of ancient Greek, archaeology and Hellenic history (Leontis 1995). This development was followed by the expression of a philhellenic political interest in the destiny of the Greeks who had been under Ottoman rule until the beginning of the nineteenth century. The substantial philhellenic aid that was provided to the Greeks, and which contributed to the liberation of part of the Greek Peninsula in the 1830s, should not be dissociated from the Western European interest in Hellenic culture. The generosity of western Philhellenes, the lovers of Greek antiquity, stemmed from their belief that the institution of modern Greece would 'resurrect' the ancient Hellenes, the forefathers of European civilization (Gourgouris 1996: 123–40). At the same time, however, modern Greece provided primary material to nascent academic disciplines in Europe: travellers, academics and amateur ethnographers swamped Greece to observe and record Modern Greek customs and ideas. In this conjunction, Greek folk culture became the key to a glorious Hellenic past for Western observers. Peasant life was deemed to preserve Hellenic traces on an unconscious level, which had to be saved from oblivion (Herzfeld 1982: 6). At the same time the recent Ottoman past of the Greeks became a means of reading what was strange and therefore 'unwholesome' in Greek mannerisms. Henceforth 'Greece' would be an ambiguous category: much like Thailand, it became just another buffer zone between the imaginary civilized world of the West and the savage non-place of the (Ottoman) Orient; much like the Thais, Greeks found themselves interpellated. Condemned to react to, but ultimately reproduce, Western cryptocolonialism (Herzfeld 2002b; Tzanelli 2003), today Greeks continue to see their cultural heritage as the 'cradle of Europe'.

The cryptocolonization of Greek culture found its continuity in foreign policies that followed independence. In the nineteenth century these policies supported temporary British occupations, and at the dawn of the twentieth century contributed to the outbreak of a Greek–Turkish war. During the Second World War British confrontation with communists within Greece fuelled a civil war (1944–9) that still burdens Greek collective memory. The Cold War era found Greece between the Western and Soviet spheres of influence. A dictatorship (1967–74) fully revived the narrative of Hellas-as-Europe, bestowing it also with Christian Orthodox, right-wing undertones (Herzfeld 2002a: 13–15). Hellenic excellence became in questions of Greek foreign and domestic policy what Diamantouros (1983) called 'underdog culture': an inward-looking, Christian-'Hellenocentric' culture, that defensively warns against foreign interventions, alien elements and cultural difference. Apparently, the 'curse of philhellenism', to borrow Stathis Gourgouris' apposite metaphor (1996), continues to cast itself on modern Greece.

The relationship between travel and amateur ethnography is crucial. Contemporary tourism preserves a practice similar to nineteenth-century travel that is implicated in the present study: the pre-established reading of alien cultural signs (Urry 1990: 12). When tourists visit countries they pack pre-conceptions about the culture that they visit with their luggage. These they use to understand what they experience in the host country. Nineteenth-century travellers were fond of this practice of reading their prejudices into their encounter with aliens, and were anxious to record them in travel books. It would not be an exaggeration to say that Western

European tourists in the Mediterranean region are very prone to a similar practice: romanticizing the sunny host country and anticipating cultural difference is, after all, what gives meaning to travel. Greece falls into this category of artificial difference: in the plane of politics it is often European (as a member of the European Union). In some cases, however, it is seen as an Oriental domain. This was a persistent theme in American politics and British newspaper commentary after the terrorist attack of the 17th of November group in 1999. The assassination of the British diplomat Steve Saunders posed serious questions concerning the safety of foreign tourists in Greece. It also invited American anti-terrorist circles and the British press to draw a parallel between Pakistani and Greek politics. The same cryptocolonial themes reappeared in the context of Athens 2004, when the Greek state was criticized for its disorganized planning of the Olympic Games and its alleged neglect of security against terrorist attacks (Tzanelli 2004). At the same time, in the tourist imaginary Greece can be Oriental (a form of European internal otherness) because of its exotic, sunny coasts and hospitable people. In fact, a set of rituals that determine tourist itineraries in Greece provides us with the essential link between the orientalist ethnographic gaze and its history: visiting ancient sights; consulting travel guides to learn about the 'Greek character'; 'experiencing' picturesque Greek folk customs; essentializing 'Greek temperament' and photographing landscapes.

The Ionian cultural encounters with colonial powers followed similar paths. The islands' strategic geographical position attracted the powerful Venetians who colonized them between 1402 and 1797, when they were 'liberated' by Napoleon Bonaparte. French occupation lasted till 1814 when it was replaced by British domination. Only in 1864, after centuries of foreign rule, were the islands granted to Greece by Britain. Representations of Ionian identity in British colonial culture had a long-lasting effect. British stereotyping of the Ionian Greeks resonated in the relationship of the latter with their Hellenic forefathers and their British rulers. Ionian Greeks would often be discussed as the 'degenerate descendants' of Hellenic civilization, disorderly bandits but also European aborigines, noble savages and 'Mediterranean Irish' (Gallant 2002: 15–45). The 'truth' of this discursive system was grounded on the British rule itself. For the British, who had almost always acted as masters of non-European races, the Ionian case was inconvenient and somehow exceptional: the Ionian Greeks were white and Christian, therefore suitable for self-mastery rather than control by other Europeans. The taxonomy in which Ionian Greeks would be simultaneously European and non-European effectively compensated for the problematic reality of British Ionian rule. Their identification with the Irish, another rebellious colonized white nation, both exacerbated and concealed the problem. The coexistence of binary opposites in this taxonomic arrangement was later mirrored in British discourses on the Kingdom of Greece, especially in British travel accounts on Greek peasant life (Tzanelli 2002b).

When the Ionian Islands were granted to Greece, the locals found themselves part of a state they knew as little as their former British masters. Four decades after liberation, the Greeks of Greece were still asking themselves who they were and where they came from. A collection of ethnic identities that the centre would not recognize coexisted under the same administrative roof but lived segregated by the peculiar geographies of the peninsula. The Greek economy was struggling to respond to foreign demands for loan repayment and internal needs for regeneration (Tzanelli 2002a). The Ionians' marginality was reproduced in the new politico-economic order and their cultural difference found a new anchor to hinge upon. This was so because not only did the Ionians never experience Oriental Ottoman occupation, but they were also under a succession of 'civilized' rulers: Venetians, French and British. Ionian perceptions of cultural superiority by association with the West became part of local mythologies, an imaginary construct that served the needs of collective memory (Connerton 1989: 13). Naturally, Ionian Greeks experienced class divides and discrimination, with the rural areas suffering from bandit raids and poverty during the nineteenth century (Gallant 2002: 4–5). However, a self-inflicted marginalization survived over the centuries and fed into local stereotypes: the Ionians still perceive themselves as defiant, inquisitive and full of 'aristocratic pride'.

The legacies of colonization and war, and the political and geographical marginality of the island, played a crucial role in Kefalonian responses to *CCM* and developing tourism. The cinematic folklorization of Kefalonian culture and the commercialization of local landscape figure throughout the film, and project the tourist desire for 'sea and sun' Mediterranean breaks and folk authenticity. Reviewers' reflections on the most pronounced issues of accent, folk dance, Greek *habitus*, landscape and history reworked this folklorization in ways similar to those of the emergent tourist industry. I will explain, however, that due to state policies and local attitudes, as well as the power of pre-established, locally generated cultural signs, *CCM* did not manage to consolidate a sign industry. *CCM* signs are mobilized in a fragmented and disorganized manner by locals without replacing firmly established cultural and geographical referents. This presents us with an entirely different case of film-induced tourism from that of *The Beach* and the *LOTR*.

Flexible categories for Mediterranean endeavours

CCM's cinematic narrative invests in the Kefalonian landscape and culture. The VHS and DVD summaries of the film conclude with reflections on how 'the harsh reality of war ultimately crashes upon the idyllic shores of Kefalonia', reinforcing the idea that we are dealing with an unspoiled natural setting, even though a crew of actors, cameramen and tourist crowds infested the island at the time of the filmmaking. This link between cinematic production of imagery and tourist consumption of place is provided by film reviewers, who commented extensively on the natural and cultural potential of Kefalonia. In this section I would like to examine the mental transition from film to tourism, already implicit in the cinematic story, and its mobilization by international tourist providers.

Several reviewers commented that the film is an exercise in tourist consumption. Not only does Madden offer us a ready-made holiday product in the form of Greek folk authenticity and nature, but he also gives us directions on how we are to experience it. Reviewers noticed the rather unusual representation of military life and found the scenes in which Corelli's fellow soldiers swim in the clear waters of the Ionian Sea while flirting with half-naked local prostitutes 'heretical'. (IMDB, 18 October 2002; see also IMDB, Athens, 31 August 2003). According to viewers, the role of Italian identity in the film is that of a 'consumer participant'. On a cinematic meta-level the Italians of *CCM* cease to be soldiers and begin to represent tourists. Representations of the tourist subject are complemented by representations of the tourist object: the Kefalonian land. The camera, with its fictional 'impartial vision' (Collier 1967: 3), 'imprisons' landscape and uses it either to complement emotional moments in the story or to distract the eye from the background of the war. The landscape is encapsulated by the camera as it is appropriated in tourist photography, becoming a commodity for mass consumption (Crawshaw and Urry 2000: 176–80). At least this is what a large group of reviewers recognizes as *CCM*'s practice. A Californian puts this into words, when he explains that 'what [the film] accomplishes superbly is to enable you to visualize the locales' (Amazon, 11 February 2004). Someone from Atlanta commented that the film's 'visual images come from photographing these majestic locations in varying light' (IMDB, 10 March 2002) and another claimed that '*Capt. Corelli* takes place on picture postcard beautiful Kefalonia' (IMDB, 18 August 2001; see also IMDB, Texas, 22 August 2004) while an English viewer stated that the film 'can be used as an advert for tourism in the Mediterranean' (IMDB, 10 June 2001; see also IMDB, North Wales, 12 September 2004). A Briton noted

Figure 4.1 The La Scala group off duty: *CCM's* Italians are mere Mediterranean tourists.

Source: Universal Pictures/Photofest. © Universal Pictures

that 'the film does have one good thing . . . and that is the photography which is stunning. The Greek Tourist Industry will be anticipating a rush on Holidays to it's [*sic*] island this summer' (IMDB, 4 May 2001), providing a link between photography and tourism (see also IMDB, Birmingham, 31 May 2004). Even more intriguing is the comment of a viewer from the touristified region of Cumbria, who remarks that the film is good to watch 'if you've been to Kefelonia [*sic*] on holiday' (13 August 2004). We note therefore that market tactics are not unknown to the audience. A reviewer takes this further, articulating a Marxist critique of the emerging *CCM* sign industry:

> Above all, the film reeks of Hollywood imperialism . . . You can easily imagine the film crew and actors' trailers plopped on the beach, setting up a camp while they make a picture on a little Greek island (make sure you get lots of shots of the ocean).
>
> (IMDB, New Haven CT, 22 August 2001)

The reviewer criticizes the reproductive element of *CCM's* photography and Hollywood's presence on the island – a critique that returns us to the discourse of lost authenticity that I examined in Chapter 2. Notably, the commentators I quoted come from two countries with developed tourist industries. Moreover, US and UK tourist itineraries are very likely to end in Greece on a sunny summer day. These reviewers draw on the standardized tourist imaginary (Kefalonia as a generic Mediterranean resort) and often reflect critically on it to discuss the film.

Photographic practices may dictate the way that nature has to be viewed as an appropriated object, but they also tend to erase the specific histories of the location to replace them with the photographer's personal memories (Mills 2003: 87). An English reviewer writes: 'after going to Kephallonia [*sic*] in 1999, I was lucky enough to experience the magic of the island. When I heard a movie was being made in the town in which I stayed, I hoped that they would bring this magic to the screen' (IMDB, England, 5 November 2001). The film is used therefore by the viewer as a surface on which they can project their own experience. A Californian recollects that he 'visited the Aegean last summer' and found himself 'addicted' to the scenery (Amazon, 11 February 2002). Both viewers discuss a generic holiday backdrop that can be enjoyed in any Mediterranean resort. Kefalonia is absorbed in their comments into a large, nebulous, category with exchange value abroad. Other times representations of Kefalonian nature generate a desire on the part of the reviewer to visit Kefalonia. 'It's a beautiful island, and the cinematography inspires me to travel to Greece some day,' claimed someone from New York (Amazon, 13 April 2002). These travelogues, whether based on actual memories or not, transform Kefalonian nature into the principal actor of the story. The natives stay in the natural background and live in a time that defies or ignores the laws of history. As someone from Atlanta claimed, the 'photographed locations' of Kefalonia are enhanced by 'Greek actors as the townspeople, giving the town an authentic feel' (Amazon, 10 March 2002). Consequently, Kefalonian culture is de-temporalized and placed at the services of the random tourist:

> Its slowness contributes to recreate the tranquil atmosphere of the stupendous Greek island of Kefalonia as it was in the forties. The photography of the island was so beautiful that I was almost able to smell the olive oil and the leaves on the trees . . . I liked Corelli and the soldiers of the opera house because their jovial character reminded me of many of my friends in Italy . . . I loved the entire atmosphere of the island, which reminded me of my father's small village in Southern Italy. These Mediterranean places have one exceptional thing in common: time seems to run slower over there, letting you fully appreciate the beauty and the serenity of the community and the scenery.
>
> (IMDB, Carlsbad, 4 October 2001)

The reviewer conflates Italy with Kefalonia, issuing a reminder of the homogenizing result of cultural representation. Time seems to stop in the narrative and the island is viewed as an ahistorical entity. Because the reviewer romanticizes the landscape and incorporates local culture into it, she erases its history altogether. In her discourse Kefalonia becomes the signifier of her personal history, which has nothing to do with the history of the island itself. She is not the only one who mobilizes Kefalonia as a word emptied of meaning, and hence ready to acquire any meaning at all. In literary reflections on the narrative structure of the film, the 'spirit of the island' (Amazon, Phillips Academy, Andover, MA; Beijing, China, 18 August 2001) is ontologized in a romantic Victorian fashion: the natural surroundings are deemed to have their own ambiance, which has a soothing effect on the visitor. The visitor engages with the landscape, not with the human beings that inhabit the place. This engagement is turned into a personal project of self-fulfilment: away from the noise, worries and distractions of everyday life, visitors re-engage with their inner self, or a part of their self that was lost and is retrieved unexpectedly. The Kefalonia of these viewers is that of the actual tourist subject who blends their senses in the natural environment (Crouch *et al.* 2001).

There are many reviews from countries other than Britain and the US that discuss the transformation of Kefalonia into an aesthetic object for personal consumption. Unlike an Athenian Greek, who claimed that 'the Greek sceneries add something special and magical to a movie', (IMDB, 31 January 2002) another Greek notes that 'all the villages on the island were partly [*sic*] filmed; there should have been a lot more emphasis on the hardships that the locals had to endeavour [*sic*]' (IMDB, North England, 5 December 2001). While the first reviewer objectifies Kefalonian landscape and severs it from its history, the latter draws attention to the pitfalls of this practice. It may not be mere coincidence that the first reviewer comes from Greece's urban centre; a Polish commentator inadvertently explains why:

> The location of the filming, in these days of lightning-sped urban-
> ization fills the heart with a longing for peaceful, level[l]ed life in
> nature's beautifully powerful company.
>
> (IMDB, Poland 2 September 2001)

According to the reviewer, urbanization has deprived modern mankind of its peace – a peace which can only be rediscovered in film images. In this discourse of demediating mediation Kefalonian nature bears the mark of a lost authenticity that, in its turn, becomes homologous to the authentic savagery of folk culture. This discourse unveils an area of modern consciousness that has not yet been subjected to rationalization but preserves a longing for genuine forms of otherness (White 1978: 153). The aesthetic value the Kefalonian landscape acquires in reviews can be read as a symptom of modern alienation.

The advertising of Kefalonian landscape became the driving force of *CCM*-related tourism. Although the websites that refer to the book and the film are numerous, it is worth mentioning a few which are an offspring of the post-*CCM* tourist industry. Villa Pelagía, a tourist complex on the island named after de Bernière's heroine, is illustrated by an enhanced image of Kefalonian coasts, just like *CCM*. Famous Locations, another website, lists CCM among the most popular films and invites readers to 'search for holidays to Greece'. Xirin.com, a site maintained by 'lovers' of the island, contains information on the film, the book and its characters. The site features travelogues by those who travelled to the Ionian Islands. We note how contemporary tourist practices reinvent the nineteenth-century travel book – yet another electronic reference to the grand tour. For all intents and purposes Kefalonian history becomes a 'good' that can be enjoyed by a mass audience/readership.

The growing tourist industry around the island followed the same strategy: various holidaymakers constructed web pages on *Captain Corelli*'s 'unspoiled Kefalonia', in which they reproduced the cinematic landscape. Shores, clear waters and Kefalonian folk decorate the special Kefalonia website Tapestry Holidays, 'experts of uncommercial Greece and Turkey'. Calypso, a Greek tourist site, has a special webpage under the title 'Filming of *Captain Corelli* puts Kefalonia on the global map'. The article describes the 'Ionian Paradise of crystalline blue waters' and depicts it above a photo of Penelope Cruz and Nicolas Cage. The same strategy is followed by the Greek Tourist Information site, which invites visitors to book luxury village houses 'near where the true story of *Captain Corelli's Mandolin* was filmed'. Like the *LOTR* advertising of the 'authentic stage', other websites recommend to tourists the towns of Sámi and Fiskárdo, where parts of *CCM* were filmed. Reiterating the discourse of lost authenticity, but always using *CCM* as a referent, other online tourist providers prefer to stress that 'Kefalonia is still virtually untouched by mass tourism' (Kefalonia Travel 2006). The Kefalonia website explains that Sámi 'received a Hollywood facelift' (Kefalonia Travel 2006) with the film, inviting virtual flâneurs to visit it. Its special page on *CCM* is decorated with a photograph from Sámi. More importantly, however, the image is accompanied by a list of books, maps and travel guides on Kefalonia that situate the island in imaginary geographies of travel. However, the webpage exceeds the film's signification because alongside the 'peaceful' travel destinations it recommends (that correspond to the cinematic story), it advertises the lively holiday resorts of Lássi (destined for mass tourist consumption). This is avoided by Thompson, one of the most famous international tourist providers. In Thompson's website a reference to CCM is followed by a reassuring description of the island that apparently 'has managed to retain a true sense of Greek life . . . lost on many other islands' (Thompson 2006). Again the description is followed by a number of radiant photographs of the island addressed to a variety of tourists, including those who are not averse to standard holiday packages. Tourist providers ignore the historical framework of *CCM*, focusing instead on the scenic beaches and good local produce.

The prominence of the landscape is followed by the mastery of the protagonists and the foreign characters in the film. There are various ways one can demarcate cultures in film, but none is as convincing as language and accent, the hallmarks of otherness. Language and accent demarcate cultures, whereas mannerisms denote social and cultural status. It may be worth recalling Pierre Bourdieu's analysis of *habitus*, a group of dispositions that originate in our social upbringing, and which we unconsciously cultivate throughout our lives (Bourdieu 1977). Bourdieu discussed *habitus* in relation to social power and classified it as a form of symbolic capital. In film, *habitus* joins the world of commodities, as it ceases simply to be what it is (to have what Marx called *use value*) and becomes just one item in a chain of constant exchanges (Bourdieu 1998: 34). Here language cannot be reduced to a mechanical structure, which is operated by a competent speaker: the Saussurian segregation of *langue* and *parole* loses its persuasiveness when put to the test (Bourdieu 1998: 30–2). The act of speaking 'Greek' in *CCM* should be seen as an authorized performance that is legitimate and plausible only in the specific context in which it is carried out: not everybody in the film speaks Greek, yet the audience is supposed to welcome the 'technologies' used to designate different languages as Greek, Italian or German. Unfortunately, *CCM*'s 'universal translator' is not always as convincing as *Star Trek*'s. An annoyed reviewer wittily observed:

> On a remote Greek island invaded first by liberal (or inept) Italian soldiers then by a big bad German army, everybody speaks English for the sake of the American audience who still feels embarrassed when Nicolas Cage (seemingly speaking some Greek, we assume) is the go-between during a 'surrender' ceremony: he reads the Greek text from the island official, translates it into Italian, I mean English, then goes to get a German soldier who doesn't appear to be disturbed

by any language barrier (actually, does the German soldier speak Italian, German or Greek? Only his director could tell).

(IMDB, New York, 18 May 2002)

Almost a third of the IMDB and Amazon.com reviewers commented on the uses of accent and language, quite a number critically. Language performance foregrounds the story but also creates a distinctive background. In the foreground, the principal characters speak English in 'phoney accents'. Richard Dyer (1982) has explained that stars work as signs in film because their career and fame precede their casting of particular roles. In *CCM* stars are consciously used as signs, because the characters that they impersonate become more 'authentic' thanks to the actors' actual cultural backgrounds. Hollywood's *doxa*, its pseudo-objective cultural order, exploits thus the actual *habitus* or cultural affiliations of actors to grant their acting with verisimilitude (Neale and Krutnik 1990: 3–4). The selection of the main protagonists was predicated upon the conviction that their cultural or ethnic background will compensate for the missing authenticity in the film's foreground (Strain 2003: 155). It is plausible that Nicolas Cage belongs to the Italian Coppola family, that is, he is an American of Italian descent; his in-betweenness was expected to be all the more appealing, according to director Madden and producer Kevin Loader (Clark 2001: 47, 50). His Italian temperament is symbolized by a deliberate overacting, singing, music playing and the ceremonial 'Ciao Bambina' addressed to women. As Madden himself admitted (*ibid.*: 64) Penelope Cruz is a Spanish brunette, and her Mediterranean demeanour will suffice for an audience that disregards arbitrary generalizations. John Hurt's British identity is also concealed in an intriguing way: a thick Greek moustache that nowadays we find only in sepia pictures complemented a fake accent and the two together 'delighted' (*ibid.*: 106) chief make-up artist Lois Burwell. Perhaps Christian Bale struggled with the Greek accent, but his darkened hair 'made his own look more Greek' (*ibid.*: 106).

The background ambiance is sustained by a number of Greek, Italian and German native-speaking actors who converse in their own language. Background speech is thus integrated into the magnificent Greek landscape, in which ethnic characters become 'picturesque'. I use the term picturesque literally to denote that these actors become part of the island picture, and metaphorically to allude to their exotic mannerisms. Only when characters such as Drosoúla (Iréne Papá), Mandrás' mother, move to the foreground do they switch to accented English. Hence, Greek and Italian speech is simultaneously instrumentalized and naturalized. Two forms of naturalization are taking place at the same time: the first one transforms social actors (the background characters) into nature (Lévi-Strauss, 1972 [1962]). The second one presents to the audience the film's 'Babel of communication' as a natural phenomenon (Lévi-Strauss, 1964: 26–7; Barthes, 1993). It would not be an exaggeration to term this kind of speech 'stolen' (from its context) and 'restored' (as natural national characters).

Language also enabled the makers of *CCM* to recreate the Greek social reality of the war. In this reality Germans, Italians and Greeks coexisted out of necessity, but the multiculturalism of the film super-imposes a version of American social reality on the Greek social life of the war. In *CCM*, Spaniards, Americans and British can become Greeks, Italians or Germans if they speak in accents, and ethnic actors can just speak in accents or in their native language as they (inevitably) do. This is expected – at least in the imaginary of an American audience – to be plausible. Bearing in mind that multiculturalism constitutes the core of American self-narration (Alba 2000), *CCM*'s pandemonium of accents and languages becomes a powerful reminder of America's multiform culture.

Reviewers who found the use of language and accent appropriate and 'believable' were mainly English native speakers. 'The acting in this movie has passion, regardless of those who did not have an authentic accent', claimed an American (IMDB, 8 July 2004). At stake was the authenticity of the whole enterprise, as an anonymous Italian stated. Mobilizing the expertise of her relatives, she stated: 'The Italian members of my family assure me that [Nicolas Cage's] accent was good' (IMDB, Anonymous, 7 July 2002). 'Nicholas [*sic*] Cage seemed to be enjoying himself. I bet he felt he was going back to his roots as an Italian,' explained a Californian (IMDB, 4 February 2002). 'Madden also uses numerous Greek actors as the townspeople giving the town an authentic feel,' claims another (Amazon, Atlanta, 10 May 2002). Reviewers who protested against the follies of language stressed the same point. A reviewer from Louisville argues:

> [I wonder] whether other cultures employ accents in drama to denote aspects of character or of the contrasts in culture between people from different places. (Would a Manchurian playing uncle Vanya essay any variety of Russian accent? Would his ear provide him the basis for a toying with relatively more limited – not to say deadened – array of western inflections?)
>
> (IMDB, 4 September 2001; see also
> IMDB, Derbyshire, 11 June 2004)

But the demediating effect of cinematic apparatuses 'pledge[s] to succeed where tourism has failed' (Strain 2003: 177): to enable the frustrated flâneur to establish contact with an unspoiled folk culture. Two very controversial scenes in *CCM* attempt to reconstruct Greek folk customs for the tourist gaze. The first one refers to a feast, invented to enhance the film narrative, which Greeks enjoy on a gloriously sunny day just before the Italian occupation. The scene is dominated by Christian Bale's lamentable effort to dance in Greek 'folk' rhythms; he is accompanied by Greek actors who also follow an obscure choreography. The second incident is situated in wartime and takes place under the surveillance of the Italian and German army officers who participate in it. In this scene multiculturalism is captured in Penelope Cruz's tango, which she performs with an army officer.

These two incidents are meant to engage the audience with Greek culture – and I stress the term 'Greek', for no indication exists that we deal with local dancing. MacCannell's analysis of 'staged authenticity' (1973) applies again, as the film itself acquires the qualities of a front region of travel performance – only this time the front is not manufactured by the hosts but by Western Hollywood outsiders *for* Western outsiders. Dancing in Greece acquired the status of front staging

Figure 4.2 Mandrás dancing in Greek folk rhythms.

Source: Universal Pictures/Photofest. © Universal Pictures

Figure 4.3 Pelagía's tango.

Source: Universal Pictures/Photofest. © Universal Pictures

in the nineteenth century, when Western travellers inundated the country. The pedagogical value of the travel for Westerners, which initially consisted of visits to archaeological sites, became progressively a quest for folk authenticity. This quest enabled the Neohellenes to identify (that is, invent) their tradition, and perform it for foreign travellers and later tourists in a crude, yet recognizable manner (Herzfeld 1992). As Herzfeld (2001: 289) has observed, 'Zorba's Dance' has also been nationalized by losing a cultural specificity that tied it to the history of dance styles and social settings. The tourist function of dancing is, therefore, part and parcel of a long and rich history of Greek encounters with 'others'. Under this theoretical umbrella we can take the two folk scenes in *CCM* as genuine reproductions of the Greek front stage for mass consumption. Even those who have not travelled to Greece can still enjoy a tourist experience through the film. As an anonymous reviewer put it:

> The story is rich with the beauty of the island, and the charm of the natives. I really enjoyed the scenes of dancing and Greek parties . . . If you are pretty sure that you're ready to travel to Greece, definitely check this out!
>
> (IMDB, 4 March 2002)

An authorized look into the film's back regions of performance confirms the importance of the folk dance scene: in order to choose the right dance for Bale, Cruz and others, choreographer Quinny Sacks spent a considerable amount of time researching Greek folk dances. However, she admitted that when she arrived at Kefalonia she 'threw most of [her] mainland search out of the window' (Clark 2001: 112), as island dances differ significantly from those of the mainland. Thereafter, she co-opted locals to show her what they dance and how, discarding thus the idea of recovering 'pure forms' of Greek performance. For a Greek with little knowledge of dancing, the cinematic outcome seems rather generic, just like any front stage performance. Interrelations of cinematic and tourist signs were also manifested in the logic of *selection* of folk customs. Thus, some genuinely Greek beliefs were foreclosed from the story because they do not fit in with idealized versions of 'Greekness'. For example, the relationship of Pelagía with her goat (which, note, is part of her small dowry) is erased from the film – a sensible choice, considering the protestations of a modern audience against such distastefully 'backward' practices. The only reference to the dowry is made in passing, when Dr Ioánnis refuses to give Pelagía any money to marry the uncouth Mandrás. This reference has a different function in the narrative economy nevertheless. First, it asserts Ioánnis' sensibility and high expectations of Pelagía: she should marry 'from love' an educated foreigner. Second, it blocks marriage preparations and secures time for Corelli's arrival.

'Pelagía's tango' is a more complex issue, and the fact that it has not been extensively commented upon by reviewers bears witness to a lack of interest in the particulars of Greek culture. Apart from a few who protested that the dance was the 'worst point in the movie' (IMDB, New York, 22 August 2001) and that the mixing of 'flamengo and tango was graceless' (IMDB, Mexico City, 4 November 2001) the scene was passed over in silence. When silence is replaced by observations one comes across amusing remarks:

> I liked the dancing . . . The movie had a scene where she did either the tango or merengue or who knows whatever dance it was, it was good.
>
> (Amazon, California, 17 April 2002)

The fact that a Spanish actress, who impersonates a Greek peasant girl, dances in exotic Argentinian rhythms did not strike the Californian reviewer as bizarre. The confusion between Argentinian tango and Cuban merengue designates an inclination to lump together a whole constellation of cultures and histories. 'Latin American' dances, a theme to which

I return in the following chapter, have formed a significant part of the American and European mass culture over the last ten years. Not only are these dances feverishly taught across the developed world, but they are also reinvented. Amateur instructors and professional dancers teach different Latin American steps and every now and then debates erupt on the authenticity of these styles. The conception of Latin America as a homogenous entity is another contemporary version of Orientalism, which encourages the consumption of appropriated others. The fact that it crept into *CCM* betrays the market-oriented nature of the film. Not only was tango not known in the 1940s in remote Greek islands, but also it was very unlikely to be 'shamelessly' performed by young unmarried women in front of the villagers and the occupiers, as two reviewers noted (IMDB, London, 8 May 2001; Amazon, Connecticut, 9 October 2001).

The same practice of folklorization is followed in other scenes, but not commented upon by viewers. The film begins and ends with a village litany during which the holy icon of Saint Gerásimos, patron Saint of the island, is taken out to bless the crippled natives. Indeed, at the beginning of the film a disabled person is cured by divine means and everybody marvels at the miracles of the Orthodox God. The camera becomes an extension of the tourist gaze that observes villagers dressed in colourful clothes like true Orientals and the priest chanting in Greek. What he actually says does not matter; it is the folkish setting that matters because it pleases the external eye. In fact, Dr Ioánnis, the voice of internalized Western reason, whispers to Pelagía when a sick man is healed: 'A purely psychological phenomenon!' The intrusion of rationality into Greek culture is also discernible in the last scenes of the film, when Pelagía, now a doctor in an enormous hospital (which emerges out of nowhere in a poverty-stricken island), is not 'cured' of her loneliness by the Saint but by Corelli who returns for her. The fact that his reappearance coincides with the second litany is simply a device to amuse a Western audience. Ultimately, the folklorization of Kefalonian culture (already present in other instances in online reviews) is an exponent of a master narrative that was not generated by *CCM* but was definitely promoted by the film. This cinematic folklorization promotes a geometry of time and space in which the Kefalonian other appears as primitive in relation to the observer (Fabian 1983, 1991).

On other occasions the scenario uses a crude but universally recognizable binarism (civilization vs. wartime savagery) to reintegrate Kefalonian folk culture into Western civilization, this time coinciding with the winners of the Second World War. When symbolic appropriations of history are passed as historical realities, we are not far away from the politics of history writing (de Certeau 1986: 200). Cinematic impositions of history and stereotyping of the film's actors go hand in hand to reinvent Kefalonia for non-Greek observers. The verbal and visual depiction of German, Italian and Greek cultures serves to realize this aim, as many viewers explained. To be more precise, viewers noted that in the film German officers are characterized by reservation, rational planning, emotional repression and cruelty. Greeks and Italians live a 'happy' life, characterized by singing, dancing, emotional self-expression and ample gesticulation (IMDB, Los Angeles, 17 August 2001; Amazon, New Jersey, 12 June 2002; IMDB, USA, 10 June 2005). Gesticulation, once upon a time regarded by evolutionists as the language of the Greek European savages (Herzfeld 1987b: 136–7), becomes here a signifier of warmth, humanity and civilization. German rationalism is thus juxtaposed to Italian–Greek emotionalism, reversing the logic of the religious scene.

The logic of this stereotyping is the product of post-war European history in which the rational Germans represent the dark side of humanity. Contrariwise, the depiction of the Italians and the Greeks 'as educated and cultured [becomes] a compliment to an educated and cultured civilization' (IMDB, Anonymous, 7 June 2002) and serves to highlight Greek's and Italian's 'natural inclination' to 'civilized manners'. Italian fascist ideology and the brutal Greek–Italian conflict on the Albanian frontier are conveniently written out of the scenario. 'The main reasons that make me like the movie were the growing appreciation of the Greeks and the Italians for each other's cultures . . . and . . . the contrast between the Latin culture of the Greeks and the Italians on the one hand and the Teutonic culture of the Germans on the other,' states a Californian (IMDB, 4 October 2001; see also Amazon, Texas, 17 January 2002). Here it is not the story's actual agents who interact, but whole cultures. Again, the reductionist principle of the reviewer's comment replicates the stereotypical narrative of German culture as different. The uses of the terms 'Latin' and 'Teutonic' are historically erroneous, but their function is to set 'Greekness' (devoid of Kefalonian specificity) and 'Italian-ness' apart from 'German-ness'. Thus the viewers consume a cluster of signs that misrepresent history, but are in accordance with post-war prejudices. These prejudices are not based merely on cinematic artifacts, but correspond to specific Second World War histories of Greek–Italian encounters. Similar attitudes guide collective imaginations within the Greek *Raum* (space). As Doumanis (1997) has noted, Dodecanese perceptions of Italian occupation (1912–43) were strikingly positive. One of the reasons why the Dodecanese Greeks remember Italian rule with nostalgia is the Italians' attachment to their ancient Greek heritage (especially regarding the colonization of the Italian south). Conversely, the German occupation, which started in 1943, was viewed by locals in a more negative light. In contrast to the Italians, the Germans were stereotyped as disciplined automata, people devoid of emotions (Doumanis 1997: 193) – just like their stereotypes in *CCM*.

The conflation of Greek and Italian mannerisms exposes the second cinematic function of Italian identity, as *an object of consumption*. The film's marriage of Italian 'happy-go-lucky' nature with Greek folk open-heartedness is often taken for granted. An Australian viewer of Kefalonian descent reconstructed her island history on the basis of *CCM*, claiming that the movie depicted folk life accurately:

> The Italians would sing, the oppression and the earthquakes that rock the island [were] so often. . . . And yes, there were plenty of Italians in love with Kefalonian women. My sketchy bits of history were filled.
>
> (IMDB, Australia, 7 May 2002)

The comments seem to reiterate Doumanis' observations on Dodecanese collective memory. Other reviewers went so far as to identify with the narrative. A Dutch viewer stated: 'as a Latin myself with ample knowledge of the Italian participation in Second World War, I state that Italian soldiers often behaved like that' (IMDB, 5 May 2002). These reviewers, and many more, treat the film as real history, an educational medium. It is forgotten that precisely such representations of Italian–Greek 'civilized' *habitus* merge the two cultures, let alone identify 'Greek' with Kefalonian history. As an American Greek put it, 'the two cultures are bound together by traditions and similarities – love of music for instance. Greeks and Italians sing together (and this did happen during the war)' (Amazon, Florida, 1 September 2001). The assumption that Greeks and Italians are still more civilized than the Germans replaces explicit references to the Greek or Italian classical past: an imagined heritage valued in Europe and beyond can guarantee the superiority of historical actors.

The fascination with these two ancient civilizations is not new, although its history is replete with breaks and discontinuities. A reference was made in the introduction to German, British and American classicism. Yet the grand tour, an offspring of classicism, began from continental countries such as France and Italy. The latter had a special place in the British imperial imagination, because it was deemed to preserve traits of the Roman Empire – yet another model of governance for Britons alongside ancient Greece (Jenkyns 1980: 331–5). In the twenty-first-century context, however, this is just a piece of scholarship unknown to most. We have to look elsewhere to understand the *raison d'être* of the reviewers' discourse on Greek–Italian cultural ancestry. It is more accurate to say that an admiration of Greek or Italian history became commonplace within the framework of a growing tourist industry. Let us not forget that travel guides on Greece begin with comments on Greek history and suggestions for visits to ancient sites. Not only does *CCM* invoke these references in the mind of the audience, it also opens up new possibilities for the tourist industry itself:

> If you want to know more about the historical incident upon which the movie is based, just search on the Internet for Kefalonia. It is one of the [six] Ionian Islands, which also happen to be the birthplace of Greek philosophy. Today, the Greeks have a shrine there for the executed Italian soldiers.
>
> (Amazon, New Jersey, 12 June 2002;
> see also IMDB, US, 10 July 2005)

The reviewer blends Italian history, classicism and contemporary tourism. The Internet reference they suggest is one of many to *CCM* and Kefalonia which progressively replace or complement the conventional travel guide. The Greek official tourist website, to which the reviewer probably alludes, is a copy of her words. We learn, for example, that Kefalonia was Homer's Ithaca because it interchanged names with Ithaca in antiquity. We also learn about the massacre of the Italian soldiers, which is narrated in *CCM*. The imaginary Hellenic and Roman civilizations acquired in Western collective imaginations the role of an appropriated past, an ideal that the West has cherished ever since. It is interesting that in this context *CCM* engages in a game of cultural amnesia that quite a few viewers endorse. As David Lowenthal noted, an ever-expanding past may have enabled an increasing awareness of our roots, but it also activated a war against its preservation (Lowenthal 1985). It is interesting that reviews happily replicate the long-forgotten past of the grand tour alongside the whole debate upon the preservation of the two poles of the European past (Roman and Hellenic culture) while favouring the repression of the more recent histories of Second World War.

This repression is consistent even with recent self-perceptions of Italy in the European arena as purified from Second World War acts of violence. We need only recall the incident that took place in the European Parliament in summer 2003 when Italy was presenting its priorities during its six-month EU presidency. Italian Prime Minister Silvio Berlusconi, responding to the criticism from a Socialist member of the EU Parliament, Martin Shulz, daringly urged the latter to 'take a movie role as a Nazi concentration camp guard' (*International Herald Tribune* 2003). The Italian Prime Minister refused to take his comment back, and was unanimously condemned by all EU members for harassing Shulz and insulting his country. What Berlusconi did, in effect, was to write out Italy's involvement in these dark pages of European history. By calling a German MEP a Nazi, he was aligning his own country with the winners of the war, foreclosing any discussion of Italian fascist history. What was, of course, silenced, was Berlusconi's alliance with the neo-Fascist Alleanza Nationale party after the 1994 national elections, and his rumoured ongoing relationship with these circles.

To the repression of the fascist past we should add the anti-communist embarrassment that permeates the film. Even English reviewers were disappointed with the excision of 'the communist villains' from the narrative (Amazon, UK, 28 January 2004; IMDB, Manchester, 5 May 2001; Cambridge 6 July 2001), although some others were upset with the homophobic refashioning of fascist Carlo (IMDB, Sussex, 11 November 2005; IMDB, Manchester, 19 July 2004; IMDB, New York, 22 August 2001; Anonymous, 28 October 2001; Minnesota, 23 August 2001; Cambridge, UK, 22 May 2001). *CCM* deals with the supposed communist other in an innovative way, because it humanizes Mandrás in the eyes of the audience. In fact, in the film narrative there is no indication that Mandrás *is* a communist, so his communist beliefs are humanized through erasure. All that is left is a resistance fighter who is against the Nazis – uncontroversial and universally palatable to just about any audience, whatever their political persuasion.

Ironically, Mandrás' humanization illuminates a dark corner of the European and American imaginary: the surviving discourse of Balkan Orientalism. Between the two World Wars, but especially after the Second World War, communism became the new demon, a new 'other' that was employed to describe Balkan difference. The Balkans 'were proclaimed "lost to the Western World" and "written off by opponents of Western civilization," as long as Russia remained strong in the peninsula, because Russian communism "was the end of Europe"' (Todorova 1997: 133). Greece, however, with its classical heritage and its eventual alliance with Britain during the Second World War and the United States after the end of the War, was an indeterminate case. It was certainly more civilized than Yugoslavia, which 'had fallen prey' to the 'claws' of Tito's communism (Bakic-Hayden and Hayden 1992). Placing *CCM*'s narrative of Greek communism in this analytical framework we realize that Mandrás becomes representative of Greece's cultural limbo. On the one hand he is the crude communist peasant who permits his comrades to hang a young Greek woman because she kissed a German officer. On the other hand he is a compassionate human being who saves his ex-fiancée's new lover from certain death, and a lively dancer who amuses his compatriots. Ultimately, whether Hollywood's American anti-communist embarrassment was assisted by Greek Kefalonian and national politics or not, the outcome remains the same: Ionian Greece was cast as a liminal other for the needs of more advanced countries.

It becomes evident now that in *CCM* we do not deal with history as such, but with its clever fabrication to fit the sociopolitical realities of the era. Hollywood rarely respects the historical record. It is wiser to expect that its producers and scriptwriters will bend and twist it, even reinvent it, to meet their commercial aims and objectives. History is thus reduced to a platform on which cultural commodities are attractively displayed. What has to be borne in mind is that the foundations of this platform are borrowed from this kind of politics that marry Orientalism with anti-communism and dehistoricize the most poignant aspects of Greece's Second World War experience.

The Kefalonian devil: othering as identity

Tourism has been accused of many social evils, among them the breakdown of social networks and the erasure of local histories that allegedly existed unspoiled before foreign capitalist interventions (Mings 1978: 343; Nash 1996: 21; Harrison 2001: xi). But does this give a complete and unprejudiced picture of modernization (through touristification) and its inevitable host–guest encounters? Whereas tourism retains the undeniable aspects of exploitation, the outcome of the cultural encounters that accompany it may extend beyond the economic rationale of the sign industries. Herzfeld insists that 'the less literally face-to-face the society we inhabit, the more obviously cultural idioms become simulacra of social relations' (1997: 6) – especially when they are enacted during cultural encounters. Kefalonians proved to be the cardinal example of this phenomenon: indeed *CCM*'s trading in local historical signs crafted its own revenge to discipline those cinematic agents who adumbrated the development of tourism on the island. *CCM*'s cinematic mispresentations of local history brought the question of Kefalonian identity to the fore, ultimately producing modes of collective representation to outsiders. I argue then that the Kefalonian 'simulacra of sociality' (to follow Herzfeld's [1997: 7] terminology) that were advertised in the international press at the time became essential aspects of local self-narration. Passing over them in silence would result in missing the complexity of Kefalonian reactions to *CCM* and all that the cinematic venture came to mean for them.

The establishment of a local relationship with the *CCM* industry dates back to the arrival of film crews on the island in the spring-summer of 2000. De Bernières, upset about what followed, gives a lengthy description of the controversy in the film's companion (Clark 2001: 14). It seems that episodes occurred when two British journalists visited left-wing war veterans in Kefalonia to interview them about the politics of the film and the belief abroad that de Bernières' novel tarnished the contribution of Kefalonian communists to Greek resistance. Immediately after the publication of their articles, in which local left-wingers expressed indignation and outrage for Hollywood's 'calumnies', the Greek press produced a series of inflammatory reports on *CCM*, describing the film crew as 'an occupation force'. The move betrays how the Greek media internalized *a foreign* discourse. From the numerous Greek reports published at the time I have chosen to concentrate on an online article by Nafsiká Papanikolátos which exemplifies the ambivalence of local attitudes towards *CCM*'s emergent sign industry. Other articles from the foreign press will complement my analysis.

In the article Papanikolátos (Papanikolátos 2000) stated that although 'the Kefalonian stubborn and aristocratic temperament' initially appeared incompatible with the 'rigid rules of competition and exploitation', the locals eventually grasped their chance to make profit from the forthcoming movie. Papanikolátos' portrayal of the Kefalonian 'character' is intriguing, as it injects into local culture an element of uniqueness, setting it apart from Greek mainland culture. While aristocratic inclinations stand metonymically for the Venetian–Italian Ionian heritage, the conviction that Kefalonians refused to conform to the rules of competition certifies how different they are from their orientalized Greek relatives, who are still notorious amongst tourists for their dubious economic transactions (Herzfeld 1991: 52; Tzanelli 2003: 36; Tzanelli 2004). Note that Papanikolátos is of Kefalonian origin although she grew up outside the Ionian Islands; her discourse of difference may resonate in her inside–outside positioning. Yet, her article reverses strategic essentializations of national identity that eliminate internal difference (Handler 1985) by presenting it as external to identity (Balibar 1994: 63).

Initially, reactions to Hollywood's use of Kefalonia for the movie focused around de Bernière's anti-communist plot in which Mandrás is slowly brutalized through his attachment to communist ideals. Because of de Bernière's problematic treatment of resistance history, a Kefalonian committee was set up to ensure that the film would not touch upon the controversies of the era. The mayor of Sámi, Gerásimos Artelánis, stated firmly that if Hollywood turned the book into an anti-communist film, they 'would take measures'. 'You can be sure we will take the issue to the international court of justice at The Hague,' he said (*Sunday Times* 4 June 2000). De Bernières criticized Artelánis for his statements. He explained that despite his protestations the rebel mayor did not hesitate to participate in the film as an extra and to invite the novelist later as a special guest, while mourning how public opinion was manipulated by a group of 'left wingers' (Clark 2001: 15). In the meantime, however, Dionísios Georgátos, elected Governor of Kefalonia and adherent of the Greek socialist party then in power (PA.SO.K.), carefully proceeded to negotiate the terms under which Madden could shoot the film on the island. Although when Madden threatened to move his crew to Turkey the locals consented to participate in some scenes (Papanikolátos September 2000), the Kefalonian veterans never stopped complaining. 'We are at war with Louis de Bernières' claimed a 72-year-old former Kefalonian journalist and campaigner against the novel, adding that the war is defensive because 'it was declared on them' (Sicilian Culture, 2000). The campaign also criticized the involvement of Shawn Slovo in the making of *CCM*, stressing that she is the daughter of murdered anti-apartheid activist Ruth First and former communist and African National Congress Leader Joe Slovo. The anti-*CCM* movement was joined by other communist societies around the world (see for example Praxis International 2000) that expressed a concern over the ways in which the media become sources of popular historical knowledge.

Perhaps the comments that all these parties made were not wide of the mark. We need only mention that de Bernières' Corelli character was based on the war adventures of a 90-year-old Florentine veteran Amos Pamploni. Pamploni, who participated in the tragic revolt of the Italian soldiers against their German allies in 1943, disclosed a number of events to de Bernières. These events were subsequently matched with accounts that we find in the recently discovered diaries of a German war veteran, Alfred Richter (*Guardian* 2001a). Quite a few controversial aspects of these accounts never made it to the cinematic narrative, or were simply shunted aside by the 'casting' of Italian occupation as a holiday experience. The distance between Madden's frenzied editing and de Bernières' meticulous – if partial – narration of events led to a conflict between the two men (*Sunday Times* 2001). Hollywood demands for a commercial success eventually won over an appreciation of personal histories.

The producers assured the Kefalonian committee that violent reactions would not be necessary, since they did not intend to offend local sensibilities. This explains why in the film Mandrás, the local communist leader, receives ammunition from the Italian fascists, and saves the life of Antonio Corelli. It also explains why the cinematic narrative is split between the fact of Italian occupation and the myth of an amiable atmosphere between Kefalonians and Italians that culminates in the provision of Kefalonian ammunition to the latter when the 'nasty' Germans disarm them. The end of this negotiation between *CCM*'s producers and the Kefalonians could be anticipated. Hundreds of locals and Greek soldiers participated in the film as extras, Kefalonian owners of boats became richer from paparazzi that hunted Cage and Cruz, and many local cafés, bars, travel agencies and restaurants were renamed 'Corelli' and 'Pelagía' (Clark 2001: 74). In August 2002, *Daily Telegraph* journalist Oliver Bennett interviewed locals to check on *CCM*'s impact on the island's economy. 'With the Corelli business we have lost a lot of the good people because they are afraid that [the island] will be swamped' said a local restaurant owner, who hated the modernization that *CCM* imposed on the island. He condemned the 'backpackers' who visit the island and 'have one salad between them' but welcomed 'the good British' (i.e. families and *bon viveurs*) who spend money. Nowadays, Kefalonia is not the island of Hellenic Gods, but that of Capitano Corelli, awaiting foreign consumers.

Perhaps after reading the restaurant owner's cunning 'welcome' comment, we should stop mourning these developments and have a closer look at them. In her article Papanikolátos discusses an episode which illustrates how Kefalonians contrived a response to Hollywood hegemonization. Papanikolátos says that some storeowners 'insisted on demanding extortionate sums' for the use of their property as a front stage by *CCM*'s producers. This is reminiscent of Greek *poniriá* or 'cleverness', which anthropologists placed in the framework of the competitive relationship of locals with foreigners (Herzfeld 1985: 25). The production company then threatened to shoot the film in Turkey – a clever move, given that in national politics Turkey is the demonized 'other' that wants to annihilate the Greek nation. The rationale of cheating and taking advantage of situations to generate profit on the margins of acceptable (or legally sanctioned) behaviour is an integral part of Greek social poetics. To be *ponirós* is to acquire the qualities of the Devil in order to cope with the challenges of the everyday life: to be cunning without being evil. Taking advantage of situations demonstrates one's ability to retain a socially acceptable self-image in the community. If a Greek manages to make a fool of someone else, then they are a good entrepreneur and the deceived becomes the object of collective derision (du Boulay 1994: 116–17). Even film crews commented upon this obstructive behaviour in a light manner (Clark 2001).

As a result, cheating became akin to practical orientalism, 'the translation of hegemonic ideology into everyday practice so that it infiltrates the habitual spaces of ordinary experience' (Herzfeld 1997: 96). In the space of a few days the Kefalonians had managed to both perform (by cheating) and contest (by calling upon the EU human rights charter) Western classifications of Greekness as semi-Oriental. The Kefalonian entrepreneurial spirit manifested itself more than once: when the *CCM* stage team reconstructed the old Argostóli (capital of Kefalonia) in Sámi, visitors and tourists began to photograph themselves in front of the cinematic façades. This confirmed that the stage exuded the essential historical authenticity for the film, as even the old generation of locals admitted (Clark 2001: 95). It was then that a Kefalonian printing company took shots of *CCM*'s stage and reproduced them as 'Old Argostóli' postcards for tourist consumption 'without bothering to explain that the images shown were of a film set that would only be there for a few weeks' (*ibid.*). Putting aside that the marketization of the cinematic front stage takes MacCannell's (1973) point a step further, the very act of trading in fake authenticity is a crystal-clear sign of *poniriá* addressed to foreign tourists.

Nowadays the contribution of EAM/ELAS to anti-Nazi resistance and subsequent civil strife fuel historiographical debates in Greece and abroad. Still, the Italian–Greek communist collaboration on which some Kefalonians pride themselves (*Guardian* 2000) is simply a piece of uncertified oral history, highly contested even locally. This immediately opens a fissure in the alleged Kefalonian solidarity against the common Corelli-led 'enemies' that the media advertised abroad. The international glamour that the Second World War episode acquired in the context of *CCM*'s filmmaking contributed to the transformation of the episode into an element of 'truthful' Kefalonian self-narration. It is significant that local communist veterans discussed the film and the novel as 'an insult to the whole Greek people' (*ibid.*), not just the Kefalonians. It matters less whether there was dissent within the island over resistance history; what truly matters is what was projected outside the island. Ultimately, the controversy enabled Kefalonians to claim a special place in the history of Greece and in Modern Greek identity.

All these Kefalonian manoeuvres suggested that local self-presentations are not immune to wider political and intellectual discourses; on the contrary, they communicate with and borrow from them (Davis 1977; Just 2000: 34). To push the analysis further, bifurcated self-presentations, in which Kefalonians figure both as proud rebels and *poniroí* entrepreneurs, command anthropological comparisons between Kefalonia and Crete. Cretan identity is still regarded as an idiosyncratic example of Greekness, both marginal and yet central to national self-narration. On the one hand, Cretans proudly discuss and are discussed for their resistance to Turkish rule and their legendary participation in the Second

World War. As a result, at a national level they are deemed to embody the ultimate Greek values of heroic self-sacrifice and patriotism. On the other hand, Cretans have become the stereotype par excellence of the untamed and uncivilized – they play, in other words, the role of the Greek 'savage' within Greek identity (see Herzfeld 1985: 9). Unlike the Cretans, the Kefalonians never became part of the Ottoman dominions; yet in the *CCM* controversy they did not hesitate to endorse orientalist stereotyping. At the same time, they defended ferociously a local version of Second World War history that depicts them as intrepid patriots. Although the cryptocolonial fashion of Kefalonian self-presentations seemed to contradict local understandings of the more recent past (the Second World War), the two together reproduced Kefalonia's self-styled symbolic status: as an island at the geographical margins of Greece but at the core of Modern Greek identity.

Kefalonian tourism today: sign capitalization and local symbols

A film might announce the generation of consumption networks, but cannot guarantee their sustainability or their nature. When I visited the island in the summer of 2004 I expected to be confronted with a picture of capitalist colonization. Reality, however, was more complex: Kefalonian tourism had begun to oscillate between a mobilization of *CCM*'s sign industry and a display of locally produced signs. This compromise was not the product of careful long-term planning but of local cultural practices and central state policies towards tourist development.

An observation that applies to some tourist sites that I visited in the eastern, central and southwestern part of the island is that local tourist economies are still largely dependent on iconographies of Kefalonian geomorphology. To offer a few examples: near Lixoúri, the second biggest town on the island, the pits that repeated earthquakes created (*katavóthres*) still constitute one of the main tourist attractions. Their sign value is totally unconnected to *CCM*, yet they are very popular with tourists who take an interest in geological phenomena or others who are attracted by the aesthetics of the site. Not far away from Sámi one finds the caves of Melissáni and Drogaráti, which are linked to the *katavóthres*. Underground water flows have created the stunning lake of Melissáni, the 'jewel of Kefalonia' as the tour guide termed it, which is open to the public. Tours to the caves and boat trips to the lake are very popular. These three natural phenomena, 'unique in Europe', are the focus of foreign and domestic tourism alike, and generate considerable profit for local entrepreneurs.

The distinctive Kefalonian wild life is another bonus for the ecotourist economy. The scarcity of some species that inhabit the island – for example locals advertise Kefalonia as the natural habitat of the almost extinct tortoise Karetta-Karetta – add charm to the place. The region of Mount Aínos and Roudí is famous for its Kefalonian pine (*Albies Cephalonica*) and other forest flora, as well as for various species of reptiles, birds and the so-called horses of Aínos that live in inaccessible parts of the mountain. Despite the declaration of the region as a national park by the Greek state in 1962, a side-road off the main road that connects the capital, Argostóli, to Sámi leads lovers of nature to a tourist pavilion at a height of 1,300 metres. Even some locations that figured in the film are not referenced as such in tours. For example, although tours include stops at Mýrtos Bay, a secluded beach in which scenes were shot with Cage and his Italian 'opera group', there is barely any mention of the film. References to *CCM* are overshadowed by the radiance of the landscape and the claim that the clear green-blue waters of the beach have acquired international fame. Stops above Mýrtos Bay facilitate the obligatory pictures. These photographs contain personal narratives of the journey and belong to no imposed sign order (Squire 1994: 6; Crang 1999: 238; Coleman and Crang 2002). In conclusion then, on Kefalonia the cinematic, tourist and local gazes may operate under independent indexical rules.

Similarly, there is a wealth of cultural referents that operate independently from the *CCM* sign industry. The Byzantine-Venetian castles (for example in the Àsos peninsula) and the museums (especially those of Argostóli) appeal to traditional cultural tourists. One would expect that at least the monastery of Saint Gerásimos would have been subjected to the needs of the *CCM* industry. An 'exploration' of the monastery is part of standard tours but with little mention of the Saint's litany that frames *CCM*'s narrative of the war. Kefalonian and foreign tour guides prefer to discuss the cultural significance of the monastery for islanders, cautioning tourists to dress modestly when they enter its premises so as not to offend religious sensibilities. As on other occasions of tourist advertising, tours to the monastery are followed by visits to the local winery in which foreign tourists are offered a glass of Rombóla, the local wine recommended in every restaurant.

The case of Fiskárdo, the fishing village at the northern tip of the island that figures in some *CCM* scenes, is illustrative of other complexities that characterize local tourist economies. The fame of this 'Mediterranean Riviera', as tourists call the village, resonates in the place's survival from the 1953 earthquake that devastated the island. The villagers have been careful enough to preserve its picturesque 'feel', constantly restoring and repainting the old buildings that ornament its small harbour. Their efforts have paid off: today the village is recommended by popular travel guides such as *Lonely Planet* and *Frommers* as an ideal holiday destination. Although Fiskárdo is popular with British and Italian tourists, it is also internal, Greek tourism of a particular type that has bolstered its economy. Hotels are very expensive for backpackers and the local cafés and restaurants charge steep prices that can drive away backpackers and 'casual' tourists. What has contributed to its international reputation is that Fiskárdo has been for decades an established resort for ship owners and yachting fraternities. Quite a few of its restaurants advertise themselves as favourites of Greek actors, ship owners and politicians, inciting a lot of jealousy in other resorts. Stories of 'relieving' ignorant foreigners of their money at local eateries circulate on the island and incite competitive gossip elsewhere. Locals involved in tourist business in the southwestern resort of Skála have remarked with envy that the little northern village is 'taking all the glory of the Corelli business', when the spoils should have been distributed fairly.

We should take a more careful look at this comment. The social awareness of jealousy may be betraying an understanding of market competition, but simultaneously becomes an expression of local values of success in the global economic arena (for comparisons see Broegger 1990: 107; Macleod 2004: 203). Like *poniriá*, 'jealousy' is addressed to visitors: its effects (profit-making and subsequent socioeconomic recognition) matter more in an interactive context. It is no coincidence that narratives of Fiskárdo's success are followed by stories of excessive charging of visitors, as on a cultural level both practices command the respect of Kefalonian compatriots. This drive for success also explains why in developing resorts such as Skála *CCM* asserts its presence in direct and indirect ways. Skála has a beautiful beach and about a dozen newly built hotels but no 'Corelli glory': no cinematic scenes were filmed there. Yet its locals often mention the film to attract the attention of tourists. Upon arrival I was repeatedly told about the blockbuster's impact on local tourism until the hotel owners realized that I was a Greek amongst a group of Britons. After that I was rarely reminded of it and was drawn instead into debates on national politics. I was led to assume that for locals *CCM* is transformed into symbolic capital (Britton 1991) when they perform the role of the host for foreigners. In fact, when in the evenings a group of Kefalonians (friends of the hotel manager) would gather in the café-bar of the hotel, they would invite me to participate in their conversations. As a *dikó mas korítsi* (our own girl), my enquiries were answered and my requests were granted. Caught in the drama of everyday host–guest exchanges, the locals needed some firm ground to step on. In their eyes I was 'one of their own', as the vocabulary of kinship that they used to classify me denoted (Just 2000: 94–5). Predictably, I was told that the *CCM* quarrel was 'the job of political fraternities' (*fatríes*) that were well-disposed towards the then socialist government and wanted to nullify right-wing propaganda in the international press. Local social life is politicized to such an extent that an interlocutor is always invited to take a political stance before any serious social commitments are made towards them. Narrowly did I escape the 'invitation' I received from my hosts to comment on PA.SO.K.'s domestic policies, claiming that I live abroad and do not follow Greek political developments.

CCM's impact was more apparent in the visual presentations of the resort, which had its own 'Corelli' tavernas and a 'Corelli' bar, which is run by an Irish woman and has no local patrons. The younger generation seemed to see the place as an oddity addressed to foreigners and considered the whole Corelli hubbub ridiculous. Attitudes towards *CCM* were overdetermined by age and occupation: the younger generation considered the film and its tourist referents a disgrace, whereas the older generation seemed to mobilize it, often for commercial purposes. An illustrative example of this ambivalent response to *CCM*'s sign value involves the ways in which a taverna in the village square lured foreign tourists. The strategy of the owner centred on the staging of dancing. I watched the same performance taking place more than once: two waiters would appear in the restaurant area, dance 'Zorba the Greek' and other 'quintessentially Greek' songs, and break some plates to the amusement of those present. The *rationale* of this performance was identical to that of the dance scenes in *CCM*: the dancing waiters were simply re-enacting a 'simulacrum of Kefalonian sociality'. '*Ksénoi eíne re, tí katalavaínoun.*' ('They are foreigners pal, they don't understand') a barman next door explained to me, intimating his thoughts on the alleged cultural myopia of the audience. I was impressed by the professional precision with which the staged event took place *every* evening. Its staging must have been an open secret in the locality and among foreign tourists, who nevertheless did not cease to visit the taverna. The appeal of social simulation might have been stronger for foreign tourists than the knowledge that the performance itself did not correspond to any social reality. It may be wrong to discuss the performance as 'fake' – after all, the enacting of Kefalonian *kéfi* (high spirits) (Cowan 1990, Papataxiarchis 1991) through dancing attained meaning *during* interaction between locals and tourists (see also Cloke and Perkins 1998: 189). As Damer has explained, authenticity 'is in the eye of the beholder': in Skála 'both locals and tourists colluded creatively . . . to construct a locally specific version' (2004: 221) of Kefalonia.

In Skála the first grievances regarding the recent tourist development were intimated to me. Not unlike his compatriots' confessions to the *Daily Telegraph* in 2002, the manager of the hotel in which I was staying explained that from the outset the Kefalonians' aspiration was to cater for the right type of tourists (*sostoús anthrópous*). When I asked for clarification, his wife 'María' drew my attention to the 'dirt' (*vromiá*) of neighbouring Zante, an established destination for young Britons, and Faliráki, a holiday resort on the island of Rhodes. A series of unpleasant incidents in Faliráki such as brawls and drug use involving British bar-crawling tourists spread considerable panic in the media about the future of Greek tourism (see for example *AIM* 2003). 'María' expressed the fear that Kefalonia may have the same fate if no attention is paid to the policing of mass holiday resorts in south Kefalonia. She was referring to Lássi, a mass tourist resort whose cosmopolitan feel and developing nightlife is attracting younger foreigners, mostly British. The language of dirt that she used to describe British tourists was strikingly similar to that of Thai locals in the case of *The Beach*. It underpinned the symbolic boundaries of Greek identity, 'deporting' foreign tourists to a polluted territory. Her reference to 'rapes' of women on Rhodes (often based on rumours and over-reaction of local police [BBC News 2002a]) had a similar symbolic meaning. The link between cleanliness (dirty tourists) and sexuality, present in other Mediterranean countries (see Goddard 1987), manifested fears of cultural intrusion. Not only are dirty (and therefore neglected) homes associated with sexual delinquency, but also as women symbolize the private sphere of domesticity, their physical violation corresponds to the symbolic violation of the community's intimate space (Herzfeld 2001: 217). 'María' also explained that she preferred the clientele of the more 'posh' holiday resorts or those addressed to families and couples, such as Fiskárdo. Although it may be incorrect to suggest that she was familiar with British class distinctions, she was certainly referring to the emerging class geographies of tourist consumption on the island.

A resort that certainly capitalized on *CCM*'s success is Agía Efimía, a village that rests on a beautiful bay in the northeastern part of the island. During the filming of *CCM* the village housed Cage, Cruz and other actors. Initially locals publicized the rooms that actors occupied as 'shrines' for *CCM* lovers. It has been reported that a few years ago a local woman even advertised her apartment 'as the venue for Nick Cage and Cruz's alleged affair' (*Kefalonia Island Guide* 2003). A local entrepreneur, Dimítrios Kalliakoúdis, set out to make his restaurant-café internationally famous: when film crews and actors began to visit his restaurant, he changed the name of his business into Capt. Corelli's. De Bernières himself lamented this development in the film guide (see Clark 2001: 15), but today Kalliakoúdis has expanded his business enough to acquire his own website. His virtual display of Agía Efimía with its alleged excellent local specialities is accompanied by Kalliakoúdis' trading in real estate. The website hosts images of idyllic locations that conform to *CCM*'s tourist gaze. Villas and land on which foreigners can 'build [their] holiday home' (Café Capt. Corelli 2006) are now available for sale via the website. On the morning that our group arrived at Agía Efimía, Capt. Corelli's was not open, but our tour guide recommended it as a *CCM* attraction and 'the best' restaurant in the village.

Although the inhabitants of Sámi appeared to be less interested in *CCM* their town was replete with banal traces of the *CCM* sign industry, such as the names of cafés that mushroomed after the film. Passing by the town on a personal tour in a taxi, I noticed that my driver did not offer to stop. 'There's nothing here to see', he explained. When I inquired about the template of the film's set that allegedly decorated the central square, he explained that even that was eventually removed. Sámi is not discussed as the town of Corelli anymore, but as a quiet port in which you can spend just a couple of hours before you sail off to Itháki, the unspoiled neighbor of Kefalonia. Many have commented upon the Sámian display of indifference to *CCM* – an indifference often attributed to Kefalonia as a whole. Some puzzled Britons tried to comprehend why even touristified locations did not try to 'cash in on the Corelli phenomenon' (This is Travel 2002), 'leaving commercial exploitation . . . largely to foreign tour operators' (*Kefalonia Island Guide* 2003). Such claims bypass the fact that non-initiative bears the Janus-like qualities of Mediterranean essentialism. During my stay I noticed that Kefalonians would be described by foreign visitors as hospitable and friendly, but totally indifferent to the development of a formalized system of tourist services. Underneath this contradiction there lies the rhetoric of reciprocity that marks the temporary supremacy of the host-'giver'. The increasing inferiority of the non-reciprocating guest 'reaches its extreme in the selfish and insensitive tourist, who finds that "the natives are friendly" but fails to understand that this friendliness masks an enduring contempt' (Herzfeld 1987a; Herzfeld 1992: 61). Kefalonian off-hand attitudes may serve to keep foreigners outside the intimate confines of everyday life, while benefiting economically from them.

Attitudes do not reflect political decision-making however, which determines the future of tourism in any resort. In 2000, during a visit to a Kefalonia bursting with optimism for its economic future, the then Minister of Culture Theódoros Pángalos 'tried to encourage filmmaking business to make investments' (Papanikolátos 2000). Similar state initiatives figured after the release of *The Beach* and the *LOTR*, but in the Greek case they were not actively encouraged to flourish by the government. The country is an established mass tourist destination and its exoticization is a tired business after centuries of intellectual and economic exploitation. Decades ago charter flights opened wide the country's gates to European working classes, contributing to the general disenchantment of the place: there is nothing more banal than going to a Greek island for a short holiday break. The absence of offers by any film industries was something to be expected, then. As an island, Kefalonia faces economic challenges that researchers have identified elsewhere – namely a limited resource base that invites tourist expansion as a compensatory mechanism (Wilkinson 1989; Conlin and Baun 1995; Briguglio *et al.* 1996). Because the Athenian core controls both capital distribution and policy planning, islands at the margins of the nation-state have little power and support to develop economically sustainable initiatives (King 1993; Sharpley 2001, 2004). Thus the Kefalonian dependency model seems to follow the logistics of the international tourist structure (Britton 1989: 161–2): it corresponds, in other words, to a 'world system' (Wallerstein 1974) in which a centre controls the periphery (see also Britton 1982). The malfunction of formal consultation apparatuses for tourist growth at a national level has left local tourism at the mercy of foreign travel agencies: as a result today Thompson and Thomas Cook are the main holiday suppliers for Kefalonia.

This arrangement encourages a constant economic leakage abroad at the expense of localities (Crick 1989). In the absence of any policy planning, hotels managed by Kefalonians were 'encouraged' to sign deals with foreign travel companies that supply them with tourists in search of sun or culture. An upshot of these formal deals that are often secretly resented by staff and managers themselves as I was told in Sámi, is the creation of informal local economies based on kinship relations. When my hosts in Skála found out that I wanted to sign up for a Thomas Cook tour of the island, they recommended instead a local taxi-driver who charges a fixed fee for 'personalized' tours. His excursion through the Kefalonian landscape and culture was followed by an analysis of the *CCM* 'communist brawls'. Obviously he was persuaded that the controversy was the outcome of a political polarization that reflects the post-civil war divides in the Greek mainland and assumed that his intimations would encourage me to take sides. As I found out later, the man was a distant relative of the hotel manager who, like many other taxi drivers on the island, runs this business alongside his regular taxi shifts. One of my hosts also turned out to be the uncle of the hotel manager (he was covering for his nephew who was on holiday). I encountered similar cases in Fiskárdo and Trapezáki near Argostóli, where a number of apartments, cafés and restaurants are supported by family networks. Under the surface of foreign economic intrusion, I discovered a microcosm of culturally informed practices that reinforce local or familial bonding. Loyalties drove local economies even in tourist resorts such as Skála, in which locals would visit only the tavernas of friends and relatives at weekends to provide 'support' (*ypstíriksi*) to 'their own' (*dikoús mas*). As a Greek, I was invited to honour this practice by eating out in recommended places run by friends and relatives – an exhibition of introspection suggesting that reciprocity is possible only within the Greek national community.

Kefalonian responses to the *CCM* industry have a surprising story to communicate to the defenders of the classical 'cultural imperialism' thesis. The island's involvement in global networks of economic exchange certainly presents locals as helpless recipients of foreign economic designs. A bitter taste of injustice may remain in one's mouth, as de Bernière's book and *CCM did* toy with ideas and histories dear to the old folk of this marginal Greek community for commercial reasons. However, underneath the surface of consumerist homogenization that economic globalizations may support, we find the obdurate survival of local custom and experience that shapes even daily economic transactions. So, even if 'the homogenisation proceeds . . . in terms of globally marketed goods' such as food, film, music and holidays, 'the development of greater heterogeneity [is] occurring simultaneously' (Macleod 2004: 218) through an injection of established sociocultural order into the global scene: local history, politics, familial solidarity and collective public performance. The ethnic and professional ethos may belong to different spheres of Kefalonian life, but their interaction bears the potential to revive local culture and identity.

5 'Welcome to the land of salsa'
Lifestyle and the curse of Orientalism

It has been almost two decades since the release of *Dirty Dancing* (1987), a film starring Jennifer Grey and Patrick Swayze set in an innocent world of rock 'n' roll passion that captured teenage imaginations. The film told the story of a young middle-class 'ugly duckling' who meets a dancer who sets her free from her inhibitions and gives her a lesson in love. Lions Gate Cinema's decision to summon the ghost of this movie by resetting it in Batista's pre-revolutionary Cuba (*c.*1958), was met with mixed feelings in the world of critics. The political background against which the cinematic narrative developed became an element of discord, as some found the ornamental use of Cuban history by Hollywood agents insulting. Although *Dirty Dancing: Havana Nights* (*DD2*) (2004, director Guy Ferland) appeared to be too frivolous and incoherent to make it to any award-winning lists and soon found itself on the shelves of HMV stores and DVD rental shops, it still retained the charm of adolescent romance. Perhaps the greatest irony of all has been the journalistic allegation that Lions Gate incorporated so-called 'Latino elements' in the plot (the male protagonist, the political scene, the music and dancing) to attract a growing Hispanic audience that currently boosts ticket sales in American cinemas (*Empire* 2002). Such remarks were countered by Tom Ortenberg, president of Lions Gate Releasing, who classified the film as a 'mainstream American movie' (*Wall Street Journal* 2004a).

The comment is not a trivial one: biographical in its nature, as film posters advise ('Based on true events'), the script was fashioned on the experiences of choreographer JoAnn Jansen as an American teenager in Cuba (*Seattle Post-Intelligencer* 2004). Before Jansen's interventions the plot was closer to the original 1980s film: after her contribution plans changed dramatically. Originally the story was set in Miami, where most of the Cuban expatriates live – hence the anticipation that it would appeal to Afro-Caribbean working class immigrants. When Miramax producer and former dancer Lawrence Bender was introduced to the production process, the fictional locale was changed to reflect Jansen's adolescent adventures (*Wall Street Journal* 2004b). So attractive were these changes that the film recently (2006) made its way to London's West End as a musical. Producer Kevin Jacobsen has described it as 'the perfect date musical . . . a really good story and as well as dirty, sexual dancing, there is Latin, tango, mambo and ballroom' (*Evening Standard* 2006). Clearly, complaints concerning the marginalization of Cuban history in favour of a spectacle pleasing to the eye had some basis.

DD2 presents 'brainy' 17-year-old Katey Miller (Romola Garai) dislocated into Havana on the eve of Castro's Revolution. Laughed at by her classmates, rich kids of American businessmen who engage in trivial gossip and vicious racist commentary about locals, she barricades herself in the world of books. One day unexpectedly she is introduced into street dancing, apparently present in every square and street of Havana. The hotel's waiter, Javier (Diego Luna), invites her to local nightclubs that white foreigners and tourists never visit, initiating her into the secret culture of salsa. Together with Javier, who single-handedly supports his family while his brother joins *La Revolution* to undermine the Batista regime, Katey enters a ballroom contest. It is decided that if the couple wins, the sought-after prize will be spent on Javier's deprived family, but in the meantime dancing creates a special bond between Javier and Katey that defies class and racial divisions and enables both to explore their sexuality. Unfortunately, the arrival of the Revolution necessitates the departure of Katey's family from Cuba. Heartbroken, the young couple bid farewell to each other – but not before a night at La Rosa Negra, the famous working class club of Havana. In dim lights Javier and Katey, now recognized as queen of salsa, dance for one last time together before they part forever.

Needless to point out that unlike *The Beach*, the *LOTR* and *CCM*, this movie did not become responsible for the touristification of Havana. As the film suggests, the origins of this phenomenon do indeed date back to the post-Second World War era, when a change in patterns of American leisure (with rumba, mambo, Daiquiri and cigars enjoying a growing popularity in the USA) bolstered tourist arrivals in Cuba (Jayawardena 2003: 52). Given the historical background of *DD2*'s plot, the cinematic narrative appears to encourage associations between the American desire for exotic pleasures and the achievement of full economic colonization. Certainly the most interesting aspect of Jansen's nostalgic recollections is the clash between the tourist paradise of Batista's corrupt Cuba with the working class 'sexy' dance culture that presumably brews social change. This tension, which drives the story from beginning to end, also guides reviews of *DD2* on IMDB and Amazon.com.

Putting the process of film production and reception aside for a while, we are free to scrutinize the choice of the actual setting itself, which is significant for the present study because it tells a compelling story about *DD2*'s implication in the Western commodification of the 'Caribbean' Cuba – this non-existent category that has guided past and present colonial imaginations. It must be clarified that *DD2* was not filmed in Miami or Cuba, but in Puerto Rico (for the authentic feel that Western audiences expect from Hollywood imagery). The inference was that the material background of the story should not lack the verisimilitude of a standard travel brochure – on the contrary, it should replicate it. The transposition of 'Cuba' into one of Puerto Rico's most touristy areas removes the specificity of Cuban history from the chain of production/ consumption and dumps it into the gutter of unpleasant geopolitics that allegedly belong to colonial *pasts*. Edward Said would have included this practice into his analysis of Western orientalist contempt for the 'other' as constitutive of political and ideological claims to supremacy (1978: 21). Following Mimi Sheller's polemics (2003: 8), I will explain how contemporary Western economies and policies constantly resurrect these pasts. The erasure of historical and cultural specificity saturates tourist imaginations as much as it informs academic and other sociopolitical fields (McClintock 1995; Sheller 2000). Placing *DD2* in this macro-sociological debate I argue that the movie hardly engages with Cuban culture and history; instead, it promotes an image of 'Caribbean' Cuba as a tourist resort paradise (Pattullo 1996). This fantastic 'Cuba' is addressed to Western aficionados of a manufactured 'Latin American' lifestyle centred on dancing and gratification akin to the liminal tourist experience. My understanding of the notion of lifestyle focuses on the aestheticized consumption of place, linking it to the active (re)construction of the identity of the host country (Chaney 1996). Learning to dance salsa as a lifestyle choice challenges traditional differentiations between tourism and leisure (Cohen 1995): both focus on the subject's renewal through a quest for 'difference', whether this involves travelling to another place or undertaking non-ordinary activities that broaden the subject's sociocultural horizons. The mastery of salsa dancing is thus a 'symbolic good' obtained though hard physical work that nevertheless retains its aura as an exotic leisure activity (Crouch 1999; Ritzer 1999).

One could argue that this approach is *very* structuralist in so far as it refuses to acknowledge the intrinsic properties of Western popular culture. Even if one does not agree with the claim that salsa 'training' and tourism is an *ekfrasis* (expression) of popular culture, a creative process of consumption, one should still examine the act of consumption as such to understand contemporary cultures and identities. For this purpose I will scrutinize the content of online reviews of *DD2* to provide theoretical observations on the multiple significance of salsa dancing and tourism in Western sociocultural orders (see also Den Tandt 2002). Still, the film I explore is by definition situated in the realm of colonial and neocolonial politics: it talks about an aspect of the 'other's' history in anodyne ways, objectifies culture and its performance without questioning the origins of this objectification, and naturalizes the racialization of ethnicity with no remorse. This symbolic appropriation of the Caribbean in *DD2* is exquisitely ambivalent, like any form of cannibalization, because it celebrates the symbolic defeat of otherness in the realm of First World consumption, but retains a cultural reverence for its properties. The element of Cuban/Caribbean culture that *DD2* primarily commodifies, salsa dancing, involves a repackaging of otherness for Western consumers but also a desired property, that of corporeal control. A central theme to this study is then that the 'culture' and 'identity' of any place is open to contestation (Massey 1994), forever adaptable to the needs and demands of the historical moment (Hall 1992: 310).

'Represent Cuba': from salsa heavens to hip-hop havens

DD2's adaptation into a musical could be anticipated, as the film constantly mediates its political messages through dancing. Katey and Javier barely know each other when they get to the dance floor to practise their steps and then to bed for their first sexual experience. In *DD2* dancing and music do not simply enhance the cinematic background but also provide the sociohistorical framework in which Cuba is being domesticated in sign industries. The global sign networks that I explore here link music, film and tourist industries in an unprecedented way. *DD2* appealed through its soundtrack and dancing routines to a predominantly young group of salsa and hip-hop fans, as well as to lovers of the Caribbean who combine their salsa exploits with travels to Cuba. Since its inception and development, the practice of ballroom salsa dancing has been part of Western imaginary topographies of exotic travel. Flourishing in the early 1990s, after the deflation of the disco balloon, salsa dancing became 'a post-national invented tradition' (Hobsbawm and Ranger 1986) worked and reworked in the laboratories of developed countries for the sake of Western consumers. The globalization of salsa dancing and music are part of a new Western lifestyle that dictates the sanitized consumption of Afro-Caribbean culture (see also hooks [1992: 22] on symbolic consumption). This involves the sexualization of the Western body, stereotypically conceived as awkward and inflexible, in nightclubs and under the sweaty beats of hybrid music. To dance salsa is to be 'hot', desirable and sexually competent – just like the imagined Afro-Caribbean subjects who live through their physical properties.

Akin to early colonial practices of domestication and aestheticization, not only does this hunting for exotic lifestyle appropriate native resources to Western ends, but 'it also appropriates the native point of view' (Spurr 1993: 34). As James Clifford (1988: 224) has explained, Western institutions have constructed taxonomies responsible for 'making authenticity', which consign value to performances and ideas that originate outside the Western world. The depiction of salsa dancing in *DD2* is the aesthetic, cultural focus of the cinematic journey – a journey that leads to the mastery of Cuban/Caribbean culture by the American protagonist of the story. In this context *DD2* can only be treated as part of a Western representational apparatus that promotes the circulation of cultural difference globally (Salvatore 1998: 74). Salsa and salsa tourism to Cuba are exponents of cultural mobility from the Caribbean 'heart of darkness' to the Western (both American and European) zone of 'civilization'. In a first stage, I will consider *both* as an extension of past modes of bodily commodification: 'the legality of the slavery, indenture, prostitution and sex work, and varieties of personal service' (Sheller 2003: 27) that defined early European orientalizations of the region. The analysis places the poetics of *DD2*'s global sign industry within the 'power-geometry of space-time compression' (Massey 1993: 61) that regulates the flows and interconnections of human beings, ideas and cultural products. It is interesting that the principal role of dancing in *DD2* was recognized by most online reviewers, especially those who aspired to join, or already belong to Western dance cultures. The motivations and understandings of dancing did not converge in them, yet diverse readings shared one point: salsa is a learning process. This process involves the mobilization of knowledge for things Cuban by Western subjects who aspire to master their own body.

If *DD2* begins with a dispirited Katey who watches the natives dancing in the streets, it certainly ends with impressions of her growing admiration for their ability to move their body in exotic rhythms. In the underground world of club dancing, allegedly a common feature of the 1950s Cuba, her white body is glowing in the darkness of the Cuban (predominantly black) crowd. The contrast between white and black, Hollywood's enduring chiaroscuro technique (Dyer 1997), demarcates cultures and highlights racial boundaries. The club scenes are full of *Habanero* couples entangled in frenzied dancing that emulates the sexual act. The scant clothing of Cuban women or the deliberate exposure of parts of their bodies amidst swinging exacerbates bodily contact. Male dancers are equally sexualized: their pronounced masculinity is communicated through movement, firm control and leadership of their partners. Cuban dancers are thus presented as archetypal specimens of contemporary dance cultures in which the male leads and the female follows. In contrast, Katey's body remains demurely hidden in elegant dresses for the greatest part of the film. Her persona both defies and reasserts the stereotypical image of the 'dumb blonde' – the white feminine identity par excellence that remains untouched by rationality and devoid of knowledge about sexuality (Dyer 1979). Katey is a bright teenager who reads literature in her spare time (as opposed to the stereotype of the dumb blonde), but is totally inexperienced when it comes to her sexuality (much like the 'dumb blonde'). Javier also partakes in this racial classification, by relativizing 'blackness'. In relation to Katey he is black, but in relation to his compatriots he is white(r) and therefore exceptional. A chain of associations visually arranged in binary oppositions is formed: whiteness vs. blackness, civilization vs. nature, innocence vs. sexuality, intellect vs. physicality.

The politics of race did not escape attention in online reviews, but the comments differed. A group of viewers recognized in salsa dancing an equal opportunities terrain (see also hooks 1992), a de-politicized zone in which people from different classes, cultures and races can meet and 'overcome their prejudices' (IMDB, 14 January 2006). A Slovenian fan says that the film 'makes you want to stand up and dance' as it proves that 'no matter what language . . . you speak or where you come from you will always understand another person through dance' (IMDB, 3 January 2006; Cambridge, MA, 23 August 2004). 'This is a sweet story of an interracial relationship in Cuba, where a white girl from America falls in love with the sexy Cuban pool boy!' exclaims someone else (IMDB, Washington, 21 November 2004). Others were more annoyed by 'the inclusion of the very white and aged Patrick Swayze' (Amazon, San Diego, CA, 10 September 2005), expecting more dark bodies to complete the spectacle. The contrast between whiteness and Cuban mulatto appearance is significant for a New Yorker who praises the transformed Katey Miller of the last scenes:

> Her golden, regal beauty and bewitching sensuality are so completely radiant and luminous in every scene, you never wonder if she'll get the guy. Instead you wonder why she wants a mere boy instead of a grown man of greater animal power and allure!
>
> (IMDB, 2 May 2005)

Recurring in these reviews is an admiration for Katey's achievement to penetrate 'indigenous' culture coupled with the tendency to treat Javier and his compatriots as objects of aesthetic value. It is this aestheticization that reconstitutes Cuba and reduces the natives to a baroque, 'parasitical function' (Barthes 1993: 37). Javier's sensuality is valuable only as an oriental fantasy, 'a sexual promise . . . unlimited desire [with] deep generative energies' (Said 1978: 188). For example, an Australian sighs at the thought of 'the hot Cuban guy [falling] for the plain American girl' (IMDB, 13 May 2005), dreaming of a similar experience. Even more blunt is a viewer from the Netherlands who finds that 'the story of someone on vacation, meeting one of the natives and having the time of there [sic] lives' is great.

This is when Cuba loses its unique attributes as a historical category. Diego Luna's casting as Javier certainly assists in it: like Cage and Cruz in *CCM* he is believable as a Cuban boy because of his actual nationality. His cultural *habitus* assists in his cinematic signification. The implication is that if he is from that hazy category of 'Latin America' then he must 'make little girls swoon with his Mexican accent and his pretty hot dance moves' (IMDB, Austria, 23 May 2004). 'I must learn to dance, then I must find a Cuban boy' plans a Turkish viewer, who obviously finds the prospect appealing. There is little notice that Luna is Mexican, not Cuban, and viewers remain satisfied with his accent, which is 'believable' (IMDB, 29 June 2005). The conflation becomes comical in other comments, in which the young actor is described as a 'young but sexier Al Pacino with a very Cuban accent' (IMDB, US, 13 June 2005). 'I have a thing for latinos [sic]' (IMDB, Illinois, 8 August 2004), admits an American who obviously is not concerned with the specificity of geographies. The oriental fantasy of a Latino sexual partner is analogous to the experiential journey of 'acculturation' (IMDB, Sweden, 3 January 2006) that Western tourists pursue in countries such as Thailand. There were other viewers who deplored this attitude. Some were angered by the hint that 'todays [sic] young girls [want] to date Hispanics' just because of their fashionable cultural background, accusing *DD2*'s scriptwriter both of reversing and reproducing racist discourse. The idea that the film is a 'mindless escapism' (IMDB, Santa Monica, 9 May 2004) guides only a small group of critically minded viewers who spot in *DD2* a consumerist logic that remains insensitive to the social realities of the Caribbean countries. Such attitudes, however, activate virtual flâneurism, transforming cinematic viewers into collectors of global tourist signs:

> The film makes me want all this to happen to me in my life, me being on holiday and I meet a sexy guy and we get to dance and kiss.
>
> (IMDB, UK, 26 December 2004;
> see also IMDB, USA, 12 August 2004)

Or, as another reviewer puts it: 'I always wanted to "dance" like that with a man . . . They were so loving each other through music [and] . . . salsa' (IMDB, Slovenia, 13 January 2006).

The persistence of this motif, through which the viewer is transformed into a sexual tourist raider of the host country, is striking. Today the Cuban tourist industry is the strongest in the Caribbean region, despite the US embargo that keeps the influx of American visitors under control. It is commonly believed that Cuba's tourist boom began after the break-up of the Soviet Union and the dissolution of the Communist Bloc. On the other hand, there is evidence that President Fidel Castro supported both the internal and external (with the promotion of black American tourism) touristification of the country from the outset (Jayawardena 2002). An inclusive agenda that countered racism and other types of discrimination in tourist services and the establishment of the National Tourist Institute in 1960 placed Cuba on the global economic map as a tourist destination. However, pre-1958 tourist trends characterized by gambling, entertainment and sex were never replaced or eradicated. Prostitution remained a major economic resource nationally (Miller and Henthorne 1997), further promoting the stereotype of the Cuban who is looking to marry a foreigner and flee the country. In the mid-1990s researchers even anticipated that the end of the Castro regime and/or the eventual lifting of the US embargo will introduce in the country political and economic changes similar to those that are taking place in Eastern Europe (see Stein and Kane-Hanan 1996), consolidating sexual trade and trafficking in women (Rubin 1975).

I am deviating from my initial focus because sexual encounters, unquestionably a defining characteristic of Cuban tourism, are implicit in this last cluster of online reviews. As Ryan and Kinder (1996) have explained, visiting prostitutes 'is an example of liminal behaviors undertaken by those who operate at social thresholds' (1996: 507), especially tourists (see also Rojek [1993] on tourism and the carnivalesque). This liminal behaviour informs online comments and reproduces the colonial order of things: Havana was notorious as the Caribbean 'brothel' in the 1950s (Pattullo 1996: 91), and still is in the eyes of twenty-first century cinematic tourists. The censored presentations of sexual intercourse that frame *DD2*'s nightclub scenes correspond to a recent resurrection of global Cuban stereotyping concerning the provision of sexual pleasures for the sake of tourist growth (Sheller 2004: 19). For the aforementioned group of *DD2* (re)viewers, dancing simply conceals the packaging of human beings as 'embodied commodities', available to affluent Westerners at a low price (see Sánchez-Taylor 1999).

Examining more online reviews, one notices that such hedonistic fantasies of Cuban romance and sex are overwhelmingly addressed to female viewers, especially Diego Luna fans. This engendering of virtual consumption mirrors changes in actual tourist contexts, whereby native working-class men and teenagers are treated as sexual objects by wealthy female visitors (Sheller 2004: 164). *DD2* itself promotes this. Javier is introduced to us as a poor waiter who struggles to earn his salary while enduring the abuse of the American patrons of the hotel. The cinematic narrative refuses to present him as anything other than a competent dancer, pushing his political sensibilities aside. This creates a gamut of repetitive observations, such as those of a Canadian who admires the 'amazing way' Luna's body moved, deciding that she will 'pay to learn to dance so Cuban' (IMDB, Canada, 12 February 2005) or of an anonymous reviewer who generalizes about 'Hispanics', 'always known for their love of dance and their festivities' (IMDB, 6 March 2004).

Another group of North American and European viewers discusses how salsa dancing has become part of a cosmopolitan 'travelling' culture (Urry 2000) that has migrated to the First World. These reviewers stress the importance of corporeal inculcation in dancing not simply as a process of acculturation but also as a way of accumulating cultural capital to display on the dance floor (Bourdieu 1977, 1984). 'Being a dancer myself I can relate to how hard it must have been 4 [*sic*] them 2 [*sic*] learn the routines', says a British viewer (IMDB, 26 December 2004). 'The dancing was great, I am learning salsa right now so it was cool to see people dancing that really know the steps' claims an American (IMDB, 13 June 2005). 'I liked the way they showed off in the club' (Amazon, 13 February 2005), admits a viewer from Atlanta. Urquía Norman's (2005) ethnography of salsa enclaves in London's clubs reveals that Western amateur dancers have a repository of aesthetic qualities that they use to judge the acceptability and felicity of performances. Salsa dancing is therefore implicated in the politics of self-presentation (Goffman 1987 [1959]): the elegance of moves, the number of spins, the complexity of the steps that dancers execute commands the respect of their peers (see also Román-Velázquez 1999: 113–49). Dancing is an act of performativity (Butler 1993: 225) that constructs the embodied self in public through regularized repetition of moves, twists and turns.

I have turned to Butler's understanding of the performative because in Western countries the decision to learn salsa and join a dance group automatically locates the subject into the realm of gender discourse. The repetition of dance routines shifts 'from the condition of the subject to its effects' (Butler, 1997: 16), ascribing to the game of power and control (of 'Caribbean' culture, of femininity and masculinity) a universal feel.

Figure 5.1 DD2's multicultural landscape: Javier and Katey in La Rosa Negra against a background of dark bodies.

In this context girls like the fictional Katey Miller have to 'discover their sensuality' (IMDB, NY, 2 May 2005), 'pull from [their] old life [and] get changed into a woman [they] want to be' (IMDB, Virginia, US, 15 September 2004) – a woman ready to be subjected to the 'sexiness of the lead male' (IMDB, 1 January 2006) and his 'animal of power' (IMDB, US, 2 May 2005), on the dance floor. Many viewers expressed the desire to undergo this pedagogical/performative procedure and internalized this discourse that enriches 'hegemonic masculinities' and 'emphasized femininities' (Connell 1987, 1995) with a 'Cuban/ethnic' flavor (IMDB, New Orleans, 6 March 2004; IMDB, US, 1 June 2005; Canada, 21 February 2006). The ability to 'dance naturally' and create a 'special bond' with one's partner is discussed in terms of 'chemistry' (IMDB, Utah, US, 1 February 2005), 'hot moves' (IMDB, 23 April 2005) and passion that 'you will never find . . . in a studio' (IMDB, 12 February 2005). For these viewers one's ability to be 'natural' on the dance floor is the proof that dancing has become part of one's cultural *habitus*. Ultimately, understandings of this *habitus* oscillate between innateness and learning. This is why Luna is favourably commented upon for his 'earthy, non-structured salsa style' (IMDB, US, 5 April 2004) and his 'sexy', 'Cuban' demeanour (IMDB, Canada, 30 January 2005), and Garai is often criticized for displaying a 'Barbie' attitude (Amazon, UK, 10 January 2005) and being unable to 'get into [the dancing]' (IMDB, Canada, 30 January 2005). Evidently some viewers related bodily competence to the ethnic origins of the performer. This tendency was encouraged by choreographer Jansen. In an interview she commented extensively on 'the difference' in the two protagonists' 'body types', describing Garai as 'statuesque' and Luna as 'funky', 'flirty' and with 'natural mannerisms' (*EtownSalsa* 2004). The same comments appeared independently in a BBC review of the film (Wilkinson 2004).

Peculiarly, there is nothing *essentially ethnic* about salsa dancing and music. As black Americans used the word 'soul' (Connell and Gibson 2004: 6), salsa (meaning sauce or spice) was mobilized mainly by Cubans and Puerto Ricans to denote an imagined cultural essence (Padilla 1990: 87). In reality, salsa comprises a mixture of music styles such as the Cuban *son* (with African-Cuban roots), the *clave* (a more experimental style) the *bomba* (a blend of Hispanic and other alien elements) and the *plena* (of Puerto Rican origins) (Duany 1992: 77, 197). Dominican, Colombian and Venezuelan influences were added to this mixture, and as a result today many different ethnic groups claim salsa as part of their own tradition. Despite the fact that salsa was associated with Cuba, it was Puerto Rican immigration to New York after the Second World War that gave birth to it. Cuban factory workers in New York and post-1958 exiles in Miami further contributed to the evolution of the style. Amidst the ugly urban realities of the US – the working-class ghettoization and social exclusion of newcomers – this new hybrid style helped migrants to establish continuity between their native and host countries (Bilby 1985: 182). But if salsa was initially a Cuban and Puerto Rican attempt to redeem the legendary authenticity of a 'pure' identity that was lost during the years of cultural dislocation, it soon grew to be a global commodity (Aparicio 1998: 100–3). Many other Caribbean styles have defied geographical and ethnic boundaries, presenting us with a 'phenomenon that has come to be called "crossover" (in the jargon of the popular music industry)' (*ibid.*: 212). The salsa genre became popular in the 1950s New York music and dance scene and at the time contributed to representations of Cuba as a tourist paradise. Immigrant musicians from Latin American countries began to define the musical style that would achieve global fame in the next two decades.

David Hesmondalgh (1996: 201) has explained that the cultural politics of music can only be properly illuminated if we combine an examination of the music's reception across cultures with the unequal distribution of power that this dissemination may conceal. In the 1990s the emergence of *salsaromantica* and ballroom salsa, both based on a blending of Caribbean and Western styles, created a club culture in the West. In countries such as Britain and the US, this was followed by the recognition of 'Latin' music as another 'ethnic' terrain to be exploited by global music industries (Scott 1994). Addressed mainly to listeners of 'world music' – the section under which it is customarily classified in music stores – today salsa is considered an example of the cosmopolitanization of taste (Román-Velázquez 1999: 69), an outcome of global mobilities of ideas and lifestyles from peripheral places to the First World (Sheller 2004: 15). In the 'ethnoscapes' (Appadurai 1990: 7) of metropolitan centres such New York and London, a new hybrid genre has been born – neither 'Cuban' nor 'Western' but both and neither of the two. Centuries ago, colonial encounters with the Caribbean on Southern American soil were deemed to breed the potential for degeneracy (Sheller 2003: 110–11): in the popular culture environments of today, hybridity has ceased to be dangerous and turned into an opportunity for profit-making and a project of self-fulfillment. Brian Turner (1994: 21–2) has argued that the orientalization of the 'other' is not always achieved through its denigration, but through rational management that transforms it into a familiar category. Both ballroom salsa and Westernized salsa music can be seen as part and parcel of this process of rationalization.

My analysis follows the observations of a group of viewers who were struck by the anachronism of *DD2*'s rhythms. Some viewers are not put off by it 'if you love Latin music' (IMDB, Australia, 15 March 2005; IMDB, Denmark, 20 April 2005), whereas others simply acknowledge the marketing potential of the 'mixing [of] different dancing rhythms' (IMDB, 8 December 2005) that 'would appeal to most of todays [*sic*] teens, what with the newer "hip" music, and the dancing' (IMDB, USA, 2 July 2005). Dancing brings young people together, 'mix[ing] Afro-Cuban rhythms with ballroom dance' (IMDB, 22 March 2005), explains a viewer from Denmark who follows the equal opportunities argument. Other viewers, however, complained because the music 'was not even trying to be the 50's [*sic*] era in many places' (IMDB, 27 February 2004). 'I doubt that people in the 50s would use "represent" and other hip hop terms in their music', one viewer points out (IMDB, Norwalk, CA, 26 March 2004). 'My father was living in Havana in the early 1960s and reports what seems pretty obvious: this film is full of modern, highly stylized and "hip-hopified" version of Cuban street dancing' says an American (IMDB, Washington DC, US, 22 July 2005). It is true that no effort was made to adapt the music style to that of the 1950s. If anything, most songs in the film soundtrack are a mixture of hip-hop, hints of salsa, lambada and other Latin American genres. The 'creolization' (Sheller 2004: 180) of music compels us to re-examine the expectation of the makers of *DD2* to produce a film that would appeal to 'Latin Americans' in the USA. All songs from the film were addressed to the thoroughly 'Americanized Latinos' while bestowing a 'Cuban/Caribbean' form that 'enjoys more authority among expatriate communities with North American and Western European acceptance and conversion' (see also Kapcia [2005: 16–17] on *mambo*). Indisputably, the archaeology of salsa points to the ways in which global sign industries turn music and its visual ambiance into key components of the distant 'tourist gaze' (Urry 1990). Such virtual flâneurism operates under the auspices of *heterotopia* – a conscious and intentional misplacement of time-levels, which enables human actors to rearrange experience and reconceptualize phenomena (Foucault 1986) such as 'the delights of travel, relaxation and remote pleasure' (Connell and Gibson 2004: 20).

After careful examination one realizes that some of *DD2*'s musical 'texts' both reflect and debate structures of tourism, especially because their lyrics become a site of contested meanings and changing community ideals (Mitchell 1996; Malbon 1999; Duffy 2000). I will argue henceforth that *DD2*'s musical terrain was turned into a battlefield of political (di)visions concerning the ethical consumption – or even noncon-sumption – of Cuban identity in the First World. The film includes a wide range of songs, some of Cuban origins and some characteristic of more recent genre fusions. Perhaps the most notable absence from the commercial CD release of *DD2* music is the classical song *Lamento Cubano* (music by Eliseo Grenet and lyrics by Teofilo Radillo), which is sung in the movie by Donato Poveda and The Troubadours. The song appears in a significant scene in *DD2*, when Katey and Javier wander in the streets of Havana. It is performed by a group of street musicians who are subsequently arrested by the police for the anti-Batista propaganda that they run through their music. 'In Cuba there is no such thing as simple singing', Javier explains to Katey while they flee the scene. But *Lamento Cubano* is sung in Spanish, so Javier's passing comment is the only reference to the fact that it has been ascribed a revolutionary content in the cinematic narrative. A makeshift translation of the lyrics confirms the suspicion that the scene is gently neutralized for the viewers through linguistic vagueness:

> Oh beautiful and dainty Cuba,
> Why are you suffering so much today?
> Oh, my beloved homeland,
> Who could imagine
> That in your blue sky
> The tears would mist

A number of other references are missing: the song was previously performed by Omara Portuondo, a world-class singer who brought to life melodic narratives of tragic love loss. Her style – reminiscent of jazz influences that defined the 1940s *mambo* fashion – but local in its emotive content and context, takes us back to the Second World War period when she started her career. Portuondo was recently discovered by Western audiences through her involvement in *Buena Vista Social Club* (1999). This documentary by Ry Cooder examined the trajectory of a group of veteran Cuban musicians (Ibrahim Ferrar, Ruben Gonzales, Compay Segundo) whose talents were forgotten after Castro's takeover of Cuba. *Buena Vista Social Club* did not become popular in Cuba mainly because their *son* romantic style did not conform to revolutionary ideological demands. Their resurrection in a Western context as 'world musicians' is telling: the invitation to hold concerts in Amsterdam and New York City's Carnegie Hall, as well as the footage of these concerts in the documentary and the narration of their lives as a social biopic of the post-1958 period, inform Western constructions of the Caribbean/Cuba as a desired other. By keeping *Lamento Cubano* as a cinematic backdrop, the makers of *DD2* emphasized the structure of the distant tourist gaze without letting too much politics to get in the way of an exciting – albeit mystifying – incident.

At the other end of the musical spectrum stand hip-hop creations such as 'Represent – Havana Nights' (lyrics by Livan Nuñez). The song was performed by the Cuban rap group Orishas, who are currently very popular among Afro-Cuban youths. Hip-hop is usually identified as a movement of Afro-American origin that includes practices such as breakdancing and rapping, DJ-ing and graffiti writing, all bestowed with the glow of resistance to the social values of hegemonic American culture (Marshall 2005). Although Orishas songs are mainstream market music, in 'Represent – Havana Nights' the group describes itself as underground – an alternative term for 'conscious' Cuban rap that proffers strong criticisms of neoliberal globalization, the consumerist logic and the supremacy of market ideologies in the West (Fernandes 2003b: 359). Following the collapse of the Soviet Union and Castro's aggressive economic policies (the so-called Período Especial that accelerated economic Americanization) the question of tourist exploitation of the locals came to the fore within and without Cuba. The prediction that the post-communist condition will introduce Western consumer lifestyles into former communist countries to fill the political void left behind (see Verdery 1996) formed a *problematique* that permeated the poetics of hip-hop music in Cuba.

Amongst the most enduring post-1989 changes was the introduction of a dollar economy in the country which resulted in the socioeconomic exclusion of, and blatant discrimination against, black Cubans (De la Fuente 1994: 322–31). Speaking the militant language of anti-establishment, Cuban rap articulated the experiences of Cuban displacement in the USA and racial discrimination within Cuba (for more see Fernandes [2003a]). Today the genre is fully commercialized, but the songs themselves often promote a socialist vision that counters consumerist practices. The Cuban government's attempt to cash in on representations of the country as a tropical paradise ready to be enjoyed by tourists (Sheller 2004: 15) has put enormous pressure on Cuban rappers to follow the dominant market logic (Pacini Hernandez 1998). The Orishas case is emblematic of these tensions: in the past the group have sung both about a Cuba as the pre-Castro land of cigars, rum and sex (Fernandes 2003b: 363–4) and the country of *jineteros* or professional hustlers who earn their living by providing sexual services to tourists and extracting money from them (Azicri 2000: 78). 'Represent – Havana Nights' is the product of the same political and artistic tensions: on the one hand the song celebrates the atmosphere of the fictional La Rosa Negra in which faceless mulattos 'dance to the tempo of love', urging the audience to 'move their body', 'bring down their last defense' and 'feel the innocence' of the music. Following the lyrics, Katey and Javier lose themselves to the music, just like any couple in the middle of a transient weekend experience in a *Cuba Libre* or Ibiza club. The other half of the lyrics, sung in Spanish and obviously addressed to Cuban communities, discusses how *rumba* and *son* tie to the specific histories of the 'homeland'. The chorus consists of the constant repetition of 'Represent Cuba, Orishas underground de Cuba, hey tu musica', emphasizing the emotional attachments of the group and raising claims to a mobile cultural heritage of global reputation. 'Represent', a typical hip-hop term, denotes Orishas' political loyalty to the values of the ethnic community it comes from and complements the hints to the poignant past of Cuban migration and identity transformation.

It seems that *DD2*'s narrative devices contain the potential to subvert the consumerist potential of Cuban cinematic simulations. I use the term 'simulation' because *DD2* already belongs to a fictional order; it is the product of Western domestic versions of Cuba mediated through dancing as virtual touring of an exotic culture whose clock has stopped in the early twentieth century. It is such multilevelled mediations that render the semiotics of Caribbean tourism structurally powerful. Layered mediations of culture can also be reversed – or, as Strain has put it, they can activate 'the mirroring of the filmic technology or other visual apparatus[es] within the travel story itself' (2003: 8). This two-way process is present in the current advertising of salsa holidays, which both borrows from and copies *DD2*'s travel narrative.

Havana Nights relived: virtual and actual tourings of a global cityscape

Havana can be regarded as a storeroom of tourist signs: its 'signature' bears the marks of trade, migration and culture that make Cuban identity itself distinctive. As Kapcia (2005: 1) has explained, cinematic accounts of Havana draw upon the same repertoire of signs (cosmopolitanism, sounds and music, blends of cultures) to construct its profile as the primary site of Cuban culture. *DD2*'s subtitle (*Havana Nights*) suggests to the viewer that everything worth observing takes place in the historic centre of the Cuban megalopolis. This complete identification of Cuba with Havana is the product of neocolonial politics, the consequence of steady Americanization of the domestic economy. The international political and economic focus on Havana supported the construction of a rather ambivalent relationship between the centre and the rest of the country, making the city a site of economic contestation. Havana was viewed internally both as the etiological cause of Cuban weakness vis-à-vis economic superpowers such as the USA (colonial powers detected in Havana the opportunities for profit-making and economic control) and

Cuba's sociopolitical panacea (with the idea that Havana bears the potential for universal modernization having a strong hold on popular imaginations) (Kapcia 2005: 3–5). Havana's cosmopolitan flair has also become complicit in academic constructions of Cubanness as decentred, fragmented and of intersecting realities and histories (Carpentier 1982: 13–14). This indeterminacy parallels uncritical uses of 'hybridity', 'syncretism' and 'creolization' (Bolland 1992; Burton 1997) that plague academic writing on the Caribbean in general (Sheller 2003: 191–6). In both cinematic and real-time worlds, Havana appears to be another cryptocolonial case (Herzfeld 2002b), an undefined cultural space produced through the history of the city's 'global iconicity' (Franklin *et al.* 2000). Even Castro's post-1989 policies of modernization focused almost exclusively on Havana, promoting its global image through tourist trade and widening the domestic gap between the better-off urban populations and the less developed rural regions. Today, Havana's cityscape is characteristic of all types of mobility – from human relocations and diasporic histories to migrations of culture and tourism (Gilroy 1993; Clifford 1997; Wardle 1999; Sheller 2004).

The opening sequence of urban images in *DD2* follows the word and the spirit of such ready-made discourses and mythifications. In a Cuban car, Katey Miller assumes the position of a Baudrillard (1988) who watches images of Havana racing in front of the car's window: colonial buildings, squares and parks with tropical plants and groups of black Cubans enjoying their street dancing under a blinding sun. As she unhappily narrates the background of the Millers' relocation, the camera begins to reproduce and frame these scenes in sepia colors, intensifying the feeling that we have truly been transported to the past. But our strategic positioning as viewers *in the present* fosters a sociocultural 'coevalness' (Fabian 1983), transforming us into the ideal type of cultural tourist who visually devours simulations of the architecture and folk culture of the host country. While we enjoy this 'Havana', Katey's father (John Slattery) appears in the car, holding a camera that he points at Katey's direction. So, while the production of simulatory imagery in *DD2* defines our identity as mobile subjects in a Cuban world fixed in the past, Katey's father assumes the position of the cinematically mediated tourist. The very first scene of the film has defined what virtual flâneurism is about as well as how we, as virtual flâneurs, are supposed to consume Havana through music, dance and sightseeing.

The cinematic immobility of Cuban culture caught the attention of many viewers. A few commented on the commercialization of revolution-ary history for the tourist gaze that favours a combination of politics with romance (IMDB, Romania, 3 January 2006; IMDB, US, 24 November

2004; Canada, 2 March 2006). 'The story gave me a brief glimpse of the history of Cuba' (IMDB, 23 February 2005), states an American who treats the film as an educational medium. 'I am glad to hear that [the Revolution] really happened' (IMDB, USA, 6 February 2005), confesses someone even less informed. The usual protests were not missing from reviews in which the use of history was described as 'superfluous' (IMDB, Vancouver, BC, 28 February 2004), because 'the complexities of Cuban revolution are glossed over in favor of a soap opera mechanics and melodramatics' (IMDB, US, 24 October 2004). The reference to 'drama', which was repeated by a few viewers (IMDB, Australia, 19 March 2005; Amazon, Canada, 12 February 2005), was in fact significant. An American nicely captures its resonance when he argues that 'with romance, a bit of drama, dancing and of course a little bit of Cuban culture, it was an all around GREAT movie' (IMDB, 28 June 2005). No space is spared for a discussion of the turbulent histories of the place. Ultimately, it is precisely the prominence of the picturesque and the melodramatic that displaces the historical dimension, 'isolating the story *as* story from the relations of political and economic power' (Spurr 1993: 48, emphasis added). Now, with the nuisance of anti-American politics out of the way, the viewer can enjoy the scenery and the cosmopolitan ambiance of the 'place'.

The choice of Puerto Rico's Old San Juan by the makers of *DD2* as a backdrop was a clever resort to an 'unspoilt' historic location. The old part of Puerto Rico's capital, architecturally reminiscent of colonial times, is very popular with the locals and tourists. To preserve the aesthetic of the period the producers secured underground parking for visitors during the filming of *DD2* (IMDB, *Trivia*, undated). Perversely, *DD2* did not make San Juan any more popular with cultural tourists than it already is. Rumba nightclub (located in San Juan's busy district), used for many club scenes in *DD2*, has nevertheless gained an international reputation after the filming of the story as a place where one can enjoy avant-garde 'Hispanic' hip-hop. The nightclub is today listed among other 'places to visit' for the devotees of the flamboyant clubbing lifestyle (*The Sunday Mail* 2005; search also Wikipedia under 'San Juan'). *DD2*'s sign industry was also assisted by Garai who, in an interview for *Cinema Confidential*, talked about her experience of learning how to dance salsa and 'other Afro-Cuban dances' and visiting San Juan's nightclubs (*Cinema Confidential* 2004). It seems that *DD2* promoted the production of signs for the 'post-tourist' (Feifer 1985; Ritzer 1996) who prefers to collect a pastiche of experiences that promote enjoyment as an end in itself.

The cinematic background was noticed by almost a fifth of IMDB and Amazon reviewers. Some displayed ignorance about the actual setting, resorting to banal comments on 'the colourful surroundings [which] bring to life a surreal feeling that captures the summer buzz of the movie perfectly' (IMDB, UK, 23 April 2005; see also IMDB, US, 5 August 2005), the 'tropical and exotic place' (IMDB, Portugal, 15 October 2005) and the desire to 'visit Cuba and learn to dance' (Amazon, Oxford, UK, 10 January 2005 and Ohio, US, 25 November 2004; IMDB, Canada, 25 September 2004). These reviews return to the generic image of the Caribbean paradise and ignore the context. Some viewers do not seem to mind the fabrication of place and history, even when they are aware of the context and the workings of the sign industry. An American mentions in total resignation that 'the city they are showing is Puerto Rico! So much for the Havana Nights' (IMDB, 22 July 2005), but moves on to discuss the film and its attractions. A number of other viewers simply find it amusing that the makers of *DD2* 'cheated a little' with the setting, which they find 'stunning' anyway (IMDB, Glasgow, Scotland, 12 December 2004; IMDB, London, 23 December 2005; Amazon, Belgium, 1 July 2005). Another viewer has recourse to mockery:

> Imagine a movie set in Cuba shot in Puerto Rico. Imagine a blonde who moves her hips in a box. Now add in a cameo by Patrick Swayze, a few hot and steamy PG-13 (blue-ball hell) scenes between Diego Luna and the fortunate Romola Garai, and about 20 minutes plotlines (including Castro's overthrow of Batista) that for the most part go completely ignored. What do you get?
> The best laugh you've had in years . . . and a free salsa lesson.
> (IMDB, New York, 29 February 2004)

The reviews replicate the post-tourist project of *DD2*'s sign industry, confirming that in global mediascapes place identities are always constructed, deconstructed and contested (Lawrence 1997). For these viewers the illusion of geographical and cultural immersion exists independently of the cinematic setting's resemblance to the actual cultural locale. Yet the quest for cultural difference is already working as 'the postulate for the voyage' (de Certeau 1986: 69) and opens up new opportunities for the sign industries. A quick search on the web reveals that the salsa culture merchants have already taken advantage of this desire for lifestyle travel focused on dancing, organizing Cuban Salsa Congresses around the world and booking flights to Havana for their members. I will present two examples here that are tied to *DD2* in particular but addressed to two distinctive categories of tourists that roughly correspond to those of our reviews: the conventional consumers of Caribbean 'sun and sea' and the 'salsa junkies'. The examples are also representative of the cultural geographies of Cuban consumption: the first comes from the USA, historically associated with the exoticization of the country, and the second from Britain, a more recent addition to the list in the wake of the salsa craze.

The first example originates in a Diego Luna fan site hosted by *Havana Journal*, a blog exclusively focused on issues concerning Cuban politics, culture, business and travel, and run by 'Americans for Americans' (*Havana Journal* 2006). The journal claims its continuity from the newspaper *Havana Journal* founded in New York in the 1800s, but is a thoroughly contemporary venture set up in 1996 by a group of Internet entrepreneurs. It principal founder and editor, Rob Sequin, a veteran of e-commerce, has previously trained individuals and businesses in how to sell their products on eBay. The blog retains its links with the famous online market, trading in 'things Cuban'. Today, *Havana Journal* is in the top ten search results for keyword 'Havana' in Google, Yahoo and MSN. The Luna subsite itself is swamped by hundreds of letters addressed directly to the young actor and written by manic teenagers who beg him to give them lessons in salsa, *mambo* and other dances or are desperate to arrange a date with him. More fans are invited to join in, sending an open letter to Luna. The fans declare their 'love' and 'dedication' to Cuba, and 'are dying' to 'find out how Cuban politics works' – all this in order to capture the young Mexican's attention. It would take a separate study to explore the content of these letters and the culture of the fan site as a whole. What immediately attracts one's attention is the aggressive advertising of Cuba through Havana, featuring in the weblog's first page. This combines 'carefree', 'tailormade', 'dream' holidays to Cuba that can be booked online, alongside a wide range of Cuban produce such as cigars and rum that transport us to previous decades. A new addition to these offers is the movies section, which is evoked by *DD2*'s virtual presence. The essential networks that ensure the healthy function of the Cuban sign industry are in place, complete with an American philosophy that crowns *Havana Journal*'s website: 'Free Speech and Free Trade are the parents of Happiness and Prosperity'. Primarily, if not exclusively, for Americans, of course.

British networks of Cuban consumption perform the same function, but distil interest in Havana through lifestyle dancing. The largest promoter of so-called Cuban-style salsa in the Midlands (based in Leicester, Nottingham and Loughborough) has been named Havana Nights and invites web surfers and salsa lovers to register and 'get access to special member benefits that you can use before, during and after your holiday'. Behind this venture we discover a holiday promoter, Club Dance Holidays, which has joined in the new salsa sign industry. The site also

Figure 5.2 The idyllic picture of Javier and Katey learning to dance figures in Diego Luna's fansite that *Havana Journal* hosts. The image is surrounded by advertisements of things Cuban.

Source: Lions Gate/Photofest. © Lions Gate Inc. Photographer: Barry Wetcher

features answers to a list of frequently asked questions for those who would like to learn how to dance but cannot overcome their inhibitions. The following is a carefully crafted answer to the last question ('Where else can I go dancing?'):

> Salsa opens up a huge social scene to you both in the UK and abroad . . . You can also combine your holiday with salsa. Particularly popular are the regular Pontins Salsa Weekenders in the UK and the Salsa Havana provided by companies such as Dance Holidays and Key to Cuba (see holidays section).
>
> (Dance Holidays-Havana Nights 2006)

A very long list of options follows, with holidays to Havana ranging from 7 to 14 nights and including intensive courses by famous dance instructors, education classes in the history and practice of *son*, *rumba*, *cha cha cha* and *mambo*, dancing in the 'ultimate clubs' of the Havana, meeting new dance partners and many more. We encountered this de-differentiation of leisure and tourism (Lash and Urry 1994) combined with an overlap of leisure and work (Butler 1995; Rojek 1995) in online reviews of *DD2*:

modern *salseros* do not want to relax on a sunny Caribbean beach, but train their body until they become more like the Cuban 'natives'.

The list of examples connected to *DD2* practices of consumption would be long and tedious, so I will stop my empirical explorations here. Through them, and through reviewers' comments, I wanted to highlight the ways in which the consumption of place and the tourist experience itself have been overtaken by global capitalist networks. In the past, film and tourism had a loose relationship: virtual, cinematic tourism has been present for decades in so far as film viewing is closely tied to the creative workings of imagination. Tourist industries have been using visual references to remote travel destinations in order to capture individual and collective imaginations, thus replicating the mechanisms of filmmaking. What has changed over the last few years is a progressive convergence of the sign repositories that film and tourist industries mobilize to achieve maximum profit. The two industries may still be independent, but a particular type of film is becoming inextricably linked to mass tourism – or, more precisely, to the foundation of new, or extension of old, tourist industries. This type of film does the imagining that used to be reserved for virtual and actual tourists and constitutes more and more the basis on which both virtual tourists and tourist industries construct other cultures and places. In the case of *DD2*, tourism to Havana/Cuba is mediated through the hunting for an alternative lifestyle that *embodies* Western encounters with other cultures. *DD2*'s suggested type of tourism retains the experiential dimension that we explored in *The Beach*, but seeks to connect the cognitive with the corporeal, performative aspects of human life. Though absorbing in its own right, this process of Caribbean or Latin American consumption reduces indigenous voices to a whisper that never reaches our ears. What we enjoy is a thoroughly Western construct of place and culture, with no auxiliary need for actual referents. In this respect, Ottenberg's claim that *DD2* is 'thoroughly American' rings louder and truer than one would like to admit.

6 Farewell to authenticity?

Capitalist/cultural hegemony and the structure of resistance

On a sunny July day I found myself outside Slovakia's main airport waiting for a taxi that would take me to my hotel in Bratislava. A courteous taxi driver approached my travel companion and me, gave us a big smile that revealed a few missing teeth, dropped a low bow and pointed to his car. Luck, then, was with us: someone was available for the much-needed lift despite the traffic. Naturally, we smiled back and using the essential paralinguistic signs, we asked for the price. The man however, had already extended his hand to me. How civilized, I thought: here is a stranger who does not forget his manners and treats tourists like human beings. The aura of the whole performance had worked its charm on me, and smiling back I gave him a firm handshake. It was only when his fellow taxi drivers laughed and he grabbed my rucksack to put in the taxi that I realized my misreading: he only wanted to get on with work and move on to the next customer. He had certainly recognized a romantic fool in me: upon arrival at our destination, he asked for what we found out to be double the amount of money for the designated distance.

It is not so much that someone managed to play on me the trick that Kefalonian Greeks had successfully tried on capitalist intrusion following the *Corelli* boom years ago – although, to have a sociologist who studies the staging of authenticity make a fool of herself in this way admittedly bears the irony of Nemesis. It is more the case that even today, narrating this incident leaves me with the same bitter taste that I get when reading Georg Lukács' (1968) gloomy elaboration on Marxist theory: has the progress of productive processes eroded our humanity? For that Slovakian taxi driver, the art of self-presentation had acquired a 'phantom objectivity' (Lukács 1968: 83), a rationalized autonomy that detached it from its fundamental nature. The intrinsic value of friendliness did not apply to his professionalism, simply because on a hot summer day a taxi driver has no time to reflect on the 'partial consciousness' that the capitalist system cultivates.

One wonders, of course, how I came across to that Slovakian man. Given the transitory nature of our encounter, I must have been less than a Thai 'wallet on legs', a pretentious tourist who tries to be 'nice' and 'interested' in the well-being of his service facilitator. A feeling of indignation and injustice might have risen in him when I became amicable. With remorse I realize that he was not the one who had exploited his positional role in the system of tourist services. It was I, the one who had misrecognized our encounter as genuine human exchange, devoid of economic imperatives. Despite my academic reflexivity, I was replicating the attitude of the average tourist that MacCannell (1973) described in his pioneering essay on staged authenticity – worse, I was denying the existence of social inequality that defined the taxi driver's positional role and mine. One wonders if the practice of cheating could be understood as a form of resistance to the structure of the economic system in which we are situated. Another issue to consider is the convergence of my cultural and economic identity: how much did my 'English front' (to him, I must have been a stereotypical Westerner) aggravate his silent resentment?

In the opening chapter of this book I clarified that this is as much a study of the ability of sign industries to spread their power globally as it is an investigation of the responses that localities and nation-states develop to the challenge. My Slovakian incident nicely encapsulates the dilemmas and consequences of such responses: first, it highlights the inevitable pressure representational apparatuses exercise on host cultures to replicate the formalized 'stage' that these apparatuses produce for them; and second, it invites a sensitive approach to cultural specificity when we examine responses by host cultures. Early on I explained that responses to representations and simulations that originate from without is conditioned by the sociohistorical experience of nation-states and localities. This concluding essay examines the nature of these responses to the calls of economic and cultural globalization from a critical perspective. Undoubtedly, the academic search for resistances to the capitalist system is as old as Marxist theory and has been under constant attack in recent years by the defenders of pluralism (for a review see Hesmondalgh 2002: 82–5). In this conflict there lies a fundamental confusion about the correlation between culture and economics, which I will attempt to address in the following pages.

In a relatively recent study, Herman and McChesney (1997) examined the globalization of culture industries, lamenting the commercialization of communication and the subsequent homogenization of culture. In fact, their study comprises a series of examples of what in media studies came to be called 'cultural imperialism', the control and elimination of cultural identities by powerful media conglomerates. Media entertainment, according to this thesis, weakens democratic dialogue and eventually replaces it. The result is a world colonized by uniformity and lack of critical voice, a *Matrix*-like state of affairs that works its way through our brain every time we plug ourselves in to the chosen medium. Sign industries simply accelerated and convoluted this process by directly introducing countries into the game of collective self-presentation: yesteryear's viewers of images generated in distant countries are now invited to enact them for a second-order audience of tourists; 'authentic stages' are raised in every part of the world to respond to this insatiable search for pure, unspoiled culture; and whole nations relegate their real self to forgotten history in order to embrace the capitalist value of identity-trading. According to this thesis, the domination of capital is unquestionable.

After considering the four cases that this book examines, we can only admit that there is an element of truth in the argument: the obstinate resistance of Thai localities to global capitalist interests and their internal representatives, the Thai state, did not bear any fruits. To be precise, the fruits it bore were rather sour, given that *The Beach* boycott was cleverly used by Hollywood and its capitalist satellites in subsequent publicity campaigns. Today anyone with an Internet connection can visit sites that trade in exotic Krabi holidays and book a room in the newly erected traditional style hotels of the Phi Phi islands. In spite of the international support from well-organized activist circles, the battle was fought and lost. Much like the Thai state, which from the outset acted like a partner of external economic interests, the New Zealand state seemed willing to adopt capitalist tactics so as not to be marginalized in the battle for brand monopolies. The glamourization of Auckland as a 'fashionable' urban destination for *LOTR* fans and the renaming of New Zealand as the new Middle Earth simply shows how the periphery 'beats' the centre by emulating it. The Mediterranean example does not deviate from this pattern: despite – if not because of – their initial protestations against the *CCM* industry, the Kefalonians accepted the commodification of their island as a way out of economic marginalization by the national centre. International tourist providers detected this lack of economic state regulation early on and stepped in to appropriate the terrain. As a result, today many Kefalonians who work in the service industry cater for foreign tourists *on behalf* of international tourist providers. So, even though the *CCM* sign industry did not manage to radically change the nature of Kefalonian tourism, it did take possession of the Kefalonian economy without encountering much local or state resistance. Perhaps more surprising has been the total absence of Cuban state control in the case of *DD2* but also the images and ideas it stands for in the global capitalist scene. But as I explained in detail, *DD2* is the product of a sign industry that reinvented 'Latin America' in political and economic networks a long time ago. The absence of any Cuban resistance to the commodification of identity and place is the consequence of a firmly consolidated Americanization, but also the internationalization and subsequent decontextualization of cultural products and practices (music, dancing) related to Cuba. It is not only that the origin of cultural products matters little to consumers (as film reviews confirm), but also that their hybridization makes legitimate claims over their origins a difficult business. As a result, in the circulation of global signs Havana and San Juan become the same imagined *topos* sold out to virtual flâneurs who constantly chase after the chimera of an authentic experience. Implicit in this failure of subaltern resistance remains the role of long-established patterns of colonialism or cryptocolonialism that the four countries endured in the past, and which crept into the products of the respective sign industries.

All four cases reveal the enormous complexity (Giddens 1990; Held *et al.* 1999; Urry 2003) of late modernity and invite us to accept that the confluence and interconnectedness of changes in the economic, cultural and political domains has reached its apogee and makes the compartmentalized study of different domains of human experience very difficult. This sounds like a de facto explanandum. In postmodern studies of globalization this interconnectedness is even imagined as a Leviathan of consumer capitalism that promulgates unprecedented market uniformity and swallows up cultural distinctiveness only to spit out a single, global culture (Jameson 1984). Five chapters into this book the argument becomes very attractive indeed; all we need is to have recourse to the Frankfurt School logic of cultural 'standardization' (Held 1980: 70–6) to put a full stop to the analysis.

I will not distance myself from this thesis altogether. For anyone who believes in social justice and equality, the economic methods of sign industries outlined in the previous chapters are too gross to ignore. To re-member the Slovakian incident, their ultimate victims are not the consumers of half a dozen movies or package holidays, but the ordinary people of the filmed and touristified localities who have to earn their living in the new order. Of course we need to note that the damage was not present in all four cases: a strong response from the New Zealand state bears the potential to regenerate communities, as has been noted in a recent study (Beeton 2005). More often than not, however, forced touristification hardens preexisting ethnic, class and gender structures of inequality, as the cases of Thailand, Greece and Cuba indicate. In other words, sign industries often act as catalysts in national or international politics to sanction unsound political orders. But behind the sociological rhetoric of economic 'incorporation' *and* subsequent loss of cultural uniqueness for those subjected to the demands of sign industries, there lies a slightly modified *problematique*. Its focal point is the *cultural* encounters of localities and states with the representatives of sign industries and their role as vehicles of sociocultural change.

Lest I am accused of confusing the social (the acclaimed terrain of sociology) with the cultural, I will explain that my combination of the two is based on correlation rather than identification. As anthropologists have explained, 'the shift from a social to a cultural idiom . . . is largely the outcome of the emergence of European nationalism' (Herzfeld 1992: 68). The cases of cinematic tourism explored in this book suggest that what happens locally constitutes a response to, or reflection of, hegemonic national discourses of identity and culture (see also Just 1989). I use the term 'hegemony' in a post-Gramscian sense (Laclau and Mouffe 1995) to describe the construction of self-understandings through an almost imperceptible but unrelenting channelling of ideas from the powerful political centres of the West to the peripheral countries that have fallen prey to the cinematic tourist gaze. Since the trajectories of cultural hegemonization that I explored are linked to early modern colonialisms, I will not pretend to be wholly indifferent to the cultural imperialism thesis. My constant movement from the local/regional to the national and international scene (and back again) was an attempt to provide a holistic account of resistances to globalization and its histories at the receiving end. But the shift from the social to the cultural also 'occurs through the generalization of what, at the local level, are relatively intimate distinctions between outsiders and "our own"' (Herzfeld 1992: 99). In our case, the designated outsiders can be either the representatives of global economic centres (Hollywood crews and production companies, tourist agencies) or, by cultural affiliation, the tourists.

The explored local and national responses were directed at both: in Thailand, localities became involved in the international boycott of *The Beach* and the commodification of Phi Phi Leh, but also mediated their opposition to Western tourist practices through language, often accompanied by action. The New Zealand state marshalled elements of nationalist practices to respond to foreign capitalist interference. The Kefalonians attempted to obstruct Hollywood production and still deny foreign tourists the right to enter the private domain of culture by serving them *CCM*'s staged authenticity. Even in products of the tourist gaze that signify Cubanness/Caribbeanness, such as popular music, the logic of resistance to Western tourist invasion persists. The four cases are obviously different in focus and background, but even across responses as variable as these interesting patterns can emerge. The pattern that marks these four cases is the recurring use of discursive practices analogous or identical to nationalist ideology. Modifying the original Foucauldian term, I use 'discourse' to refer to language constitutive of *praxis*, the conscious reworking of the subaltern's experience into a meaningful whole (Lukács 1968). Such discursive practices enable large groups that are caught in the mechanics of master–slave relationships to resist power while simultaneously asserting their solidarity and cohesion. In the face of encounters characterized by inequality, the 'imagined communities' (expatriate groups, localities and nation-states) of this study needed a protective shield to preserve themselves from what they recognized as the road to 'incorporation' by global sign industries.

What is *actually* protected from 'corruption' is a different question. As a number of theorists have consented, cultures – especially cultures that experienced direct or symbolic colonization at some point in their life course – should be viewed as relational products. I will limit my references to nationalism and colonialism studies, as they better relate to the subject matter of the book. Commenting on the production of mechanical solidarity, Anderson points out that the conditions of collective self-narration are potentially intersubjective, because 'through language the nation presents itself as simultaneously open and closed' (Anderson 1991). Partha Chatterjee (1986) may be critiquing Anderson for his Eurocentric model of nationalism, but he also supports the idea that formerly colonized nations develop a dialogue with colonial powers. The domain of anti-colonial nationalism becomes that of culture (what he calls the 'spiritual'), to which the colonizer is denied access (Chatterjee 1993: 3–5). A number of other writers before and after Chatterjee have developed the same take on post-colonial nationalism: as opposed to the 'material' world of colonial rule (the political and economic terrain), 'culture' should be viewed as the private sphere of the nation (Fanon 1967, 1970; Bhabha 1990, 1994; Gilroy 1987; Herzfeld 1997). Undoubtedly, any 'imagined community' and its members wish to forget that their commitment to a nationalist ideal is the product of colonial violence. However, before imagining oneself, someone else imagined one; selfhood is the synthetic product of conflict between the desire for a uniform, independent self and external representations. To transfer these reflections back to tourist studies: culture and authenticity should be viewed as the outcome of interactions between hosts and guests, 'in which tourees attempt to mirror tourists' desires and vice versa' (Cohen 1988a; Ryan 1991; Kroshus Medina 2003: 355). Discursive practices of staged authenticity in tourist encounters are based on patterns of incorrigible misrecognition: of one's own identity as pure and free of alien intervention; of host identities as pure and untouched by visiting 'others' – whether these be global televised simulacra of identity or projected tourist desires for demediating mediation 'on location'.

Here the analysis begins to provide useful insights into the reasoning, rather than the structure, of misrecognition. From the outset (the production and release of tourism-inspiring movies) cinematic tourist encounters are destined to facilitate exchange – put simply and through a rather unwelcome pun, to secure value for money. In Bourdieu's terms (1984), cinematic tourism makes possible the exchange of different forms of symbolic capital: money that tourists bring into the host country with what is locally and nationally *valued* most, culture and identity. Because Bourdieu circumnavigated the politics of social inequality that his Marxist muse (Marx 1973: 256) aspired to expose over a century ago (for a critique see Sayer [1999]), I have to stress again that in the context of cinematic tourism *capital* is forcefully equated with cultural *values*. This equation is not to be dismissed, as the signifying potential of economic practices can be both cultural and material (Ray and Sayer 1999). It is precisely this conflation of one thing for another that will provide us with the social reasoning of resistance.

We may begin by acknowledging that Thailand, New Zealand, Greece and Cuba are somehow tied to political discourses that place them in the developing world. So much is obvious from the background analysis provided in the respective chapters. All four countries have industrialized economies and operate within global capitalist structures, albeit at the margins. Yet in spite of their urgency to catch up with the economic pace of the centre, the resistance they display to its representatives assumes the form of an angry frustration for their cultural misrecognition. Implicitly or not, all four localities and states accuse the agents of cinematic tourism of one form of exploitation or another: local Thais call tourists 'white bird shit' because of their inability to recognize the value of host services; the New Zealand state's struggle to secure the monopoly of the *LOTR* was firmly based on the conviction that the *LOTR* simulation of New Zealand belonged to New Zealanders after all. The Kefalonians expressed their anger against the Hollywood agents and subsequent tourists with monetary extortion and a staging of their 'culture'. The rhetoric of cheating as resistance to foreign appropriation also dictates the content of 'Cuban' products of *DD2*'s sign industry that record actual tourist encounters. In all four cases there is a wilful expression of the belief that foreigners who enter the country to make it 'theirs' deserve neither humane treatment *nor* consideration as clever entrepreneurs. All responses exhibit the same ambivalence: they reiterate *and* contest the conventions of capitalist exchange which licenses free competition regardless of the distribution of power in the social field. This is so because cheating in any form (from demanding payment of exorbitant amounts of money for tourist services and hustling, to claiming trade monopoly on emotional grounds) bypasses these market conventions and subverts power.

In a fashion similar to critical theory's renunciation of the emergent culture industry, Karl Polanyi (1944) has claimed that the industrialization of economy posed a threat to culture, as it led to the prioritization of the material conditions of sociality and contributed to the emergence of a market society. We note that in the system of host–guest exchange the practice of cheating representatives of sign industries challenges norms of social conduct (see also Jessop 2000) that are considered to be 'unfair' (Sayer 2000). This is hardly surprising, as the practice of cheating articulates the conviction that the host is morally allowed to take by any means what is expected in any reciprocal relationship, but what is not delivered in this instance: gratitude for the provision of good services. The basic function of hospitality is the recognition that hosts and guests share the same moral universe or 'the construction of a moral universe to which both host and guest agree to belong' (Lashley and Morrison 2000: 6). When one side in the reciprocal system is placed in the position of the subordinate, like our four countries are, the norm of reciprocity is challenged (see Gouldner 1960; Bell 1991). Not only are the hosts constrained by their duty to offer plenty in emotional and physical labour without – at least explicitly – asking anything back, but they are also not sufficiently recognized for who they think they were before touristification.

It could be argued that cheating returns the hosts to the Hobbesian state of nature, where they legitimate their demand to be reciprocated on the basis of self-interest (Berking 1999: 124). Two comments are in order here: the struggle for recognition does not take place 'at the level of appearances' (O'Neill 1999: 80) and self-regard 'is very difficult to sustain without external confirmation' (Offer 1997: 452). I will refuse to regard the calculative nature of exchange as somehow different or opposed to the spirit of pure reciprocity (Malinowski 1922; for an update see Cheal 1988). As anthropologists and sociologists have shown, in many societies the monetary calculation that openly characterizes formalized exchange finds its informal expression in the cultivation of moral indebtedness (Firth 1983: 102–3; Strathern 1983). A number of scholars from different disciplines have challenged analytical differentiations of societies on the basis of solidarity versus calculation (see Baudrillard 1973, 1975; Sahlins 1974, 1976; Douglas and Isherwood 1979; Sayer 2001, 2003) – differentiations that, as Appadurai (1986: 11) has diligently explained, derive from theoretical attempts to divorce Marxist and Maussian approaches to exchange and reciprocity. To be more precise, at stake for our four host countries is the gesture of recognition as autonomous agents in the global scene and in cultural terms – a recognition that can never be fully expressed by tourists, the faceless representatives of media conglomerates or the various managers of tourist agencies who are tied to the sign orders that they produce and maintain (Barth 1981: 40). An *exactly* balanced exchange of economic and cultural capital is never feasible, as the two forms of capital are not identical (Sahlins 1974: 193; Ardener 1989) and the exchange does not satisfy both parties. And there is more: in the context of such imbalanced relationships as the ones I have explored, the possibility of an alternative partner would naturally alter the situation. As Bell has pointed out (1991: 254) 'two-party relationships can be understood only by reference to the large number of non-activated relations that are feasible within that social context'. Unfortunately, here there is no alternative at all, as all optional partners operate within the same system of capitalist values. The absence of any alternatives however can be detrimental for the weak: preferences in reciprocal partnerships are overdetermined by 'social definitions of value vis-à-vis material and non-material resources, as well as on socially derived representations of self' (Bell 1991: 235). As a result, guest countries are left with nothing more than the symbolic capital (the 'island of *Corelli*', the 'home of Middle Earth') that has been allocated to them from without, stranded between submission to the calls of global capitalism and the need to salvage what they can from an identity in the process of transformation.

This is a sad conclusion to draw in the midst of decades-long attacks on social rights. The patterns of globalization progressively associated with the global telecommunications scene favour a particular type of global citizenship that 'benefit[s] mobile capital, manifested in the rights of the "corporate person"' (Calabrese 2005: 301). The rights of these groups that provide the essential labour for transnational sign industries to spread their control are as marginal as ever for corporate capital and even global consumers. Undoubtedly global communications have figured, and will figure again, as the instruments of both capitalism and global justice movements, but the negligence displayed on the human and social rights front may help us understand the rational grounds of the moral outrage that anonymous people from eponymous cinematic corners of the world express every time a new sign industry is in its birth throes. Hopefully, in the process of understanding this anger, the present study has managed to crack open a door to academic research that will address the issue in its specificity. More able scholars are now invited to open the door wide.

Bibliography

Abercrombie, N. and Longhurst, B. (1998) *Audiences*, London: Sage.

Adler, J. (1989) 'The origins of sightseeing', *Annals of Tourism Research*, 16(1): 7–29.

Adler, J. (1992) 'Mobility and the creation of the subject: theorizing movement and the self in early Christian monasticism', *International Tourism – Between Tradition and Modernity Colloquium*, pp. 407–15.

Adorno, T. (1991) *The Culture Industry: Selected Essays on Mass Culture*, translated by J. M. Bernstein, London: Routledge.

Adorno, T. and Horkheimer, M. (1993) *The Dialectic of Enlightenment*, New York: Continuum.

Agarwal, S., Ball, R., Shaw, G. and Williams, A. M. (2000) 'The geography of tourism production: uneven disciplinary development?', *Tourism Geographies*, 2(3): 241–63.

AIM (2003) 'British police head for Faliraki', 25 August, online. Available at http://www.hri.org/cgi-bin/brief?/news/greek/apeen/2003/03-08-25.apeen.html#03 (accessed 20 February 2006).

Alba, R. D. (2000) 'Assimilation's quiet tide', in S. Steinberg (ed.) *Race and Ethnicity in the United States: Issues and Debates*, Oxford: Blackwell.

Althusser, L. (1971) *Lenin and Philosophy and Other Essays*, London: New Left Books.

Anderson, B. (1991) *Imagined Communities*, London: Verso.

Aparicio, F. (1998) *Listening to Salsa: Gender, Latin Popular Music and Puerto Rican Cultures*, Hanover, NH: Wesleyan University Press.

Appadurai, A. (1986) 'Introduction: commodities and the politics of value', in A. Appadurai (ed.) *The Social Life of Things: Commodities in Cultural Perspective*, Cambridge: Cambridge University Press, pp. 3–63.

Appadurai, A. (1990) 'Disjuncture and difference in the global cultural economy', *Public Culture*, 2(2): 1–24.

Ardener, E. (1989) *The Voice of Prophecy and Other Essays*, Oxford: Basil Blackwell.

Arnould, E. and Price, L. (1993) 'River magic: extraordinary experience and the extended service encounter', *Journal of Consumer Research*, vol. 20, 24–45.

Asiaweek (1999) 'Postcards from *The Beach*'. 19 February.

Ateljevic, I. (2000) 'Circuits of tourism: stepping beyond the "production/consumption" dichotomy', *Tourism Geographies*, 2: 369–88.

Azicri, M. (2000) *Cuba Today and Tomorrow: Reinventing Socialism*, Gainesville: University of Florida Press.

B&T (2004). 'Middle Earth airline unveils latest livery', online. Available at http://www.bandt.com.au/news/fd/0c01c1fd.asp (accessed 28 April 2004).

Backpackers' Ultimate Guide (2005) 'Waikato Destinations', online. Available at www.bugpacific.com/destinations/nz-waikato.html (accessed 11 January 2006).

Bakic-Hayden, M. and Hayden, R. M. (1992) 'Orientalist variations on the theme "Balkans": symbolic geography in recent Yugoslav cultural politics', *Slavic Review* 51(1): 1–15.

Balibar, E. (1994) *Masses, Classes, Ideas: Studies on Politics and Philosophy Before and After Marx*, translated by S. James, London and New York: Routledge.

Bangkok Post (1999a) 18 February.

Bangkok Post (1999b) 2 February.

Bangkok Post (2000) 'Face to face with Leonardo', 26 January.

Barth, F. (1981) *Process and Form in Social Life: Selected Essays of Fredrik Barth*, vol. I, London: Routledge and Kegan Paul.

Barthes, R. (1993) *Mythologies*, translated by A. Lavers, London: Vintage.

Baudrillard, J. (1973) *Toward a Critique of the Political Economy of the Sign*, St Louis, MO: Telos.

Baudrillard, J. (1975) *The Mirror of Production*, St Louis, MO: Telos.

Baudrillard, J. (1983) *Simulations*, New York: Semiotext.

Baudrillard, J. (1988) *America*, translated by C. Turner, London: Verso.

Baudrillard, J. (1991) 'The reality gulf', *Guardian*, 11 January.

Baudrillard, J. (1998) *The Consumer Society: Myths and Structures*, translated by C. Turner, London: Sage.

Baym, N. K. (2000) *Tune in, Log On: Soaps, Fandom and Online Community*, Thousand Oaks, CA: Sage.

BBC News (2002a) 'Rome's gladiators make a killing', 3 September, online. Available at http://news.bbc.co.uk (accessed 20 February 2006).

BBC News (2002b) 'Faliraki police over-reacted', 2 July 2002, online. Available at http://news.bbc.co.uk (accessed 20 February 2006).

The Beach (1999–2000). Online. Available at www.thebeachmovie.com (accessed 7 March 2005).

The Beach, Amazon.com reviews, online. Available at http://www.imdb.com (accessed January 2006).

The Beach, IMDB reviews, online. Available at http:///www.imdb.com (accessed February 2006).

Becker, H. (1999) 'Visual sociology, documentary photography and photo-journalism: it's (almost) all a matter of context', in J. Prosser (ed.), *Image-Based Research: A Sourcebook for Qualitative Researchers*, London: Falmer, pp. 84–96.

Beeton, S. (2005) *Film-Induced Tourism*, Clevendon, Buffalo, Toronto: Channel View Publications.

Belich, J. (1986) *The New Zealand Wars and the Victorian Interpretation of Racial Conflict*, Auckland: Auckland University Press.

Bell, C. (2002) 'The big OE: young New Zealand travellers as secular pilgrims', *Tourist Studies*, 2(2): 143–58.

Bell, D. (1991) 'Reciprocity as a generating process in social relations', *Journal of Quantitative Anthropology*, 3: 251–60.

Benjamin, W. (2002) *The Arcades Project*, Cambridge, MA: Harvard University Press.

Bennett, A. (1999) 'Subcultures or neotribes? Rethinking the relationship between youth style and musical taste', *Sociology* 33(3): 599–617.

Bennett, A. (2005) *Culture and Everyday Life*, London: Sage.

Berking, H. (1999) *Sociology of Giving*, translated by P. Camiller, London, Thousand Oaks, CA and New Delhi: Sage.

Bernal, M. (1991) *Black Athena: The Afroasiatic Roots of Classical Civilisation*, vol. I, *The Fabrication of Ancient Greece*, London: Vintage.

Best, S. and Kellner, D. (1997) *The Postmodern Turn*, London: Guilford Press.

Bhabha, H. K. (1990) 'DissemiNation: time, narrative and the margins of the modern nation', in H. K. Bhabha (ed.), *Nation and Narration*, Westport, CT, London and New York: Routledge, pp. 291–322.

Bhabha, H. K. (1994) *The Location of Culture*. London and New York: Routledge.

Bilby, K. (1985) 'The Caribbean as a musical region', in S. W. Mintz and S. Price (eds), *Caribbean Contours*, Baltimore, MD and London: Johns Hopkins University Press, pp. 181–218.

Billig, M. (1995) *Banal Nationalism*, London: Sage.

Bolland, N. (1992) 'Creolization and creole societies: a cultural nationalist view of Caribbean social history', in A. Hennessy (ed.), *Intellectuals in the Twentieth-Century Caribbean*, vol. I, London: Macmillan Caribbean.

Boorstin, D. (1962) *The Image*, Harmondsworth: Penguin.

Bourdieu, P. (1977) *Outline of a Theory of Practice*, translated by R. Nice, Cambridge: Polity Press.

Bourdieu, P. (1984) *Distinction: A Social Critique of the Judgement of Taste*, translated by R. Nice, Cambridge, MA: Harvard University Press.

Bourdieu, P. (1998) *Practical Reason: On the Theory of Action*, translated by R. Johnson, Cambridge: Polity.

Boycott the Beach (undated). Online. Available at www.1worldcommunication. org/boycottthebeach.htm (accessed 23 March 2005).

Briguglio, L., Archer, B. V., Jafari, J. and Wall, G. (1996) *Sustainable Tourism in Islands and Small States: Issues and Policies*, London: Pinter.

Britton, S. G. (1982) 'The political economy of tourism in the Third World', *Annals of Tourism Research*, 9(2): 331–58.

Britton, S. G. (1989) 'Tourism, dependency and development: a model of analysis' in Y. Apostolopoulos, S. Leivadi and A. Yannakis (eds), *The Sociology of Tourism: Theoretical and Empirical Investigations*, London: Routledge, pp. 155–72.

Britton, S. G. (1991) 'Tourism, capital and place: towards a critical geography', *Environment and Planning D: Society and Space*, 9(4): 451–78.

Brodie, I. (2003[2002]) *The Lord of the Rings Location Guidebook.* New Zealand: Harper Collins.

Brodsky-Porges, E. (1981) 'The Grand Tour: travel as an educational device, 1600–1800', *Annals of Tourism Research*, 8(2): 171–86.

Broegger, J. (1990) *Pre-Bureaucratic Europeans: A Study of a Portuguese Fishing Community*, Norway: Norwegian University Press.

Brooker, W. (2003) 'Rescuing *Strange Days*: fan reaction to a commercial failure', in D. Jermyn and S. Redmond (eds), *Hollywood Transgressor: The Cinema of Kathryn Bigelow*, London and New York: Wallflower Press, pp. 198–219.

Brunner, E. M. (1991) 'Transformation of self in tourism', *Annals of Tourism Research*, 18(2): 238–50.

Burch, W. Jr. (1969) 'The social circles of leisure competing explanations', *Journal of Leisure Research*, 1(2): 125–45.

Burton, R. (1997) *Afro-Creole: Power, Opposition and Play in the Caribbean*, Ithaca, NY: Cornell University Press.

Butler, J. (1993) *Bodies that Matter: On the Discursive Limits of 'Sex'*, London: Routledge.

Butler, J. (1997) *The Psychic Life of Power: Theories in Subjection*, Stanford, CA: Stanford University Press.

Butler, R. (1995) 'Introduction', in R. Butler and D. Pearce (eds), *Change in Tourism: People, Places, Processes*, London: Routledge, pp. 1–15.

Café Capt. Corelli (2006) Online. Available at http://www.captaincorelli.com/aboutus.html (accessed 25 January 2006).

Calabrese, A. (2005) 'Communication, global justice and the moral economy', *Global Media and Communication*, 1(3): 301–15.

Calhoun, C. J. (1980) 'Community: toward a variable conceptualization for comparative research', *Social History*, 5(1): 105–29.

Captain Corelli's Mandolin, Amazon.com reviews. Online. Available at http://www.imdb.com (accessed February 2006).

Captain Corelli's Mandolin, IMDB reviews. Online. Available at http://www.imdb.com (accessed February 2006).

Carpentier, A. (1982) *Le cuidad de las columans*, Havana: Letras Cubanas.

Carrier, J. (1995) 'Introduction', in J. Carrier (ed.) *Occidentalism: Images of the West*, Oxford: Oxford University Press, pp. 1–32.

Castells, M. (1996) *The Rise of the Network Society*, Oxford: Blackwell.

Cavanagh, A. (1999) 'Behaviour in public? Ethics in online ethnography', *Cybersociology* 6, online. Available at http//www.socio.demon.co.uk (accessed 20 May 2002).

Caves, R. (2000) *Creative Industries: Contrasts Between Arts and Commerce*, Cambridge, MA: Harvard University Press.

Cere, R. (2002) 'Digital counter-cultures and the nature of electronic social and political movements', in Y. Jewkes (ed.), *Dot.cons: Crime, Deviance and Identity on the Internet*, Tavistock, Devon: Willan, pp. 147–63.

Chaney, D. (1996) *Lifestyles*, London: Routledge.

Chaney, D. (2002) *Cultural Change and Everyday Life*, Basingstoke: Palgrave.

Chard, C. (1999) *Pleasure and Guilt on the Grand Tour: Travel Writing and Imaginative Topography 1600–1830*, Manchester: Manchester University Press.

Chatterjee P. (1986) *Nationalist Thought and the Colonial World: A Derivative Discourse?* Minneapolis, MN: University of Minnesota Press.

Chatterjee P. (1993) *The Nation and its Fragments: Colonial and Postcolonial Histories*, Princeton, NJ: Princeton University Press.

Cheal, D. (1988) *The Gift Economy*, New York: Routledge.

Chhabra D., Healy R. and Sills E. (2003) 'Staged authenticity and heritage tourism', *Annals of Tourism Research*, 30(3): 702–19.

Cinema Confidential (24 February 2004) 'Romola Garai of "Dirty Dancing: Havana Nights"', online. Available at http://www.cinecon.com/news.php?id=0402241 (accessed 18 March 2006).

Clark, S. (2001) *Captain Corelli's Mandolin: The Illustrated Film Companion*, London: Headline.

Clifford, J. (1988) *The Predicament of Culture: Twentieth-Century Ethnography, Literature and Art*, Cambridge, MA: Harvard University Press.

Clifford, J. (1992) 'Travelling cultures', in L. Grossberg, C. Nelson and P. Treichler (eds), *Cultural Studies*, New York: Routledge, pp. 96–116.

Clifford, J. (1997) *Routes: Travel and Translation in the Twentieth Century*, Cambridge, MA: Harvard University Press.

Clifford, J. and Marcus, G.E. (1986) *Writing Culture: The Poetics and Politics of Ethnography*, Berkeley, CA: University of California Press.

Cloke, P. and Perkins, H. C. (1998) '"Cracking the canyon with the awesome foursome": representations of adventure tourism in New Zealand', *Environment and Planning: Society and Space*, 16(2): 185–218.

CNN (2001a) 'Captain Corelli's Mandolin', 3 May, online. Available at http://www.cnn.com/2001/SHOWBIZ/Movies/05/04/captain.corelli/ (accessed 10 October 2003).

CNN (2001b) 'Review of *Captain Corelli's Mandolin*', 22 May, online. Available at http://www.cnn.com/2001/SHOWBIZ/Movies/05/04/captain.corelli/ (accessed 10 October 2003).

CNN (2004) 'Ringing in the changes', 22 March, online. Available at http://www.cnn.com (accessed 30 April 2004).

CNN (2005) 'Backpackers help rebuild Phi Phi', 8 March, online. Available at http://cnn.worldnews.com (accessed 23 March 2005).

Cohen, E. (1973) 'Nomads from affluence: notes on the phenomenon of drifter tourism', *International Journal of Comparative Sociology*, 14(1–2): 89–103.

Cohen, E. (1974) 'Who is a tourist? A conceptual classification', *Sociological Review*, 22(4): 527–55.

Cohen, E. (1979) 'A phenomenology of tourist experiences', *Sociology*, 13: 179–201.

Cohen, E. (1988a) 'Authenticity and commoditization in tourism', *Annals of Tourism Research*, 15(3): 371–86.

Cohen, E. (1988b) 'Traditions in the qualitative sociology of tourism', *Annals of Tourism Research*, 15(1): 29–46.

Cohen, E. (1995) 'Contemporary tourism: trends and challenges', in R. Butler and D. Pearce (eds), *Changes in Tourism: People, Places, Processes*, London: Routledge, pp. 12–29.

Cohen, E. (1996) 'A phenomenology of tourist experiences', in Y. Apostolopoulos, S. Leivadi and A. Yannakis (eds), *The Sociology of Tourism: Theoretical and Empirical Investigations*, London: Routledge, pp. 90–114.

Coleman, J. and Crang, M. (2002) *Tourism: Between Place and Performance*, New York: Berghahn.

Collect Tolkien (2004) 'New Zealand Lord of the Rings coins sets', online. Available at http://www.collecttolkien.com/CoinsNewZealandSets02.htm (accessed 18 January 2006).

Collier, J. (1967) *Visual Anthropology: Photography as a Research Method*, New York: Holt, Reinhart and Winston.

Concorde International (2004) 'Air New Zealand press release', 3 February, online. Available at http://www.concorde.com.au/news/pres040203.asp (accessed 28 April 2004).

Conlin, M. and Baun, T. (1995) *Island Tourism: Management Principles and Practice*, Chichester: John Wiley and Sons.

Connell, J. and Gibson, C. (2004) 'Vicarious journeys: travels in music', *Tourism Geographies*, 6(1): 2–25.

Connell, R. W. (1987) *Gender and Power: Society, the Person and Sexual Politics*, Cambridge: Polity.

Connell, R. W. (1995) *Masculinities*, Cambridge: Polity.

Connerton, P. (1989) *How Societies Remember*, Cambridge: Cambridge University Press.

Correll, S. (1995) 'The ethnography of an electronic bar: the lesbian café', *Journal of Contemporary Ethnography*, 24(3): 270–98.

Cowan, J. (1990) *Dance and the Body Politic in Northern Greece*, Princeton, NJ: Princeton University Press.

Craig-Smith, S. and French, C. (1994) *Learning to Live with Tourism*, Melbourne: Pitman.

Crang, M. (1997) 'Picturing practices: research through the tourist gaze', *Progress in Human Geography*, 21(3): 359–73.

Crang, M. (1999) 'Knowing, tourism and practices of vision', in D. Crouch (ed.), *Leisure/Tourism Geographies: Practices and Geographical Knowledge*, Oxford: Blackwell, pp. 238–56.

Crang, P. (1997) 'Performing the tourist product', in C. Rojek and J. Urry (eds) *Touring Cultures: Transformations of Travel and Theory*, London and New York: Routledge, pp. 137–54.

Crary, J. (1992) *Techniques of the Observer: On Vision and Modernity in the Nineteenth Century*, Cambridge, MA: Massachusetts Institute of Technology Press.

Crawshaw, C. and Urry, J. (2000) 'Tourism and the photographic eye', in C. Rojek and J. Urry (eds), *Touring Cultures: Transformations of Travel and Theory*, London and New York: Routledge, pp. 176–95.

Crick, M. (1989) 'Representations of international tourism in the social sciences: sun, sex, savings and servility', *Annual Review of Anthropology*, 18: 307–44.

Crouch, D. (1999) 'Encounters in leisure/tourism', in D. Crouch (ed.), *Leisure/Tourism Geographies*, London: Routledge, pp. 1–16.

Crouch, D. and Lübbren, N. (2003) 'Introduction', in D. Crouch and N. Lübbren (eds) *Visual Culture and Tourism*, Oxford: Berg, pp. 1–20.

Crouch, D., Aronsson, L. and Wahlstrom, L. (2001) 'Tourist encounters', *Tourist Studies*, 1(3): 253–70.

Crouch, D., Jackson, R. and Thompson, F. (2005) 'Introduction', in D. Crouch, R. Jackson and F. Thompson (eds), *The Media and the Tourist Imagination: Converging Cultures*, New York: Routledge, pp. 1–13.

Culler, J. (1988) *Framing the Sign: Criticism and its Institutions*, Oxford: Blackwell.

Cunningham, S. (2005) 'Creative enterprises', in J. Hartley (ed.), *Creative Industries*, Oxford: Blackwell, pp. 282–98.

Daily Telegraph (2001) 'Italy to privatise Colosseum and Pompeii's ruins', 11 November.

Daily Telegraph (2003) '"Gladiators" meet their match over tourist rip-off', 11 March.

Damer, S. (2004) 'Signifying Sami: setting and performance on a Greek island', *Ethnography*, 5(2): 203–28.

Dance Holidays-Havana Nights (2006). Online. Available at http://www. danceholidays.com/Holidays (accessed 22 March 2006).

Dann, G. M. S. (2002) 'The tourist as a metaphor of the social world', in G. M. S. Dann (ed.), *The Tourist as a Metaphor of the Social World*, Wallingford: CAB International, pp. 1–17.

Davis, J. (1977) *People of the Mediterranean: An Essay in Comparative Social Anthropology*, London: Routledge and Kegan Paul.

Daye, M. (2005) 'Mediating tourism: an analysis of the Caribbean holiday experience in the UK national press', in D. Crouch, R. Jackson and F. Thompson (eds), *The Media and the Tourist Imagination: Converging Cultures*, New York: Routledge, pp. 14–26.

De Bernières, Louis (1997) *Captain Corelli's Mandolin*, London: Minerva.

De Certeau, M. (1986) *Heterologies: Discourse on the Other*, translated by B. Massumi, Manchester: Manchester University Press.

De Certeau, M. (1988a) *The Practice of Everyday Life*, translated by S. Rendell, Berkeley and Los Angeles, CA: University of California Press.

De Certeau, M. (1988b) *The Writing of History*, translated C. Tom, New York: Columbia University Press.

De Kadt, E. (1979) 'Social planning of tourism in the developing countries', *Annals of Tourism Research*, 6(1): 36–48.

De la Fuente, A. (1994) *A Nation for All: Race, Inequality and Politics in Twentieth-Century Cuba*, Chapel Hill, NC and London: University of North Carolina Press.

Den Tandt, C. (2002) 'Globalization and identity: the discourse of popular music in the Caribbean', in R. Young (ed.), *Music, Popular Culture Identities*, Critical Studies 19, Amsterdam and Kenilworth, NJ: Rodopi, pp. 75–88.

Dewailly, J.M. (1999) 'Sustainable tourist space: from reality to virtual reality?', *Tourism Geographies* 1(1): 41–55.

158 *Bibliography*

Diamantouros, N. (1983) 'Greek political culture in transition: historical origins, evolution, current trends', in R. Clogg (ed.) *Greece in the 1980s*. London: Macmillan, pp. 43–69.

Dirty Dancing: Havana Nights, Amazon.com Reviews. Online. Available at http:// www.imdb.com (accessed 17 March 2006).

Dirty Dancing: Havana Nights, IMDB Reviews. Online. Available at http:// www.imdb.com (accessed 17 March 2006).

DiscoveryThailand.com (2005) 'Phi Phi islands in Krabi', online. Available at http://www.discoverythailand.com (accessed 30 November 2005).

Douglas, M. (1993) *Purity and Danger: An Analysis of the Concepts of Pollution and Taboo*, London: Routledge.

Douglas, M. and Isherwood, B. (1979) *The World of Goods*, New York, London: Routledge.

Doumanis, N. (1997) *Myth and Memory in the Mediterranean: Remembering Fascism's Empire*, New York: St. Martin's Press.

Du Boulay, Juliet (1994) *Portrait of a Greek Mountain Village*. Evia: Denise Harvey.

Duany, J. (1992) 'Popular music in Puerto Rico: toward an anthropology of salsa', in V. Boggs (ed.), *Salsiology: Afro-Cuban Music and the Evolution of Salsa in New York City*, New York: Exelsior Music Publishing Company, pp. 74–80.

Dudley, A. (1992) 'Adaptation', in G. Mast, M. Cohen and L. Braudy (eds), *Film Theory and Criticism*, Oxford: Oxford University Press, pp. 420–8.

Duffy, M. (2000) 'Lines of drift: festival participation and performing a sense of place', *Popular Music*, 19(1): 51–64.

Dunn, D. (2005) 'We are *Not* here to make a film about Italy, we are here to make a film about ME . . .', in D. Crouch, R. Jackson and F. Thompson (eds), *The Media and the Tourist Imagination: Converging Cultures*, New York: Routledge, pp. 154–69.

Dyer, R. (1979) *The Dumb Blonde Stereotype*, London: British Film Institute.

Dyer, R. (1982) *Stars*, London: British Film Institute.

Dyer, R. (1997) *White*, London: Routledge.

Eco, U. (1987) *Travels in Hyperreality*, London: Picador.

Edensor, T. (2005) 'Mediating William Wallace: audio-visual technologies in tourism', in D. Crouch, R. Jackson and F. Thompson (eds), *The Media and the Tourist Imagination: Converging Cultures*, New York: Routledge, pp. 105–18.

Empire (2002) *Dirty Dancing*, January.

Empire (2006) 'Heavenly features', February.

EtownSalsa (22 February 2004) 'The Catskills meets Castro: "Dirty Dancing" in Cuba', online. Available at http://www.etownsalsa.com/newsarchives.asp (accessed 22 March 2006).

Evening Standard (2006) 'Dirty Dancing set to step from big screen to stage', 23 February.

Fabian J. (1983) *Time and the Other: How Anthropology Makes its Object*, New York: Columbia University Press.

Fabian, J. (1991) *Time and the Work of Anthropology*, Chur, Switzerland and Reading: Harwood Academic Publishers.

Fanon, F. (1967) *The Wretched of the Earth*, Harmondsworth: Penguin.

Fanon, F. (1970) *Black Skins, White Masks*, London: Paladin.

Featherstone, M. (1991) *Consumer Culture and Postmodernism*, London: Sage.

Feifer, M. (1985) *Going Places*, London: Macmillan.

Feifer, M. (1986) *Tourism in History: From Imperial Rome to the Present*, New York: Stein and Day.

Fernandes, S. (2003a) 'Fear of a black nation: local rappers, transnational crossing and state power in contemporary Cuba', *Anthropological Quarterly*, 76(4): 575–608.

Fernandes, S. (2003b) 'Island paradise, revolutionary utopia or hustler's haven? Consumerism and socialism in contemporary Cuban rap', *Journal of Latin American Cultural Studies*, 12(3): 359–75.

Fernback, J. (1999) 'There is a there there: notes toward a definition of cyber-community', in S. Jones (ed), *Doing Internet Research: Critical Issues and Methods for Examining the Net*, Thousand Oaks, CA: Sage, pp. 203–20.

Film Factory (2004) 'New Zealand: a world-class film making destination', 20 October, online. Available at http://www.filmfactorynz.co.nz/film_factorynews.htm (accessed 17 January 2006).

Film South NZ 1 (2002) 'Film and TV enquiries', June.

Film South NZ 3 (2003) 'Shooting from the hip', July.

Film South NZ 6 (2005a) 'LA behind the scenes', June.

Film South NZ 7 (2005b) 'Canterbury stars in big screen battle', December.

Film South-Latest News (2005) 'Our land speaks volumes', 9 December, online. Available at http://www.filmsouth.com/index.cfm/News (accessed 17 January 2006).

Firat, F. A. and Venkatesh, A. (1993) 'Postmodernity: the age of marketing', *International Journal of Research in Marketing*, 10(3): 227–44.

Firth, R. (1983) 'Magnitudes and values in kula exchange' in J.W. Leach and E. Leach (eds), *The Kula: New Perspectives on Massim Exchange*, Cambridge: Cambridge University Press, pp. 89–102.

Fish, R. (2003) 'Mobile viewers: media producers and the televisual tourist'. In D. Crouch, R. Jackson and F. Thompson (eds), *The Media and the Tourist Imagination: Converging Cultures*, New York: Routledge, pp. 119–34.

Fiske, J. (1989) *Understanding Popular Culture*, London: Routledge.

Forest Lodge (2005) 'The Lord of the Rings tours', online. Availableat http://www. forest-lodge.co.nz/ (accessed 11 January 2006).

Forsyth, T. (1995) 'The Mu'ang and the mountain: perceptions of environmental degradation in upland Thailand', *South East Asia Research*, 3(2): 169–92.

Forsyth, T. (2002) 'What happened on "The Beach"? Social movements and government of tourism in Thailand', *International Journal of Sustainable Development*, 5(3): 326–37.

FortuneCity (2000) '20 questions with Peter Jackson', online. Available at http://members.fortunecity.com (accessed 11 May 2004).

Foster, R. J. (1991) 'Making national cultures in the global ecumene', *Annual Review of Anthropology*, 20: 235–60.

Foucault, M. (1979) *Discipline and Punish: The Birth of the Prison*, New York: Vintage.

Foucault, M. (1986) 'Of other spaces', *Diacritics*, 16(1): 26–7.

Foucault, M. (1997) *The Archaeology of Knowledge*, translated by S. M. Sheridan, London: Routledge.

Franklin, S., Lury, C. and Stacey, J. (eds) (2000) *Global Nature, Global Culture*, London: Sage.

Friedberg, A. (1993) *Window Shopping: Cinema and the Postmodern Condition*, Berkeley, CA: University of California Press.

Friedberg, A. (1995) 'Cinema and the postmodern condition', in L. Williams (ed.), *Viewing Positions: Ways of Seeing Film*, Brunswick, NJ: Rutgers University Press, pp. 59–86.

Fruehling Springwood, C. (2002) 'Framing, dreaming and playing in Iowa: Japanese mythopoetics and agrarian utopia', in S. Coleman and M. Crang (eds), *Tourism: Between Place and Performance*, Oxford: Berghahn.

Gallant, T. W. (2002) *Experiencing Dominion: Culture, Identity and Power in the British Mediterranean*, Notre Dame, IN: University of Notre Dame Press.

Garland, A. (1996) *The Beach*, London: Penguin.

Garnham, N. (1990) *Capitalism and Communication*, London: Sage.

Geertz, C. (1973) *The Interpretation of Culture*, New York: Basic Books.

Geertz, C. (1986) *Works and Lives: The Anthropologist as Author*, Cambridge: Polity Press.

Germann Molz, J. (2004) 'Playing online and between the lines: round-the-world websites as virtual places to play', in M. Sheller and J. Urry (eds), *Tourism Mobilities: Places to Play, Places in Play*, London: Routledge, pp. 169–80.

Ghosh, N. (2003) 'Thailand may find movie-making pie hard to bite into', *Straits Times*, 9 August.

Gibson, R. and Ward, S. (1999) 'Party democracy on-line: UK parties and ICTs', *Information, Communication and Society*, 2(3): 340–67.

Giddens, A. (1990) *The Consequences of Modernity*, Stanford, CA: Stanford University Press.

Giddens, A. (1994) 'Living in a post-traditional society', in U. Beck, A. Giddens and S. Lash (eds), *Reflexive Modernisation, Politics, Tradition and Aesthetics in the Modern Social Order*, Cambridge: Polity, pp. 56–109.

Giddens, A. (1999) *Runaway World: How Globalisation is Shaping our Lives*, London: Profile Books.

Gilroy, P. (1987) *There Ain't No Black in the Union Jack*, London: Hutchinson.

Gilroy, P. (1993) *The Black Atlantic: Modernity and Double Consciousness*, London and New York: Verso.

GINZ.com (2004) '15 Days Lord of the Rings New Zealand Tour – North and South Island', online. Available at http://www.ginz.com/new_zealand/lord_of_the_rings_new_zealand_tour (accessed 28 April 2004).

Gitlin, T. (1998) 'The anti-political populism of cultural studies', in M. Ferguson and P. Golding (eds) *Cultural Studies in Question*, London: Sage, pp. 25–38.

Gluckman, R. (1999a) 'Andrew Macdonald talks about *The Beach*', 19 February, online. Available at http://www.gluckman.com/Beach.html (accessed 10 March 2005).

Gluckman, R. (1999b) 'Footsteps on *The Beach*', 19 February, online. Available at http://www.gluckman.com/Beach.html (accessed 29 November 2005).

Gluckman, R. (1999c) 'Hip author Alex Garland talks about *The Beach*', 19–20 February, online. Available at http://www.gluckman.com/Beach.html (accessed 29 November 2005).

Goddard, V. (1987) 'Honour and shame: the control of women's sexuality and group identity in Naples'. In P. Caplan (ed.), *The Cultural Construction of Sexuality*, London: Routledge, pp. 166–92.

Goffman, E. (1987 [1959]). *The Presentation of Self in Everyday Life*, Harmondsworth: Penguin Books.

Golding, P. and Murdock, G. (2000) 'Culture, communications and political economy'. In J. Curran and M. Gurevitch (eds), *Mass Media and Society*, 3rd edn, London: Arnold, pp. 70–92.

GoNomad (2003) 'More than middle earth: New Zealand for the kids', online. Available at http://www.gonomad.com/family/0503/NorthernislandNZ.html (accessed 18 December 2006).

Gottlieb, A. (1982) 'Americans' vacations', *Annals of Tourism Research*, 9: 165–87.

Gouldner, A. (1960) 'The norm of reciprocity: a preliminary statement', *American Sociological Review*, 25(2): 161–78.

Gourgouris, S. (1996) *Dream Nation: Enlightenment, Colonisation and the Institution of Modern Greece*, Stanford, CA: Stanford University Press.

Graburn, N. H. H. (1977) 'Tourism: the sacred journey', in V. Smith (ed.), *Hosts and Guests: The Anthropology of Tourism*, Philadelphia, PA: University of Pennsylvania Press, pp. 21–36.

Graik, J. (2000) 'The culture of tourism', in C. Rojek and J. Urry (eds), *Touring Cultures: Transformations of Travel and Theory*, London and New York: Routledge, pp. 113–36.

Greenwood, D. J. (1997) 'Culture by the pound', in V. L. Smith (ed.), *Hosts and Guests: The Anthropology of Tourism*, Philadelphia, PA: University of Pennsylvania Press, pp. 171–85.

Gregson, N. (1995) 'And now it's all consumption?', *Progress in Human Geography*, 19: 135–41.

Guardian (2000) ' 'Greek myth', 29 July.

Guardian (2001a) 'The real Captain Corelli', 11 April.

Guardian (2001b) 'The ring cycle', 7 December.

Guardian (2002) 'Fans flock to New Zealand's Tolkien trail', 6 January.

Guardian (2003a) 'Wellington boosts', 5 September.

Guardian (2003b) 'National elf service', 22 October.

Guardian (2003c) 'Star attractions', 13 December.

Habermas, J. (1989) *The Structural Transformation of the Public Sphere*, Oxford: Polity Press.

Hajer, M. (1995) *The Politics of Environmental Discourse*, Oxford: Clarendon.

Hall, C. M. (1995) *Tourism in the Pacific Rim: Developments, Impacts and Markets*, Melbourne: Longman.

Hall, S. (1992) 'The question of cultural identity', in S. Hall, D. Held and A. MacGrew (eds), *Modernity and its Futures*, Cambridge and Milton Keynes: Polity and Open University Press, pp. 274–325.

Handler, R. (1985) 'On dialogue and destructive analysis: problems in narrating nationalism and ethnicity', *Journal of Anthropological Research*, 41: 171–82.

Harrison, D. (2001) *Tourism and the Lesser Developed Countries: Issues and Case Studies*, New York: Cognizant.

Harrison, J. (2001) 'Thinking about tourists', *International Sociology*, 16(2): 159–72.

Hartley, J. (2005) 'Creative industries', in J. Hartley (ed.), *Creative Industries*, Oxford: Blackwell, pp. 1–40.

Hassle-Free Holidays (undated). Online. Available at http://www.hasslefree.co.nz/lord-of-the-rings-tour.htm (accessed 28 April 2004).

Havana Journal (2004) 'From "*Y Tu Mama Tambien*" to "*Dirty Dancing – Havana Nights*" Diego Luna', 15 February, online. Available at http://havanajournal.com/culture/entry/from_y_tu_mama_tambien_to_dirty_dancing_ . . . (accessed 17 March 2006).

Held, D. (1980) *Introduction to Critical Theory*, London: Hutchinson.

Held, D. (2000) 'Introduction', in D. Held (ed.), *A Globalising World? Culture, Economics and Politics*, London: Routledge, pp. 1–15.

Held, D., McGrew, A., Goldblatt, D. and Perraton, J. (1999) *Global Transformations*, Cambridge: Polity Press.

Herman E. S. and McChesney R. W. (1997) *The Global Media*, London: Cassell.

Herring, S. (1996) *Computer-Mediated Communication: Linguistic, Social and Cross-Cultural Perspectives*, Amsterdam: John Benjamin's Publishing.

Herzfeld, M. (1982) *Ours Once More: Folklore, Ideology, and the Making of Modern Greece*, Austin, TX: University of Texas Press.

Herzfeld, M. (1985) *The Poetics of Manhood: Contest and Identity in a Cretan Mountain Village*, Princeton, NJ: Princeton University Press.

Herzfeld, M. (1987a) '"As in your own house": hospitality, ethnography, and the stereotype of Mediterranean society', in D. Gilmore (ed.), *Honour and Shame and the Unity of the Mediterranean*, American Anthropological Association Special Publication 22, pp. 75–89.

Herzfeld, M. (1987b) *Anthropology through the Looking-Glass: Critical Ethnography in the Margins of Europe*, Cambridge: Cambridge University Press.

Herzfeld, M. (1991) *A Place in History: Social and Monumental Life in a Cretan Town*, Princeton, NJ: Princeton University Press.

Herzfeld, M. (1992) *The Social Production of Indifference: Exploring the Symbolic Roots of Western Democracy*, Oxford: Berg.

Herzfeld, M. (1997) *Cultural Intimacy: Social Poetics in the Nation-State*, New York and London: Routledge.

Herzfeld, M. (2001) *Anthropology: Theoretical Practice in Culture and Society*, Oxford: Blackwell.

Herzfeld, M. (2002a) 'Ethnographic phenomenology of the Greek spirit', in J. Revel and G. Levi (eds), *Political Uses of the Past: The Recent Mediterranean Experience*. Portland, OR, London: Frank Cass, pp. 13–26.

Herzfeld, M. (2002b) 'The absent presence: discourses of crypto-colonialism', *South Atlantic Quarterly*, 101(4): 899–926.

Herzfeld, M. (2003) 'Pom Mahakan: humanity and order in the historic centre of Bangkok', *Thailand Human Rights Journal*, 1(1): 101–19.

Hesmondalgh, D. (1996) 'Popular music after rock and soul', in J. Curran, D. Morley and V. Walkerdine (eds), *Cultural Studies and Communications*, London: Arnold.

Hesmondhalgh, D. (2002) *The Cultural Industries*, London, Thousand Oaks, CA, New Delhi: Sage.

Hetherington, K. (1998) 'Vanloads of uproarious humanity: New Age travellers and the utopics of the countryside', in T. Skelton and G.Valentine (eds), *Cool Places: Geographies of Youth Cultures*, London and New York: Routledge, pp. 328–43.

Hibbert, C. (1969) *The Grand Tour*, London: Weidenfeld and Nicolson.

Hill, M. (2002) *Fan Cultures*, London: Routledge.

Hine, C. (2000) *Virtual Ethnography*, London: Sage.

Hirsch, P. (1990) 'Processing fads and fashions', in S. Firth and A. Goodwin (eds), *On Record*, New York: Pantheon, pp. 127–39.

Hirsch, P. and Lohmann, L. (1989) 'Contemporary politics of environment in Thailand', *Asian Survey*, 89(4): 439–53.

Hobsbawm, E. and Ranger, T. (eds) (1986) *The Invention of Tradition*, Cambridge: University of Cambridge Press.

Homan, R. (1991) *The Ethics of Social Research*, Harlow: Longman.

hooks, b. (1992) 'Eating the Other: desire and resistance', in b. hooks (ed.), *Black Looks: Race and Representation*, Boston, MA: South End Press, pp. 21–40.

IMDB Trivia for *Dirty Dancing: Havana Nights* (2004) Online. Available at http:// www.imdb.com (accessed 17 March 2006).

In Depth Adventures (undated) 'Facts and fancy: it's not all destruction on set of "The Beach"', online. Available at http://www.indepthadv.com (accessed 11 November 2005).

Inglis, D. (2000) *The Delicious Story of the Holiday*, London: Routledge.

Institute of Economic Research, NZ (2002) *Scoping the Lasting Effects of The Lord of the Rings*, Auckland, NZ: Institute of Economic Research.

International Herald Tribune (2000) 'Tourism lobby in defence of "The Beach"', 8 February 2000.

International Herald Tribune (2003) 'As Italy takes over the presidency, he likens German MP to a Nazi guard: Berlusconi at EU sets off an uproar', 3 July.

Jackson, P. (1995) 'Changing geographies of consumption', *Environment and Planning A*, 27: 1875–6.

Jackson, P. (2002) 'Interview', at *The Lord of the Rings Net*, online. Available at http://www.thelordofthe rings.net/index_filmmakers (accessed 11 May 2004).

Jafari, J. (1987) 'Tourism models: the sociocultural aspects', *Tourism Management*, 8(2): 151–9.

Jameson, F. (1984) 'Postmodernism: on the cultural logic of late capitalism', *New Left Review*, 146: 53–92.

Jayawardena, C. (2002) 'Future challenges for tourism in the Caribbean', *Social and Economic Studies*, 51(1): 1–23.

Jayawardena, C. (2003) ' Revolution to revolution: why is tourism booming in Cuba?', *International Journal of Contemporary Hospitality Management*, 15(1): 52–8.

Jenkins, H. (1992) *Textual Poachers: Television Fans and Participatory Culture*, New York: Routledge.

Jenkyns, R. (1980) *The Victorians and Ancient Greece*, Oxford: Blackwell.

Jessop, B. (2000) 'Regulationist and autopoeticist reflections on Polanyi's account of market economies and the market society', *New Political Economy*, 6(2): 213–32.

Joseph, C. A. and Kavoori, A. (2001) 'Mediated resistance: tourism and the host community', *Annals of Tourism Research*, 28(4): 998–1009.

Just, R. (1989) 'The triumph of the ethnos', in E. Tonkin, M. Chapman and M. McDonald (eds), *History and Ethnicity*, London: Routledge and Kegan Paul, pp. 71–88.

Just, R. (2000) *A Greek Island Cosmos: Kinship and Community on Meganisi*, Oxford: James Curry and Santa Fe, NM: School of American Research Press.

Kapcia, A. (2005) *Havana: The Making of Cuban Culture*, Oxford and New York: Berg.

Kefalonia Island Guide (2003) 'No strings attached', 8 February, E. Brockes, online. Available at http://www.travel-to-kefalonia.com/article.php?article_id=3 (accessed 25 January 2006).

Kefalonia Travel (2006) 'Welcome to Kefalonia . . . the magical Greek island', online. Available at http://www.kefaloniatravel.com/ (accessed 25 January 2006).

Kellner, D. (1989) *Critical Theory, Marxism and Modernity*, Cambridge, Baltimore, MD: Johns Hopkins University Press.

Kellogg, W. A., Carroll, J. M. and Richards, J. T. (1991) 'Making reality a cyberspace', in M. Benedikt (ed.), *Cyberspace: First Steps*, Cambridge, MA: MIT Press, pp. 411–31.

King, R. (1993) 'The geographical fascination of islands', in D. Lockhart, D. Drakakis-Smith and J. Schembri (eds), *The Development Process in Small Island States*, London: Routledge, pp. 13–37.

Kopytoff, I. (1986) 'The cultural biography of things: commodification as process', in A. Appadurai (ed.), *The Social Life of Things: Commodities in Cultural Perspective*, Cambridge: Cambridge University Press, pp. 64–91.

Kozinets, R. (1999) 'E-tribalized marketing? The strategic implications of virtual communities of consumption', *European Management Journal*, 17(2): 252–64.

Kozinets, R. V. (2001) 'Utopian enterprise: articulating the meaning of *Star Trek's* culture of consumption', *Journal of Consumer Research*, 28(2): 67–88.

KrabiTourism.com (2005) 'Phi Phi islands', online. Available at http://www.krabi-tourism.com/phiphi-whattosee.htm (accessed 21 November 2005).

Kroshus Medina, L. (2003) 'Commoditising culture: tourism and Maya identity', *Annals of Tourism Research*, 30(2): 353–68.

Lac, S. (2004) 'The internet and democracy', in D. Gauntlett and R. Horsley (eds), *Web Studies*, 2nd edn, London: Arnold, pp. 217–29.

Laclau, E. and Mouffe, C. (1985) *Hegemony and Socialist Strategy: Towards a Radical Democratic Politics*, New York and London: Verso.

Langkeek, J. (2001) 'Leisure experience and imagination: rethinking Cohen's modes of tourist experience', *International Sociology*, 16(2): 173–84.

Lash, S. and Urry, J. (1987) *The End of Organised Capitalism*, Madison, WI: University of Wisconsin Press.

Lash, S. and Urry, J. (1994) *Economies of Signs and Space*, London, Thousand Oaks, CA, New Delhi: Sage.

Lashley, C. and Morrison, A. (2000) *In Search of Hospitality: Theoretical Perspectives and Debates*, Oxford: Butterworth Heinemann.

Lawrence, M. (1997) 'Heartlands or neglected geographies? Liminality, power and the hyper-real rural', *Journal of Rural Studies*, 13(1): 1–18.

Lax, S. (2004) 'The internet and democracy', in D. Gauntlett and R. Horsley (eds), *Web Studies 2*, 2nd Edition, New York: Oxford University Press, pp. 217–20.

Leadbeater, C. and Oakley, K. (2005) 'Why cultural entrepreneurs matter', in J. Hartley (ed.), *Creative Industries*, Oxford: Blackwell, pp. 299–311.

Leiper, N. (1979) 'The framework of tourism: towards a definition of tourism, tourist and the tourist industry', *Annals of Tourism Research*, 6(4): 390–407.

Leontis, A. (1995) *Topographies of Hellenism: Mapping the Homeland*, Ithaca, NY and London: Cornell University Press.

Lévi-Strauss, C. (1964) *Totemism*, translated by N. Rodney, London: Merlin Press.

Lévi-Strauss, C. (1972 [1962]) *The Savage Mind*, London: Weidenfeld and Nicolson.

Liebes, T. (2003) *American Dreams, Hebrew Subtitles: Globalization from the Receiving End*, Cresskill, NJ: Hampton Press.

Logan, B. (1995) *Hong Kong Action Cinema*, London: Titan Books.

The Lord of the Rings I–III, Amazon.com reviews, online. Available at http://www.amazon.com (accessed 15 January 2006).

The Lord of the Rings I–III, IMDB reviews, online. Available at http://www.imdb.com (accessed 16 January 2006).

Los Angeles Times (2005) 'Phi Phi's charm is entirely intact', 12 June.

Lowenthal, D. (1985) *The Past is a Foreign Country*, Cambridge: Cambridge University Press.

Lukács, G. (1968) *History and Class Consciousness*, translated by R. Livingstone, London: Merlin.

Lury, C. (2004) *Brands: The Logos of the Global Economy*, London and New York: Routledge.

MacCannell, D. (1973) 'Staged authenticity: arrangements of social space in tourist settings', *American Journal of Sociology*, 79(3): 589–603.

MacCannell, D. (1989) *The Tourist*, London: Macmillan.

MacCannell, D. (2001) 'Tourist agency', *Tourist Studies*, 1(1): 23–37.

McClintock A. (1995) *Imperial Leather: Race, Gender and Sexuality in the Colonial Context*, New York: Routledge.

MacKenzie, D. and Wajcman, J. (1985) 'Introductory essay', in D. MacKenzie and J. Wajcman (eds), *The Social Shaping of Technology: How the Refrigerator Got its Hum*, Milton Keynes: Open University Press, pp. 2–25.

Macleod, D. V. L. (2004) *Tourism, Globalisation and Cultural Change: An Island Community Perspective*, Clevendon, Buffalo, Toronto: Channel View Publications.

McGuigan, J. (1992) *Cultural Populism*, London: Routledge.

McLuhan, M. (1964) *Understanding Media*, New York: McGraw.

Maffesoli, M. (1996) *The Time of the Tribes: The Decline of Individualism in Mass Society*, London: Sage.

Mail on Sunday (2005) 'San Juan is a charmer', January.

Malbon, B. (1999) *Clubbing: Dancing, Ecstasy, Vitality*, London: Routledge.

Malinowski, B. (1922) *Argonauts of the Western Pacific: An Account of Native Enterprise and Adventure in the Archipelagoes of Melanesian New Guinea*, Studies in Economics and Political Science, no. 65, London: Routledge and Kegan Paul.

Mann, C. and Stewart, F. (2000) *Internet Communication and Qualitative Research*, London: Sage.

Marshall, W. (2005) 'Hearing hip-hop's Jamaican accent', *Institute for Studies in American Music Newsletter*, 34(2), online. Available at http://depthome. brooklyn.cuny.edu/ isam/NewsletS05/Marshall.htm (accessed 12 April 2006).

Marx, K. (1973) *Capital*, vol. I, translated by B. Fowkes, New York: Vintage.

Massey, D. (1993) 'Power-geometry and a progressive sense of place', in B. Curties, G. Robertson and L. Tickner (eds), *Mapping the Futures: Local Cultures, Global Change*, London and New York: Routledge, pp. 59–69.

Massey, D. (1994) *Space, Place and Gender*, Cambridge: Polity.

Mauss, M. (1954) *The Gift: The Form and Reason of Exchange in Archaic Societies*, London: Free Press.

Mayne, J. (1995) 'Paradoxes of spectatorship', in L. Williams (ed.), *Viewing Positions: Ways of Seeing Film*, New Brunswick, NJ: Rutgers University Press, pp. 55–183.

Media-Culture Organisation (2000) 'Cybersmear, cybersmother: Internet PR and "The Beach" protests', online. Available at http://reviews.media-culture. org.au/sections.php?op=viewarticle&artid=55 (accessed 12 February 2005).

Melucci, A. (1996) *Challenging Codes: Collective Action in the Information Age*, Cambridge: Cambridge University Press.

Miège, B. (1987) 'The logics at work in the new cultural industries', *Media, Culture and Society*, 9(2): 273–89.

Miller, M. and Henthorne, T. L. (1997) *Investment in the New Cuban Tourist Industry*, Westport, CT: Quorum Books.

Miller, T., Govil, N., McMurria, J., Maxwell, R. and Wang, T. (2005) *Global Hollywood 2*, London: British Film Institute.

Mills, S. F. (2003) 'Open-air museums and the tourist gaze', in D. Crouch and N. Lübbren (eds), *Visual Culture and Tourism*, Oxford: Berg, pp. 75–90.

Mings, R. C. (1978) 'The importance of more research on the impacts of tourism', *Annals of Tourism Research*, 5(3): 340–44.

Ministry of Economic Development, NZ (10 November 2003) Online. Available at http://www.med.govt.nz (accessed 30 April 2004).

Mitchell, T. (1996) *Popular Music and Local Identity*, London: Leicester University Press.

Mitra, A. and Cohen, E. (1999) 'Analyzing the web: directions and challenges', in S. Jones (ed.), *Doing Internet Research: Critical Issues and Methods for Examining the Web*, London: Sage, pp. 179–202.

Moore, F. (2002) 'Telling it like it is: news website and online newspapers', *Global Networks*, 2(2): 171–7.

Murray, S. (2004) 'Celebrating the story the way it is: cultural studies, corporate media and the contested utility of fandom', *Continuum: Journal of Media and Cultural Studies*, 18(1): 7–25.

Museum of Science, Boston (2004) 'The Lord of the Rings exhibition', online. Available at http://www.mos.org/lotr/ (accessed 21 May 2004).

Nash, D. (1977) 'Tourism as a form of imperialism', in V. Smith (ed.), *Hosts and Guests: An Anthropology of Tourism*, Philadelphia, PA: University of Philadelphia Press, pp. 33–47.

Nash, D. (1981) 'Tourism as an anthropological subject', *Current Anthropology*, 22(5): 461–81.

Nash, D. (1996) *Anthropology of Tourism*, Oxford: Pergamon.

Nation, The (1999) 'Cyberspace campaigns slam "The Beach" protests', 24 and 25 November.

Nation, The (2000) 'Tourism lobby in defence of "The Beach"', 30 January.

National Geographic (undated) 'Creating a mythological identity for England', online. Available at http://www.nationalgeographic.com/ngbeyond/rings/myth.html~myth (accessed 12 May 2004).

Neale, S. and Krutnik, F. (1990) *Popular Film and Television Comedy*, London: Routledge.

New Zealand Herald (2004a) 'Peter Jackson most powerful', 12 February

New Zealand Herald (2004b) 'Lord of the Rings world tour', 22 May.

Nora, P. (1989) 'Between memory and history: *les lieux de memoire*', *Representations*, 26(2): 7–25.

Norman, U. (2005) 'The re-branding of salsa in London's dance clubs: how an ethnicised form of cultural capital was institutionalised', *Leisure Studies*, 24(4): 385–97.

Norval, A. J. (1936) *The Tourist Industry: A National and International Survey*, London: Pitman.

Observer (1997) 'Burma's junta goes green', 23 March.

Observer Magazine (2006) 'Generation next', 28 May.

Offer, A. (1997) 'Between gift and the market: the economy of regard', *Economic History Review*, L (3): 450–76.

O'Neill, J. (1999) 'Economy, equality and recognition', in L. Ray and A. Sayer (eds), *Culture and Economy after the Cultural Turn*, London: Sage, pp. 76–91.

Pacini Hernandez, D. (1998) 'Dancing with the enemy: Cuban popular music, race, authenticity, and the world-music landscape', *Latin American Perspectives*, 25(3): 101–25.

Padilla, F. M. (1990) 'Salsa: Puerto Rican and Latino music', *Journal of Popular Culture*, 24(1): pp. 87–104.

Papanikolátos, N. (2000) 'Captain Corelli, the contradictions of Greek resistance, Hollywood and Cephallonia', AIM, 24 September, online. Available at http://www. aimpress.org/dyn/trae/archive/data.200009/00924–005-trae-ath.htm (accessed 25 January 2006).

Papataxiarchis, E. (1991) 'Friends of the heart: male consensual solidarity', in P. Loizos and E. Papataxiarchis (eds), *Contested Identities: Gender and Kinship in Modern Greece*, Princeton, NJ: Princeton University Press, pp. 156–79.

Parsons, D. (2000) 'Nationalism or continentalism? Representing heritage culture for a New Europe', *Yearbook of European Studies*, 15: 1–22.

Pattullo, P. (1996) *Last Resorts: The Cost of Tourism in the Caribbean*, London: Cassell-Latin American Bureau.

Pearce, P. L. (1980) 'Host community acceptance of foreign tourists', *Annals of Tourism Research*, 7(2): 224–33.

Pearce, P. L. (1982) *The Social Psychology of Tourist Behaviour*, New York: Pergamon.

Pearse, D. and Simons, D. (1997) 'Tourism in New Zealand: the challenges of growth', in F. M. Go and C. L. Jenkins (eds), *Tourism and Economic Development in Asia and Australasia*, London: Cassell, pp. 199–200.

Peleggi, M. (1996) 'National heritage and global tourism in Thailand', *Annals of Tourism Research*, 23(2): 432–48.

Perkins, H.C. and Thorns, D.C. (2001) 'Gazing or performing? Reflections on Urry's tourist gaze in the context of contemporary experience in the Antipodes', *International Sociology*, 16(2): 185–204.

Pinney, C. (1994) 'Future travel: anthropology and cultural distance in an age of virtual reality or, a past seen from a possible future', in L. Taylor (ed.), *Visualizing Theory*, New York: Routledge, pp. 410–28.

Polanyi, K. (1944) *The Great Transformation*, New York: Basic Books.

Porteous, D. (1996) *Environmental Aesthetics: Ideas, Politics and Planning*, London: Routledge.

Porter, R. (1993) 'Baudrillard: history, hysteria and consumption', in C. Rojek and B. S. Turner (eds), *Forget Baudrillard?* London: Routledge, pp. 1–22.

Positively Wellington Tourism (2003) 'The Lord of the Rings location itinerary', online. Available at http://wellingtonnz.com/Sights and Activities/ Lordoftherings.thm (accessed 28 April 2004).

Pratt, M. L. (1992) *Imperial Eyes: Travel Writing and Transculturation*, London and New York.

Praxis International (2000). Online. Available at http://praxisinternational. tripod.com/MediaHP.htm (accessed 10 October 2003).

Private Islands Online (undated) 'The Beach', online. Available at http://www. privateislandsonline.com/movie.2000.the_beach.htm (accessed 26 March 2005).

Prudishan, J. and Maneerat, M. (1997) 'Non-governmental development organization: empowerment and environment', in K. Hewison (ed.), *Political Change in Thailand*, London and New York: Routledge.

Ray, L. (2002) 'Crossing borders? Sociology, globalisation and immobility', *Sociological Research Online*, 7(3): 1.1.–6.4, online. Available at http://www. socresonline.org.uk/7/3/ray.html (consulted 4 October 2004).

Ray, L. and Sayer, A. (eds) (1999) *Culture and Economy after the Cultural Turn*, London: Sage.

Review Centre (undated). Online. Available at http://www.reviewcentre.com/reviews19209.html (accessed 12 May 2004).

Rheingold, H. (1994) *The Virtual Community*, London: Secker and Warburg.

Rings Scenic Tours (2005) 'The Shire's rest', online. Available at http://www. hobbitontours.com (accessed 16 January 2006).

Ritzer, G. (1996) *The McDonaldization of Society*, revised edn, Thousand Oaks, CA: Pine Forge Press.

Ritzer, G. (1999) *Enchanting a Disenchanted World*, Thousand Oaks, CA: Pine Forge Press.

Ritzer, G. and Liska, A. (1997) '"McDisneyisation" and "post-tourism": complementary approaches on contemporary tourism', in C. Rojek and J. Urry (eds), *Touring Cultures: Transformations of Travel and Theory*, London and New York: Routledge, pp. 96–112.

Rojek, C. (1993) *Ways of Escape: Modern Transformations in Leisure and Travel*, Basingstoke: Macmillan.

Rojek, C. (1995) *Decentering Leisure: Thinking Leisure Theory*, London: Sage.

Rojek, C. (1997) 'Indexing, dragging and the social construction of tourist sights', in C. Rojek and J. Urry (eds), *Touring Cultures: Transformations of Travel and Theory*, London and New York: Routledge, pp. 52–74.

Rojek, C. (2000) *Leisure and Culture*, Basingstoke, Hants: Macmillan.

Román-Velázquez, P. (1999) *The Making of Latin London: Salsa Music, Place and Identity*, Aldershot: Ashgate.

Rose, G. (2001) *Visual Methodologies: An Introduction to the Interpretation of Visual Material*, London: Sage.

Ruapehu Tourism (undated) 'The Ruapehu experience', online. Available at http://www.visitruapehu.com/promotions (accessed 11 January 2006).

Rubin, G. (1975) 'Traffic in women: notes on the "political economy" of sex', in R. Reiter (ed.), *Toward an Anthropology of Women's Liberation*, New York: Monthly Review Press, pp. 157–210.

Ryan, B. (1992) *Making Capital from Culture*, New York: Walter de Gruyter.

Ryan, C. (1991) *Recreational Tourism*, London: Routledge.

Ryan, C. (2002) 'The politics of branding cities and regions: the case of New Zealand', in N. Morgan, A. Pritchard and R. Pride (eds), *Destination Branding: Creating the Unique Destination Proposition*, Oxford: Butterworth Heinemann, pp. 66–86.

Ryan, C. and Kinder, R. (1996) 'Sex, tourism and sex tourism: fulfilling similar trends?', *Tourism Management*, 17(7): 507–18.

Ryan, M. and Kellner, D. (1990) *Camera Politica: The Politics and Ideology of Contemporary Hollywood Film*, Bloomington, IN: Indiana University Press.

Sahlins, M. (1974) *Stone Age Economics*, London: Tavistock Publications.

Sahlins, M. (1976) *Culture and Practical Reason*, Chicago, IL: University of Chicago Press.

Sahlins, M. (1996) 'The sadness of sweetness: the native anthropology of Western cosmology', *Current Anthropology* 37(3): 395–415.

Said, E. (1978) *Orientalism*, London: Penguin.

Salvatore, R. (1998) 'The enterprise of knowledge: representational machines of informal empire', in G. Joseph, C. Legrand and R. Salvatore (eds), *Close Encounters of Empire: Writing the Cultural History of U.S.–Latin American Relations*, Durham, NC and London: Duke University Press, pp. 69–104.

Sánchez-Taylor, J. (1999) 'Tourism and "embodied" commodities: sex tourism in the Caribbean', in S. Clift and S. Carter (eds), *Tourism and Sex: Culture, Commerce and Coercion*, London and New York: Pinter, pp. 168–78.

Sayer, A. (1999) 'Valuing culture and economy', in L. Ray and A. Sayer (eds), *Culture and Economy after the Cultural Turn*, London: Sage, pp. 53–75.

Sayer, A. (2000) 'Moral economy and political economy', *Studies in Political Economy*, 61(2): 79–103.

Sayer, A. (2001) 'For a critical cultural political economy', *Antipode*, 33(4): 687–708.

Sayer, A. (2003) '(De-)commodification, consumer culture and moral economy' *Environment and Planning D: Society and Space*, 21(3): 341–57.

Schwartz, R. (1991) 'Travellers under fire: tourists in the Tibetan uprising', *Annals of Tourism Research*, 18: 588–603.

Scott, A. (1994) 'Latin America and the focus in the nineties swings south', *Music Business International*, 4(1): 11–3.

Seaton, A. V. (1998) 'The history of tourism in Scotland: approaches, sources and issues', in R. MacLellan and R. Smith (eds), *Tourism in Scotland*, London: International Thompson Business Press, pp. 209–39.

Seattle Post-Intelligencer (2004) 'Hot music drives "Dirty Dancing: Havana Nights" beyond the ordinary', 27 February, online. Available at www.seattlepi.nwsource.com/movies/162249_dirty27q.html (accessed 17 March 2006).

Sharpley, R. (2001) 'Sustainability and the political economy of tourism in Cyprus', *Tourism*, 49(3): 241–54.

Sharpley, R. (2004) 'Islands in the sun: Cyprus', in M. Sheller and J. Urry (eds), *Tourism Mobilities: Places to Play, Places in Play*, London: Routledge, pp. 22–31.

Shaw, G. and Williams, A. M. (2004) *Critical Issues in Tourism: A Geographical Perspective*, 2nd edn, Oxford: Blackwell.

Sheller, M. (2000) *Democracy After Slavery: Black Publics and Peasant Radicalism in Haiti and Jamaica*, London: Macmillan.

Sheller, M. (2003) *Consuming the Caribbean: From Arawaks to Zombies*, Abingdon and New York: Routledge.

Sheller, M. (2004) 'Demobilizing and remobilizing Caribbean paradise', in M. Sheller and J. Urry (eds), *Tourism Mobilities: Places to Play, Places in Play*, London: Routledge, pp. 13–21.

Shields, R. (1991) *Places on the Margin: Alternative Geographies of Modernity*, London: Routledge.

Sicilian Culture (2000) 'The real Captain Corelli', online. Available at http://sicilian culture.com/news/corelli.htm (accessed 20 October 2003).

Slater, D. (1997) *Consumer Culture and Modernity*, Cambridge: Polity Press.

South Orchid (2005) 'Phi Phi islands', online. Available at http://www.nature-travel. org/phiphilanta.htm (accessed 20 November 2005).

Spurr, D. (1993) *The Rhetoric of Empire: Colonial Discourse in Journalism, Travel Writing and Imperial Administration*, Durham, NC and London: Durham University Press.

Squire, S. (1994) 'Accounting for cultural meanings: the interface between geography and tourism studies re-examined', *Progress in Human Geography*, 18(1): 1–16.

Stein, M. and Kane-Hanan, L. (1996) 'Cuba-tourism as a replacement industry', in *Ideas and Trends* (Arthur Andersen), online. Available at http://hotel-online.com/Trends/Andersen/Cuba_TourismIndustry_Spring1996.html (accessed 17 May 2006).

Stocking, G. W. (1987) *Victorian Anthropology*, New York: Free Press.

Strain, E. (2003) *Public Places, Private Journeys: Ethnography, Entertainment and the Tourist Gaze*, Brunswick, NJ: Rutgers University Press.

Strathern, A. (1983) 'The kula in comparative perspective', in J.W. Leach and E. Leach (eds), *The Kula: New Perspectives on Massim Exchange*, Cambridge: Cambridge University Press, pp. 73–89.

Sum, N.-L. (2003) 'Information capitalism and U.S. hegemony: resistance and adaptations in East Asia', *Critical Asian Studies*, 35 (3): 373–98.

Sunday Times (2000) 'Louis de Bernière's novel', 4 July 2000.

Sunday Times (2001) 'Corelli's comrades', 19 August.

Sunday Times (2005) '*The Beach* to yourself: return to Thailand', 13 February.

Sydney Morning Herald (2004) 'Quiet holidays turn to terror and despair', 27 December.

Talking Pictures 1 (2003a) 'Rings exhibition welcomes 100,000 visitors', online. Available at http://www.talkingpix.co.uk/ReviewsLordOfRingsTrilogy.html (accessed 20 April 2004).

Talking Pictures 2 (2003b) 'First official New Zealand *The Lord of the Rings* coins', online. Available at http://www.talkingpix.co.uk/ReviewsLordOf RingsTrilogy.html (accessed 20 April 2004).

Taylor, J. P. (2001) 'Authenticity and sincerity in tourism', *Annals of Tourism Research*, 28(1): 7–26.

Te Papa National Museum (7 April 2003) 'The Lord of the Rings exhibition', online. Available at http://www.tepapa.govt.nz/communications/Press_ Releases/pr_LOTR.html (accessed 21 May 2004).

Thaipro.com (2005) 'Koh Pha Ngan island, Thai paradise on a shoestring', online. Available at www.thaipro.com/thailand_00/0252_koh-pha-ngan-island.htm (accessed 18 March 2005).

Thai Students.com (2000) 'Phi Phi Le island', online. Available at http://www. thaistudents.com/thebeach/release11.html (accessed 12 January 2006).

Third World Network (2000) *New Frontiers*, 4 (6) (1998) and 5(1) (1999) '"The Beach" war', online. Available at http://www.twnside.org.sg/title/beach-cn.htm (accessed 17 March 2005).

This is Travel (2002) 'Captain Corelli: loved the book – liked the island', A. De Smith, 21 February, online. Available at http://www.thisistravel.co.uk/ (accessed 25 January 2006).

Thompson (2006) 'Kefalonia – an overview', online. Available at http://www.thompsonbeach.com (accessed 30 January 2006).

Thompson, J. (1995) *The Media and Modernity*, Cambridge: Polity.

Thorns, D. C. (1997) 'The global meets the local: tourism and the representation of the city', *Urban Affairs Review*, 33(2): 189–208.

Todorova, M. (1997) *Imagining the Balkans*, New York and Oxford: Oxford University Press.

Tolkien, J. R. R. (1999) *The Lord of the Rings: The Fellowship of the Ring*, London: Harper Collins.

The Tolkien Society (undated) 'J. R. R.Tolkien: a biographical sketch', by D. Doughan. Online. Available at http://www.tolkiensociety.org/tolkien/biography.html (accessed 11 May 2004).

Tomlinson, J. (1999) *Globalization and Culture*, Cambridge: Polity Press.

Toronto Sun (2000) 'Leonardo DiCaprio unhappy with movie rumours', 18 January.

Tourism Guide Christchurch – Attractions and Maps (2006). Online. Available at http://www.christchurchnz.net/canterbury/filmportfolio/ (accessed 17 January 2006).

Tourist Authority of Thailand (2005) Online. Available at http://expo.nectec.org.th (accessed 18 September 2005).

Towner, J. (1985) 'The Grand Tour: a key phase in the history of tourism', *Annals of Tourism Research*, 12(3): 293–333.

Travelfish.org (2005) 'Phi Phi travel guides', online. Available at http://www.travelfish.org (accessed 22 November 2005).

Tulloch, J. (1995) '"We're only a spek in the ocean": the fans as a powerless elite', in H. Jenkins and J. Tulloch (eds), *Science Fiction Audiences: Watching* Doctor Who *and* Star Trek, London: Routledge, pp. 144–72.

Turner, B. (1994) *Orientalism, Postmodernism and Globalism*, London and New York: Routledge.

Turner, B. S. (1993) 'Cruising America', in C. Rojek and B. S. Turner (eds), *Forget Baudrillard?* London: Routledge, pp. 146–61.

Turner, G. (1999) *Film as a Social Practice*, London: Routledge.

Turner, V. (1969) *The Ritual Process: Structure and Anti-Structure*, Chicago, IL: Aline.

Turner, V. (1974) 'Liminal to liminoid, play flow and ritual: an essay in comparative symbolology', *Rice University Studies*, 50: 53–92.

Tzanelli, R. (2002a) 'Haunted by the "enemy" within: brigandage, Vlachian/Albanian Greekness, Turkish "contamination" and narratives of Greek nationhood in the Dilessi/Marathon affair (1870)', *The Journal of Modern Greek Studies*, 20(1): 47–74.

Tzanelli, R. (2002b) 'Unclaimed colonies: Anglo-Greek identities through the prism of the Dilessi (Marathon) Murders (1870)', *Journal of Historical Sociology*, 15(2): 169–91.

Tzanelli, R. (2003) '"Disciplining" the Neohellenic character: records of Anglo-Greek encounters and the development of ethnological–historical discourse', *History of Human Sciences*, 16(3): 21–50.

Tzanelli. R. (2004) 'Giving gifts (and then taking them back): identity, reciprocity and symbolic power in the context of *Athens 2004*', *The Journal of Cultural Research*, 8(4): 425–46.

Urry, J. (1990) *The Tourist Gaze: Leisure and Travel in Contemporary Societies*, London and New Delhi: Sage.

Urry, J. (1992) 'The tourist gaze and the environment', *Theory, Culture and Society*, 9(1): 1–26.

Urry, J. (1995) *Consuming Places*, London: Routledge.

Urry, J. (1996) 'Tourism, culture and social inequality', in Y. Apostolopoulos, S. Leivadi and A. Yannakis (eds), *The Sociology of Tourism: Theoretical and Empirical Investigations*, London: Routledge, pp. 114–33.

Urry, J. (2000) *Sociology Beyond Societies*, London: Routledge.

Urry, J. (2001) 'Globalising the tourist gaze', online. Available at http://www.lancs.ac.uk/fss/sociology/papers/urry-globalising-the-tourist-gaze.pdf (accessed 31 May 2005).

Urry, J. (2003) *Global Complexity*, Cambridge: Polity Press.

USA Today (31 March 2004) '"The Lord of the Rings" lures climbers to death mountain', online. Available at http://www.usatoday.com/travel/news/2004–03– 31-death-mountain_x.htm (accessed 27 April 2004).

Van Gennep, A. (1906) *Rites of Passage*, Chicago, IL: The University of Chicago Press.

Van Maanen, J. (1988) *Tales of the Field: On Writing Ethnography*, Chicago, IL: University of Chicago Press.

Verdery, K. (1996) *What Was Communism and What Comes Next?*, Princeton, NJ: Princeton University Press.

Wagner, U. (1977) 'Out of time and place mass tourism and charter flights', *Ethnos*, 42: 38–52.

Wall Street Journal (*Weekend*) (2004) 'Missing the Latin beat: new "Dirty Dancing" skips appeal to Latino viewers; Catskills then, Cuba now', 6 February.

Wallerstein, I. (1974) *The Modern World System*, New York: Academic Press.

Wanaka Sightseeing Lord of the Rings Tours (undated). Online. Available at http://www.lordoftheringstours.co.nz (accessed 22 April 2004).

Wanderlust Salon (1999) 'Storming the Beach', online. Available at www.salon.com/wlust/feature/1999/02/cov_09feature.htm (accessed 10 March 2005)

Wang, N. (1999) 'Rethinking authenticity in tourist experience', *Annals of Tourism Research*, 26(2): 349–70.

Wang, N. (2000) *Tourism and Modernity: A Sociological Analysis*, Oxford: Pergamon.

Wardle, H. (1999) 'Jamaican adventures: Simmel, subjectivity and extraterritoriality in the Caribbean', *Journal of the Royal Anthropological Institute*, 5(4): 523–39.

Watson, J. (1993) 'The history of leisure, recreation and tourism in New Zealand', in H. C. Perkins and J. Cushman (eds), *Leisure, Recreation and Tourism*, Auckland: Longman Paul, pp. 15–29.

Webster, F. (1995) *Theories of the Information Society*, London: Routledge.

Weiner, A.B. (1992) *Inalienable Possessions: The Paradox of Keeping-While-Giving*, Berkeley and Los Angeles, CA: University of California Press.

Westerhausen, K. (2002) *Beyond the Beach: An Ethnography of Modern Travellers in Asia*, Bangkok: Thai Lotus Press.

White, Hayden (1978) *Tropics of Discourse: Essays in Cultural Criticism*, Baltimore, MD: Johns Hopkins University Press.

Wikipedia (undated) 'San Juan', online. Available at http://en.wikipedia.org/wiki/San_Juan (accessed 3 March 2006).

Wilkinson, M. (2004) 'Dancing in circles', BBC Collective , 27 May, online. Available at http://www.bbc.co.uk/dna/collective/A26716423 (accessed 22 March 2006).

Wilkinson, P. (1989) 'Strategies for tourism in island microstates', *Annals of Tourism Research*, 16: 153–77.

Williams, A. M. and Shaw, G. (1998) *Tourism and Economic Development: European Experiences*, Chichester: Wiley.

Williams, L. (1995) 'Introduction', in L. Williams (ed.), *Viewing Positions: Ways of Seeing Film*, Brunswick, NJ: Rutgers University Press, pp. 1–22.

Williams, R. (1958) *Culture and Society*, London: Chatto and Windus.

Williams, R. (1974) *Television: Technology and Cultural Form*, London: Fontana Press.

Willis, P. (1990) *Common Culture*, Buckingham: Open University Press.

Wittel, A. (2001) 'Towards a network sociality', *Theory, Culture and Society*, 18: 51–86.

Women's Voice for the Earth (2000) Online. Available at http://www.womenandenvironment.org/search?SearchableText=Thailand&x=13&y=9 (accessed 4 March 2002).

Zelizer, V. (1983) *Morals and Markets*, New Brunswick, NJ: Transaction.

Zelizer, V. (1988) 'Beyond the polemics on markets: establishing a theoretical and empirical agenda', *Sociological Forum*, 3: 614–34.

Index

In this index the following abbreviations have been used:
CCM   *Captain Corelli's Mandolin*
DD2   *Dirty Dancing: Havana Nights*
LOTR   *Lord of the Rings*

accents, use of 96–7
activism 29–30, 48–9, 53
Adler, J. 43, 71
Adorno, T. 7, 9, 37
adventure tourism 58, 71
aesthetic reflexivity 17
Agía Efimía (Kefalonia) 115–16
Air New Zealand 68–9
alienation 33, 44, 94
Amazon.com 19, 20
Anderson, B. 12, 146
Anderton, Jim 78, 79
Asia, travel to 34
authenticity (*see also* staged
    authenticity) 24, 27, 58, 66; fake
    37, 110, 114; language and 97;
    marketization of 13; quest for 5,
    30; travel and 28, 30–1, 33, 37

backpack travel 28, 31, 34, 41, 58
Bale, Christian 96, 98
Baudrillard, J. 8–9, 16, 44, 135, 148
Baym, N. 20
The Beach 27–8, 30; boycott of 29, 50,
    143, 145; cinematic representations
    42; impact on Thai tourism 28–30,
    46–7; marketing 43–4; online
    reviews 30–4, 35–8, 41, 42–3;
    promotion of fantasies of Eden 46;

reactions to production/distribution
    of 48–56
Beeton, S. xii, 6, 10, 57, 69, 73, 78,
    144
Bell, D. 149
Benjamin, W. 16, 17
Bennett, O. 109
Berlusconi, Silvio 104–5
Best, S. 9
Bloom, Orlando 77
Bollywood 10
Bourdieu, P. 53, 95, 127, 147
Brace, Matthew 73
brands/branding: competition for
    77–8; control of 58, 72–3, 75–7;
Brodie, Ian 80; *The Lord of the Rings
    Location Guidebook* 69–70
Brunner, E.M. 55
Buena Vista Social Club 132
Butler, J. 127

Cage, Nicolas 83, 96, 97
Canterbury (Kent) 75; appropriation
    of *LOTR* culture 76–7
capitalism 140, 143, 147; competition
    58, 78, 80, 109–10, 113
Captain Corelli's Mandolin 83–4, 90;
    anti-communism in 105–6, 107–9;
    local resistance to 107–9, 110, 116;